THE ART OF EXPERIMENTAL ECONOMICS

Applying experimental methods has become one of the most powerful and versatile ways to obtain economic insights, and experimental economics has especially supported the development of behavioral economics. *The Art of Experimental Economics* identifies and reviews 20 of the most important papers to have been published in experimental economics in order to highlight the power and methods of this area, and provides many examples of findings in behavioral economics that have extended knowledge in the economics discipline as a whole.

Chosen through a combination of citations, recommendations by scholars in the field, and voting by members of leading societies, the 20 papers under review – some by Nobel prize-winning economists – run the full gamut of experimental economics from theoretical expositions to applications demonstrating experimental economics in action. Also written by a leading experimental economist, each chapter provides a brief summary of the paper, makes the case for why that paper is one of the top 20 in the field, discusses the use made of the experimental method, and considers related work to provide context for each paper. These reviews quickly expose readers to the breadth of application possibilities and the methodological issues, leaving them with a firm understanding of the legacy of the papers' contributions.

This text provides a survey of some of the very best research in experimental and behavioral economics and is a valuable resource for scholars and economics instructors, students seeking to develop capability in applying experimental methods, and economics researchers who wish to further explore the experimental approach.

Gary Charness is a Professor of Economics and the Director of the Experimental and Behavioral Economics Laboratory at the University of California, Santa Barbara, USA.

Mark Pingle is a Professor of Economics at the University of Nevada, Reno, USA.

Routledge Advances in Behavioural Economics and Finance
Edited by **Roger Frantz**

Traditionally, economists have based their analysis of financial markets and corporate finance on the assumption that agents are fully rational, emotionless, self-interested maximizers of expected utility. However, behavioural economists are increasingly recognizing that financial decision makers may be subject to psychological biases, and the effects of emotions. Examples of this include the effects on investors' and managers' decision-making of such biases as excessive optimism, overconfidence, confirmation bias, and illusion of control. At a practical level, the current state of the financial markets suggests that trust between investors and managers is of paramount importance.

Routledge Advances in Behavioural Economics and Finance presents innovative and cutting-edge research in this fast-paced and rapidly growing area, and will be of great interest to academics, practitioners, and policymakers alike.

All proposals for new books in the series can be sent to the series editor, Roger Frantz, at rabeandf@gmail.com.

Trusting Nudges
Toward a Bill of Rights for Nudging
Cass R. Sunstein and Lucia A. Reisch

Social Neuroeconomics
Mechanistic Integration of the Neurosciences and the Social Sciences
Edited by Jens Harbecke and Carsten Herrmann-Pillath

The Art of Experimental Economics
Twenty Top Papers Reviewed
Edited by Gary Charness and Mark Pingle

For more information about this series, please visit: www.routledge.com/Routledge-Advances-in-Behavioural-Economics-and-Finance/book-series/RABEF

THE ART OF EXPERIMENTAL ECONOMICS

Twenty Top Papers Reviewed

Edited by Gary Charness and Mark Pingle

Routledge
Taylor & Francis Group

LONDON AND NEW YORK

First published 2022
by Routledge
2 Park Square, Milton Park, Abingdon, Oxon OX14 4RN

and by Routledge
605 Third Avenue, New York, NY 10158

Routledge is an imprint of the Taylor & Francis Group, an informa business

British Library Cataloguing-in-Publication Data
A catalogue record for this book is available from the British Library

Library of Congress Cataloging-in-Publication Data
A catalog record has been requested for this book

ISBN: 978-0-367-89431-3 (hbk)
ISBN: 978-0-367-89430-6 (pbk)
ISBN: 978-1-003-01912-1 (ebk)

DOI: 10.4324/9781003019121

Typeset in Times New Roman
by codeMantra

Gary dedicates his work on this book to his beautiful wife Wendy and their three children – Jacob, Emma, and Benjamin.

Mark dedicates his work on this book to Melissa, wife and love of his life, and to his three great girls – Rachel, Rebekah, and Leah.

CONTENTS

List of figures   *xiii*
List of tables   *xv*
List of contributors   *xvii*
Foreword   *xxvii*
Preface   *xxix*
Acknowledgments   *xxxiii*

1 Introducing 20 top papers and their reviewers   1
  Gary Charness and Mark Pingle

2 An experimental study of competitive market behavior
  (by Vernon L. Smith)   20
  Charles A. Holt

3 The strategy method as an instrument for the
  exploration of limited rationality in oligopoly game
  behavior (Strategiemethode zur Erforschung des
  eingeschränkt rationalen Verhaltens im Rahmen eines
  Oligopolexperimentes) (by Reinhard Selten)   30
  Claudia Keser and Hartmut Kliemt

4 An experimental analysis of ultimatum bargaining (by
  Werner Güth, Rolf Schmittberger, and Bernd Schwarze)   37
  Brit Grosskopf and Rosemarie Nagel

5 The winner's curse and public information in common-
value auctions (by John H. Kagel and Dan Levin)   53
Gary Charness

6 Group-size effects in public goods provision: the
voluntary contributions mechanism (by R. Mark Isaac
and James M. Walker)   65
James Andreoni

7 Rational expectations and the aggregation of
diverse information in laboratory security markets
(by Charles R. Plott and Shyam Sunder)   76
Mark Isaac

8 Experimental tests of the endowment effect and
the Coase theorem (by Daniel Kahneman, Jack L.
Knetsch, Richard H. Thaler)   85
John A. List

9 Bargaining and market behavior in Jerusalem,
Ljubljana, Pittsburgh, and Tokyo: an experimental
study (by Alvin E. Roth, Vesna Prasnikar, Masahiro
Okuno-Fujiwara, and Shmuel Zamir)   103
Armin Falk

10 Unraveling in guessing games: an experimental study
(by Rosemarie Nagel)   109
John H. Kagel and Antonio Penta

11 Trust, reciprocity, and social history (by Joyce Berg,
John Dickhaut, and Kevin McCabe)   119
Vernon L. Smith

12 Cooperation and punishment in public goods
experiments (by Ernst Fehr and Simon Gächter)   134
Yan Chen

13 A fine is a price (by Uri Gneezy and Aldo Rustichini)   144
Alex Imas

14 Giving according to GARP: an experimental test of
the consistency of preferences for altruism (by James
Andreoni and John Miller)   152
   Catherine Eckel

15 Risk aversion and incentive effects (by Charles Holt and
Susan Laury)   162
   Kevin McCabe

16 Does market experience eliminate market anomalies?
(by John A. List)   176
   Matthias Sutter

17 Promises and partnership (by Gary Charness and
Martin Dufwenberg)   182
   Urs Fischbacher and Franziska Föllmi-Heusi

18 The hidden costs of control (by Armin Falk and
Michael Kosfeld)   191
   Laura Razzolini and Rachel Croson

19 Do women shy away from competition? Do men
compete too much? (by Muriel Niederle and
Lise Vesterlund)   198
   Katherine B. Coffman and Alvin E. Roth

20 Group identity and social preferences (by Yan Chen
and Sherry X. Li)   210
   Marie Claire Villeval

21 Lies in disguise – an experimental study on cheating (by
Urs Fischbacher and Franziska Föllmi-Heusi)   220
   Uri Gneezy and Marta Serra-Garcia

Index   *229*

FIGURES

2.1 Symmetric value and cost arrays and contract price
    sequence (Smith, 1962)   22
6.1 Percent of endowment given   70
8.1 Linear indifference curves and WTA/WTP   93
8.2 Convex to the origin indifference curves and WTA/WTP   93
8.3 Endowment effects and the WTA/WTP disparity   95
10.1 Choices in first round of Nagel (1995) experiment: Panel A
    p = 1/2; Panel B p = 2/3; Panel C p = 4/3   111
10.2 Choice frequencies from three newspaper experiments   112
15.1 Example of subject decision sheet   166
18.1 Cumulative distribution of agents' choices in treatment
    C5 (panel a), C10 (panel b), and C20 (panel c) (Falk and
    Kosfeld, 2006)   196

TABLES

2.1   Average contract price in trading periods 4 and 5 by
subject group and trading condition (Smith, 1964)   25

5.1   Profits and bidding: Kagel and Levin (1986), Table 3   54

5.2   Effects of winner's curse: Kagel and Levin (1986), Table 6   55

6.1   Parameters of the experimental design   69

15.1   Holt-Laury price list for low payoff   165

CONTRIBUTORS

James Andreoni is a Distinguished Professor of Economics at the University of California San Diego. He is a Sloan Foundation Fellow, a Fellow of the Econometric Society, a Research Associate at the National Bureau of Economic Research, and past President of the Economic Science Association. He served as Co-Editor of the *Journal of Public Economics*, on the Editorial Boards of *Econometrica* and the *American Economic Review*, and is co-founder of the Association for the Study of Generosity in Economics. Andreoni has published in the fields of public finance, law and economics, environmental economics, experimental and behavioral economics, economic decision-making, and measuring risk and time preferences. Over the years, Andreoni has maintained an interest in altruism, fairness, and charitable giving. He has contributed to economic theory of altruistic behavior, using both lab and field-experiments to test these theories, and has written extensively on tax policy in the charitable sector.

Gary Charness is the Director of the Experimental and Behavioral Economics Laboratory at the University of California, Santa Barbara. He entered a PhD program at the age of 41 and published his first journal article at 50 years; he now has 100 published articles. In the 20-year period preceding his academic career, he traveled the world, was an options trader on the floor of the Pacific Exchange, a white-water guide, and a real-estate investor and lender. Charness is a creative experimental researcher who considers human behavior in light of economic theory, and is frequently cited for his works in the areas of social preferences, communication, networks, labor economics, and individual decision-making. He has published in many prominent journals (including *Econometrica*, *American Economic Review*, *Quarterly Journal of Economics*, *Science*, *Nature Human Behavior*, *Journal of Finance*, and *Management Science*). He is a main editor at *Games and Economic Behavior* and is on the board of editors of several other journals.

Yan Chen is the Daniel Kahneman Collegiate Professor in the School of Information at the University of Michigan, and a Distinguished Visiting Professor of Economics at Tsinghua University. She also holds an appointment as a Research Professor with the U-M Institute for Social Research. Her research interests are in behavioral and experimental economics, market and mechanism design, information economics, and public economics. She conducts both theoretical and experimental research. She is a former President of the Economic Science Association, an international organization of experimental economists. Chen has published in leading economics and management journals, such as the *American Economic Review, Journal of Political Economy, Journal of Economic Theory,* and *Management Science,* and in general interest journals such as the *Proceedings of the National Academy of Sciences.* She serves as a Department Editor of *Management Science,* an advisory editor of *Games and Economic Behavior,* and an associate editor of *Experimental Economics.*

Katherine B. Coffman is an Assistant Professor of Business Administration at Harvard Business School, as a part of the Negotiations, Organizations & Markets unit. Before joining Harvard Business School, she was an Assistant Professor of Economics at The Ohio State University. Her work focuses on understanding the sources of gender gaps in educational and labor market outcomes, and on designing and evaluating policies aimed at closing them. She has published her research in *Management Science,* the *American Economic Review, the Quarterly Journal of Economics,* the *Proceedings of the National Academy of Sciences,* and *Social Choice and Welfare.* She is an associate editor of the *Journal of the European Economic Association.*

Rachel Croson is an economist currently serving as Executive Vice-President and Provost of the University of Minnesota. Her research spans economics, psychology, sociology, and business and focuses on bargaining and negotiation, voluntary contribution to public goods and charitable giving, risk-taking, and behavioral finance. After receiving her PhD in 1994 at Harvard, she served as a faculty member at the Wharton School at the University of Pennsylvania, as a Center Director at the University of Texas – Dallas, Dean of the College of Business at the University of Texas – Arlington and Dean of the College of Social Science at Michigan State University, as well as Division Director for Social and Economic Sciences at the National Science Foundation. She is especially known in the discipline for her mentorship to junior faculty, and was the winner of the 2017 Carolyn Shaw Bell Award from the Committee on the Status of Women in the Economics Profession.

Catherine Eckel is the Sara and John Lindsey Professor and a University Distinguished Professor in the Department of Economics at Texas A&M University, where she directs the Behavioral Economics and Policy program. As an experimental economist, her contributions span many topics, including financial decision-making, altruism and fundraising, preferences and behavior of the urban poor, coordination of counter-terrorism policy, gender differences, racial/ethnic identity, and undergraduate academic achievement. Her work is supported by the National Science Foundation and many private foundations. Professor Eckel is the past President of the Economic Science Association and Southern Economic Association. She served as an NSF program director, was co-editor of the *Journal of Economic Behavior and Organization*, and has been on the editorial boards of 12 journals. She received the Carolyn Shaw Bell Award, given by the American Economic Association Committee on the Status of Women in the Economics Profession, for developing and participating in mentoring programs for women faculty.

Armin Falk is a Professor of Economics at the University of Bonn. His main research fields are behavioral, experimental, and labor economics. Professor Falk's research focuses on determinants and consequences of time, risk and social preferences, sources of inequality, early childhood development, and the malleability of moral behavior. He has received two ERC grants and was awarded the Gossen Prize in 2008, the Leibniz Prize in 2009, and the Yrjö Jahnsson Award in 2011. As an organizer or keynote speaker, he has been involved in numerous conferences and summer schools. He is Fellow of the European Economic Association and Director of the Bonn Laboratory for Experimental Economics, and he is affiliated with Hausdorff Center for Mathematics, Institute for New Economic Thinking, Institute of Labor Economics (IZA), German Institute for Economic Research (DIW), Centre for Economic Policy (CEPR), CESifo, and the Max Planck Institute for Research on Collective Goods.

Urs Fischbacher is a Professor of Applied Economic Research at the University of Konstanz and Director of the Thurgau Institute of Economics. After finishing his doctoral thesis in mathematics at the University of Zurich in 1985, he worked as a software developer in the industry and as a researcher at the Swiss Federal Institute WSL. In 1995, he moved to economics as a scientific programmer and later as a lecturer at the Institute for Empirical Research in Economics. There, he developed z-Tree, a programming language for interactive laboratory experiments that is used worldwide in numerous research institutions. His research resulted in the habilitation in economics at the University of Zurich in 2006 on the topics of human motivation and cooperation. His research interests include experimental economics, behavioral economics with a focus on social norms, social preferences, and the processes of human decision-making.

Franziska Föllmi-Heusi holds a Master's degree in political science and economics from the University of Zurich as well as an Executive Master in Business Administration from the University of St. Gallen. She is now a research associate affiliated with the SIAW institute of the University of St. Gallen.

Her research area is behavioral and experimental economics with a focus on honesty and distributive justice. After several years as lab manager and researcher at the Department of Economics at the University of Zurich and at the University of Konstanz, she worked as a consultant before she started as Managing Director of the Faculty of Business and Economics at the UZH. She is now Director (CEO) of a hospital in Switzerland and serves on the governing body of the family-owned construction firm.

Uri Gneezy is a Professor of Economics and Strategic Management at the Rady School of Management, UC San Diego. As a researcher, Professor Gneezy's focus is on putting behavioral economics to work in the real world, where theory can meet application. Topics of interest to him include incentive-based interventions to increase good habits and decrease bad ones, Pay-What-You-Want pricing, and the detrimental effects of small and large incentives. In addition to traditional laboratory and field studies, he works with several firms, conducting experiments in which they use basic findings from behavioral economics to help companies achieve their traditional goals in non-traditional ways. Before joining the Rady School, Gneezy was a faculty member at the University of Chicago, Technion, and the University of Haifa.

Brit Grosskopf is a Professor of Economics and the current Head of Department at the University of Exeter. She previously was a Professor of Experimental Economics at the University of Birmingham, where she founded the Birmingham Experimental Economics Laboratory (BEEL) of which she was the Director until she joined Exeter. She was an Associate Professor (with tenure) at Texas A&M University. Brit's research interests lie at the intersection of economics and psychology. She uses experimental methods to study individual and group behavior, with a particular interest in social preferences, reasoning, learning, reputation, identity, and happiness. Brit has obtained research support from the National Science Foundation, the British Academy, and the Russell Sage Foundation. Her research has been published in the *American Economic Review, Management Science, Games and Economic Behaviour, Experimental Economics, Journal of Economic Behaviour and Organization*, and the *Journal of Public Economics*, among others.

Charles A. Holt is the A. Willis Robertson Professor of Political Economy at the University of Virginia. He is a founding co-editor and current advisory editor of *Experimental Economics*, and has served as the President for both the Economic Science Association and the Southern Economic Association. His research pertains to measures of risk aversion and subjective beliefs, and studies of strategic behavior, using a mix of Game Theory and laboratory experimentation. He has written or co-authored three Princeton Press Books: *Experimental Economics* (with Doug Davis, 1993), *Quantal Response Equilibrium: A Stochastic Theory of Games* (with Jacob Goeree and Tom

Palfrey, 2016), and, most recently, *Markets, Games, and Strategic Behavior: An Introduction to Experimental Economics* (2019). He has worked extensively on auction design projects for the Federal Communications Commission, the Regional Greenhouse Gas Initiative, and the New York Federal Reserve Bank. His current research is focused on asset market bubbles and on strategic behavior with bounded rationality. He is the Director of the Veconlab (Google "veconlab admin") and does all programming for that free online site. He received the 2018 Thomas Jefferson Award for Scholarship and the 2008 Southern Economic Association Kenneth G. Elzinga Teaching Award.

Alex Imas is an Assistant Professor of Behavioral Science and Economics at the University of Chicago's Booth School of Business, where he has taught negotiations and behavioral economics. Previously, he was the William S. Dietrich II Assistant Professor of Behavioral Economics at Carnegie Mellon University, where he taught behavioral economics and human judgment and decision-making. Imas' research spans a variety of topics across economics and psychology. He has explored the role of incorrect beliefs in discrimination, the prevalence of behavioral biases among expert and non-expert investors, and how to better motivate performance by incorporating psychology into incentives. His research has been published in the *American Economic Review*, *Proceedings of the National Academy of Sciences*, and *Management Science*, among others.

Mark Isaac is a Professor of Economics and the John and Hallie Quinn Eminent Scholar at Florida State University, where he is also on the Executive Board of the Experimental Social Science Laboratory. He has served as Department Chair both at Florida State and at the University of Arizona. He is an editor of the series Research in Experimental Economics and has served on editorial boards of many journals, including the *American Economic Review* and *Experimental Economics*. He was the founding Treasurer of the Economic Science Association, a position he held for about 25 years. He has published over 50 refereed articles and book chapters utilizing experimental methods and says that in that process he has been blessed with the finest co-authors that one could imagine.

John H. Kagel is a University Chaired Professor of Applied Economics and Director of the Economics Laboratory at The Ohio State University. He also holds a faculty appointment in the Mershon Center for International Studies at Ohio State. He is a Fellow of the Econometric Society and past President of the Economic Science Association (aka the Society for Experimental Economics). He has served as a panelist for the National Science Foundation in the Economics Division and in the Decision, Risk, and Management Division. He has served on the editorial boards of the *American Economic Review* and *American Economic Journal: Microeconomics*. He currently serves on the editorial board of *Experimental Economics*. He has won awards for outstanding research at the University of Pittsburgh and The Ohio State University. He currently focuses on group decision-making and learning in strategic interactions, auction design and performance, industrial organization issues, and legislative bargaining. He has published over 90 articles in peer-reviewed journals including the *American Economic Review, Econometrica, Journal of Political Economy, Quarterly Journal of Economics, Psychological Review, American Political Science Review,* and *Management Science.* He co-edited (with Alvin Roth) the highly influential *Handbook of Experimental Economics (1995)* and *Handbook of Experimental Economics, vol. 2* (2016) (Princeton University Press). His most recent book, *Common Value Auctions and the Winner's Curse* (Princeton University Press, 2002), with Dan Levin, has been translated into Chinese.

Claudia Keser is a Professor of Economics and Chair of Microeconomics at Georg-August-Universität Göttingen. She is an experimental economics specialist with a Ph.D. from the University of Bonn (Rheinische Friedrich-Wilhelms-Universität Bonn), and a habilitation from the Technische Universität Karlsruhe in Germany. Her recent research has examined a wide range of topics including reputation, trust, morality, negotiation, regulation, social preferences, and public good provision.

Hartmut Kliemt was a Professor of Practical Philosophy at the University of Duisburg-Essen from 1988 to 2006. He then was Chair of Philosophy and Economics at the Frankfurt School of Finance & Management until 2016. Since 2017, he has been a Visiting Professor of Institutional and Behavioral Economics at the University of Giessen. His research interests are in the PPE (Politics, Philosophy, and Economics) area.

John A. List is the Kenneth C. Griffin Distinguished Service Professor of Economics at the University of Chicago. He received his Ph.D. in Economics from the University of Wyoming. Professor List joined the UChicago faculty in 2005, and served as Chairman of the Department of Economics from 2012 to 2018. Prior to joining UChicago, he was a Professor at the University of Central Florida, University of Arizona, and University of Maryland. His research focuses on questions in microeconomics, with a particular emphasis on using field-experiments to address both positive and normative issues. He has focused on issues related to the inner-workings of markets, the effects of various incentives schemes on market equilibria and allocations, how behavioral economics can augment the standard economic model, early childhood education and interventions, and, most recently, the gender earnings gap in the gig economy (using evidence from rideshare drivers). His research includes over 200 peer-reviewed journal articles and several published books, including the 2013 international best-seller, *The Why Axis: Hidden Motives and the Undiscovered Economics of Everyday Life* (with Uri Gneezy).

Kevin McCabe is a Professor of Economics and Law at George Mason University and is affiliated with the Interdisciplinary Center for Economic Science (ICES), the Krasnow Institute of Advanced Study, the Mercatus Center, and the Center for the Study of Neuroeconomics. Professor McCabe serves as a distinguished research scholar for the International Foundation for Research in Experimental Economics (IFREE). He researches the application of experimental methods to economics including experimental economics, economics system design, neuroeconomics, and the use of virtual world technology for experimentation.

Rosemarie Nagel is an ICREA Research Professor of Experimental, Behavioral, and Neuroeconomics and Director of BESlab at Universitat Pompeu Fabra and Barcelona GSE. In 1994, Nagel gained her doctoral degree in economics under Reinhard Selten (University of Bonn) and was Alvin Roth's postdoc (University of Pittsburgh) in 1994–1995. Her research builds bridges between economic theory and human behavior through experimental designs, and cognitive models with game theory, psychology, and laboratory, field, and neuroscientific tools. Nagel originated structuring bounded rationality with the strategy method in simple games, and via a step-level reasoning model (also called level-k) in Keynesian Beauty-Contest laboratory-, fMRI-, and large-scale field-experiments. She co-organizes experimental and macro or computational-economics workshops and summer schools. Her approaches are applied in micro-, macro-, and computational-economics; finance; neuroeconomics; management; psychology; and computer science. Her publications have appeared in a number of journals, including the *American Economic Review, Econometrica, Review of Economic Studies, Proceedings of the National Academy of Sciences, Nature Human Behavior,* and *Strategic Management Journal,* and in the popular press, like the *Financial Times* and *Spektrum der Wissenschaft.*

Antonio Penta (Ph.D., University of Pennsylvania, 2010) is an ICREA Research Professor at Universitat Pompeu Fabra and an Affiliated Professor at the Barcelona GSE. Prior to that, he was an Assistant Professor (2010–2016) and then a tenured Associate Professor (2016–2018) at the University of Wisconsin-Madison. He is currently a member of the Editorial Board of the *American Economic Review* and the *Review of Economic Studies,* an Associate Editor of the *Journal of Economic Theory* and *Journal of Theoretical Economics,* Associate Faculty at the Toulouse School of Economics, and a member of the TSE Digital Center. His research – which has been published in journals such as the *American Economic Review, Econometrica, Review of Economic Studies, Journal of Economic Theory, Theoretical Economics,* and *Management Science* – focuses on game theory, mechanism design, online auctions, and bounded rationality, and involves both theoretical and experimental work.

Mark Pingle is a Professor of Economics at the University of Nevada, Reno. His research has focused on behavioral economics, experimental economics, and macroeconomics. His work has appeared in *Journal of Economic Behavior and Organization, Economic Theory, Journal of Economic Dynamics and Optimal Control, Theory and Decision, Journal of Macroeconomics, Journal of Economic Psychology, Journal of Behavioral and Experimental Economics, Journal of Behavioral Economics for Policy*, and more. He is Book Editor for *Journal of Behavioral and Experimental Economics* and is a past President of the Society for the Advancement of Behavioral Economics.

Laura Razzolini is a Professor of Economics and Department Head at the University of Alabama. Her primary research areas are experimental economics and public finance. Her research has appeared in the *Journal of Economic Theory, Journal of Public Economics, Economic Theory, Public Choice, Journal of Economic Behavior and Organization*, and *Experimental Economics*. Before joining UA, Laura was at Virginia Commonwealth University for 13 years and before that at the University of Mississippi for ten years. She served as Program Director at the National Science Foundation from 2001 to 2003.

Alvin E. Roth is the Craig and Susan McCaw Professor of Economics at Stanford and the Gund Professor Emeritus of Economics and Business Administration at Harvard. He was the President of the American Economic Association in 2017, and is a member of the National Academy of Science. Roth's work is in game theory, market design, and experimental economics. With John Kagel, he edited the *Handbook of Experimental Economics* (volumes 1 and 2). He is known for redesigning "the Match" of medical residents to positions, for school choice systems in several American cities, and as a builder of kidney exchange networks that increase the availability of kidney transplants. He wrote *Who Gets What – and Why: The New Economics of Matchmaking and Market Design*. In 2012, he shared the Nobel Memorial Prize in Economic Sciences with Lloyd Shapley "for the theory of stable allocations and the practice of market design."

Marta Serra-Garcia is a Professor of Economics and Strategic Management at the University of California San Diego. She conducts research in behavioral and experimental economics. Her research focuses on how individuals acquire and transmit information and how this, in turn, affects their preferences and behavior. Among others, her research studies how the desire to preserve a positive self-image shapes individuals' ethical decision-making, such as lying and charitable giving. Serra-Garcia has been published in leading academic journals and has been featured in the *Wall Street Journal*. She has also been recognized as one of the Best 40 under 40 MBA Professors in 2020.

Vernon L. Smith is a Professor of Economics at Chapman University's Argyros School of Business and Economics and School of Law in Orange,

California, a research scholar at George Mason University's Interdisciplinary Center for Economic Science, and a Fellow of the Mercatus Center, all in Arlington, Virginia. Professor Smith has authored or co-authored more than 300 articles and books on capital theory, finance, natural resource economics, and experimental economics. He serves or has served on the board of editors of the *American Economic Review, The Cato Journal, Journal of Economic Behavior and Organization, the Journal of Risk and Uncertainty, Science, Economic Theory, Economic Design, Games and Economic Behavior*, and the *Journal of Economic Methodology*. He is a distinguished fellow of the American Economic Association, an Andersen Consulting Professor of the Year, and the 1995 Adam Smith Award recipient, conferred upon him by the Association for Private Enterprise Education. He was elected a member of the National Academy of Sciences in 1995, and received CalTech's distinguished alumni award in 1996. Vernon Smith was awarded the Nobel Prize in Economic Sciences in 2002 for his groundbreaking work in experimental economics.

Matthias Sutter has been Director at the Max Planck Institute for Research on Collective Goods since August 2017. He is also part-time Professor of Experimental Economics at the Universities of Cologne and Innsbruck. His research focuses on the experimental analysis of team decision-making, credence goods markets, and the development of economic decision-making with age. He is currently an associate editor for *Management Science, European Economic Review, Journal of the European Economic Association*, and *Economics Letters*. His work has earned him several prizes, including the Hans Kelsen Prize of the University of Cologne (2017), the Exeter Prize for Research in Experimental Economics, Decision Theory and Behavioral Economics (2015), Science Prize of the State of Tyrol (2009), the Honorary Prize for Science of the State of Vorarlberg (2008), and the Oberbank Science Prize (2004).

Marie Claire Villeval is a Research Professor of Economics at the National Center for Scientific Research (CNRS). She is affiliated with the GATE research institute at the University of Lyon, France. She obtained her Ph.D. in Economics from the University Paris X Nanterre. She is the President Elect of the Economic Science Association (ESA). She was the President of the French Economic Association (AFSE) and the Founding President of the French Association of Experimental Economics (ASFEE). She is co-editor-in-chief of Experimental Economics. She is a member of the Academia Europaea, Fellow of the European Association of Labour Economists and Fellow of IZA, Bonn. She has been awarded the Silver Medal of CNRS. Her main research interests focus on moral behavior and cheating, motivated beliefs, incentives and motivation, punishment and cooperation, peer effects and teamwork, status seeking, and self-image.

FOREWORD

Twenty carefully chosen papers in experimental economics, reviewed and put in context by veteran experimenters, provide an excellent, close-up introduction to the richness and diversity of the field, and where it is coming from. These 20 papers appeared over a period of half a century, from 1962 to 2013, during which experiments went from being quite rare to taking their place among the standard tools of economic research.

When John Kagel and I edited the *Handbook of Experimental Economics*, volumes 1 and 2 (1995 and 2016), we encouraged the chapter authors not to try to tell readers how to do good experiments, but to show them. And so it is with these papers: there are lots of ways to do good experiments, and here is a collection of 20 that have been influential. The reviews make clear that a successful, influential experiment is part of a scientific conversation that began well before the experiment was designed and conducted, and continued well after it was published and replicated. These conversations aren't only among experimenters, nor are they only among economists: experiments add to scientific conversations of all sorts, answering some questions and raising others – often questions that couldn't even be posed with equal precision in naturally occurring environments.

Reader, beware. After reading this volume, you will want to read more, and, your curiosity aroused, may find yourself on the slippery slope of designing and conducting your own experiments.

Alvin E. Roth, Stanford University, December 2020

References

Kagel, J.H., Roth, A.E., 1995. *Handbook of Experimental Economics: Volume 1.* Princeton, NJ: Princeton University Press.

Kagel, J.H., Roth, A.E., 2016. *Handbook of Experimental Economics: Volume 2.* Princeton, NJ: Princeton University Press.

PREFACE

We are pleased you have chosen to examine the art of experimental economics through the lens of 20 top experimental papers, reviewed by prominent experimental economists.

One good way to learn is to identify excellence and then seek to emulate it. We have identified 20 excellent applications of experimental methods, papers that demonstrate the versatility and power of using experiments to obtain insights. While experimental methods evolve and improve, the papers chosen for this book are top papers in large part because they contain excellent methods that others have chosen to emulate.

Another good way to learn is to observe the thinking of a talented, experienced thinker and seek to understand how they think. This book largely consists of reviews of the 20 top papers, written by very experienced experimental economists. By reading different reviews, one can see the thinking of a variety of talented and experienced experimental researchers.

A book aimed at identifying 20 top papers in experimental economics begs the question, "What criterion should be used?" Our starting point was the number of citations. We obtained citation counts for experimental papers we could identify using the Web of Science database.

Knowing we missed some significant contributions, we nonetheless sent a list of highly cited papers to a small group of experimental scholars and asked for two responses: (1) choose up to 20 top papers from the list and (2) identify any papers not included on the list that you would consider a top 20 paper. The responses to this initial "survey" were helpful. Some feedback was positive and encouraging: "This is an impressive list of papers and an interesting project," and "I think this is a great idea." Other responses echoed our inkling that using citations alone for identifying the top papers would be insufficient: "You will chide a lot of people for no good reason to create a stilted list of what a small subset of people define as experimental economics," "You really short-shrifted early producers," and "It is not clear to me whether you are looking for 'classic' relevant papers or somehow 'current' ones."

Based upon this feedback, we took a second step aimed at broadening the set of papers under consideration. We emailed a large group of experimental scholars, asking them to identify up to 20 top papers in experimental economics *without presenting to them any list of possible candidates*. A total of 233 papers were identified. The paper that was noted the most was independently identified by 17 different scholars.

By combining the "scholar identification method" and the "citation method," we arrived at a list of 96 papers. We started with 37 papers that were highly ranked using each method. We then added 19 papers recognized by at least three scholars from the scholar identification method. The remaining 40 papers we added all ranked highly using the citation method. We then sent this list of 96 papers to the email groups for the Economic Science Association and Society for the Advancement of Behavioral Economics, providing the ability for each respondent to vote on up to 20 papers to be included as a top paper. We received 271 responses.

We were able to identify ten papers we felt we could include as top papers without much controversy, but rounding out the list was necessarily subjective. The top ten were highly cited, independently identified by numerous experimental scholars, and received more survey votes than most other papers. To complete our list, we considered strictly applying some weighting criterion. However, we rather quickly discarded that idea, recognizing that any choice of criteria and weights is subjective and any strictly imposed approach will tend to yield odd results.

To round out our list, we decided to use our own judgment, along with input from scholars who had written one of the papers already selected. We continued to place significant weight on the ranking of the paper using our scholar identification and citation methods. However, we wanted to add works that complemented those already chosen. Scholars have applied many different experimental methods to many different topics, so in looking for complements we placed more weight on papers using a method or addressing a topic not already present in the works already chosen. None of the top ten papers had duplicate authors, so we also moved forward by placing more weight on papers written by scholars not already recognized.

Surely, we have left out many great papers. We considered publishing our rankings and considered presenting a list of "honorable mention" papers, so we would recognize more good scholars and more good papers. However, we decided against that because we inevitably would still have marginal cases. No doubt, there are reasonable criticisms concerning which papers we have not chosen, and reasonable criticisms concerning those that we have chosen. However, we hope and trust that the set of 20 papers we have chosen provides a meaningful look at the state-of-the-art of experimental economics.

To identify reviewers, we started by asking those who had written the papers selected. Thankfully, most of these top scholars responded positively. For the remaining reviewers, we sought out a well-published and well-known experimental economist with an interest that matched the theme of the paper needing a review. We very much appreciate the participation of these fine scholars in this project.

Because our reviewers are extremely talented, we did not provide a strict set of guidelines for their contributions, though we did make some suggestions. We asked reviewers to use their own judgment about how to best illustrate the usefulness of experimental methods. We suggested that the review explain why the chosen paper is a top one. We are pleased with the result. Reading these reviews should help you understand how to do experimental economics well.

> *Gary Charness, University of Santa Barbara*
> *Mark Pingle, University of Nevada – Reno*

ACKNOWLEDGMENTS

We acknowledge Roger Frantz for the discussion that motivated us to produce this book.

We acknowledge Jason Lim for his research and editorial assistance. Jason's database work, survey construction, and formatting work greatly facilitated the completion of this book.

We acknowledge Cameron Xu for assembling draft bios of our list of contributors, for working on the tables and figures, for helping create the index, and for reading through the manuscript.

We acknowledge and thank James Wynes for his artwork on the front book cover.

We acknowledge the many fine contributors to this book, who have written the reviews, and with whom we have had many enlightening discussions.

1

INTRODUCING 20 TOP PAPERS AND THEIR REVIEWERS

Gary Charness and Mark Pingle

Smith, V. L., 1962. An experimental study of competitive market behavior. *Journal of Political Economy* 70, 111–137. *(Reviewed by Charles A. Holt)*

Smith (1962) considers the question, "To what extent does competitive market theory predict the behavior and outcomes of heterogeneous buyers and sellers freely trading with each other in an oral double auction?" To examine this question, Smith conducted a series of experiments in which human subject buyers and sellers can interact and trade. Buyers are heterogeneous because they are endowed with a maximum willingness to pay that differs across the population. Sellers are heterogeneous because they are endowed with a minimum willingness to pay that differs across the population. A buyer earns consumer surplus by buying at a price below the reservation price, and a seller earns profit by selling at a price above her reservation price. Competition is instituted through an oral double auction where, during a trading period, a buyer can seek a seller by calling out "buy at __" and a seller can seek a buyer by calling out "sell at __." In general, Smith finds that competitive market theory predicts extremely well the price and quantity bought and sold by the experimental human subjects, and repeated interactions in a stable environment lead to a reduction in the variability of prices agreed upon by subjects.

In his review, Charles Holt notes how Smith's framework was comparable to but also different from an earlier version provided by Edward Chamberlin. While Smith (1962) is known for demonstrating the mechanism of the competitive market, Holt identifies one of the Smith (1962) treatments as being especially interesting for demonstrating how a change in the market institution can change the results. Holt provides examples of how Smith and other scholars, including Holt himself, have provided insight for policy by

DOI: 10.4324/9781003019121-1

learning how experimental results vary when the market institution is varied. More generally, this work has evolved into what experimentalists now call "mechanism design."

Holt also describes how the early work of Smith has influenced the experimental methods used today, contributing to Smith deserving the Nobel prize.

Finally, Holt contrasts the earlier work of Smith, which demonstrates the efficiency of markets for experimental goods analogous to consumer nondurables, to later work, which demonstrates the inefficiency of markets for experimental goods that are analogous to durable assets. This contrast demonstrates the power of experimental economics in terms of examining how changes in the decision environment can yield changes in behavior that provide theoretical and policy insights.

Selten, R., 1967. Die Strategiemethode zur Erforschung des eingeschrankt rationalen Verhaltens im Rahmen eines Oligopolexperimentes. In: Sauermann, H. (Ed.). *Beiträge zur experimentellen Wirtschaftsforschung*, Vol. I. Tübingen: J.C.B. Mohr (Paul Siebeck), 103–168.
(Reviewed by Claudia Keser and Hartmut Kliemt)

The Selten (1967) paper is the only one chosen for this volume that does not have a translation available in English. Its title in English is "The strategy method for researching boundedly rational behavior in the context of an oligopoly experiment." In this paper, Reinhardt Selten considers the question,

> How can we identify a decision maker's decision criteria that might arise in the play of a game when all contingencies are not explicitly presented, and in particular how will an oligopolist tend to price its product contingent upon the choices of other oligopolists?

To answer this question, Selten had students play an oligopoly game he designed. His primary concern was not the results. His focus was on how the human subjects made their decisions. To identify the strategies used, Selten instructed the student subjects on how to present their strategies in flow charts. He found subjects tended to focus on pricing their product near those of competitors – a boundedly rational action.

In their review, Claudia Keser and Hartmut Kliemt (hereafter KK) begin by providing context for the Selten paper. Selten and his colleague Heinz Sauermann had been studying bounded rationality for years. KK explain that Selten developed the strategy method as part of an effort to identify and understand the processes by which people make decisions.

KK emphasize that the strategy method introduced in Selten's (1967) paper was not as refined as most applications of the strategy method are today. Selten's (1967) game was not precisely defined, so the strategies expressed by subjects were not chosen from a limited set of possibilities. A primary purpose of Selten, whose interest was bounded rationality, was to see what elements of the environment subjects would use and what elements they would ignore. For Selten, KK emphasize, the strategy method was a tool for how decision makers represent information. Modern variants of the strategy method, in contrast, amplify information collection by asking subjects to provide contingent responses for the varying possible decision situations.

KK note that researchers often cite the Selten (1967) paper in contexts where the research is seeking to identify the plans of the decision maker and not just the choices, but KK suggest researchers underappreciate the contribution the paper makes to understanding bounded rationality. The strategy method facilitates the development of bounded rationality theories that are data-driven, based upon how people actually make decisions, an attractive alternative compared to developing as-if theories derived entirely from simplified assumptions.

Güth, W., Schmittberger, R., Schwarze, B., 1982. An experimental analysis of ultimatum bargaining. *Journal of Economic Behavior and Organization* 3(4), 367–388. (Reviewed by Brit Grosskopf and Rosemarie Nagel)

Guth et al. (1982), hereafter GSS, consider the question, "Will human subjects behave optimally in an ultimatum bargaining situation, and if they do not then why not?" An ultimatum bargaining situation is one where an amount of wealth is to be split between two parties and the last decision-maker in the bargaining process has the choice of either accepting or rejecting the split offered by the other party.

To examine their question, GSS introduce and examine variations of what experimental economists now call the "ultimatum bargaining game." The first mover in this game decides how much of a bargaining surplus to keep for themselves, and how much to offer to the second mover. The second mover then decides whether to accept or reject the proposed split. If the proposed split is accepted, then the two players receive what was proposed. If the proposal is rejected, then both players receive nothing. Since something is better than nothing, the assumption of material self-interest indicates the second mover should accept any split where they receive a positive amount. Knowing this, the predicted proposal for the first mover is that which offers the second mover the minimum possible amount. GSS found that actual decision behavior was not as extreme as optimizing pure material self-interest indicates. They interpret second mover willingness to reject small positive amounts as a willingness to punish unfairness. First mover offers that are not as extreme as self-interest predicts can then be explained as first movers recognizing that second movers care about fairness, in addition to wealth.

In their review, Grosskopf and Nagel, hereafter GN, emphasize the importance of the ultimatum bargaining game and GSS' contribution to motivating further research. GN note that the ultimatum game is especially useful because it effectively captures the final-stage ultimatum aspect of every more complicated multi-stage bargaining process. GN then proceed to describe the methodology of the GSS experiments, usefully critiquing some of the methods GSS used then, explaining why they may not be used today. Conversely, GN also recognize some methods GSS used then that experimentalists today should perhaps use more often.

GN describe in some detail the results of the GSS experiments. They then review much subsequent, related research, drawing upon insights they obtained from direct communication with Werner Güth. GN identify studies that vary the GSS experimental procedures, that use the ultimatum game in neuroeconomics and psychology studies, that vary the subject pool, and that use the ultimatum game to develop behavioral theories and examine learning. In their conclusion, GN identify many other important games in experimental economics directly inspired by the ultimatum game, or indirectly related. They emphasize that the ultimatum game has attained lasting importance because of its simplicity and its ability to shed light on important behavioral phenomena.

Kagel, J. H., Levin, D., 1986. The winner's curse and public information in common value auctions. *American Economic Review* 76(5), 894–920.
(Reviewed by Gary Charness)

Kagel and Levin (1986), hereafter KL, consider the question, "Can we provide evidence of the winner's curse in the laboratory with experienced bidders?" To examine this question, KL conduct a lab experiment using a pool of human subjects who have previously played a first-price common value auction game and who have done reasonably well (i.e., not gone bankrupt). Other issues include how increasing the number of experienced bidders or providing public information affect the outcomes of a first-price common value auction. The subjects play the auction game in a smaller group of three to four subject bidders but also in a larger group of six to seven bidders.

In a first-price auction, the winner earns the difference between the common value of the item and the winner's high bid. The outcomes of auctions for real world oil leases and auctions conducted with inexperienced subjects in labs suggest that this winner's curse often occurs, with poor results for the bidders. Nash Equilibrium theory indicates that experience and public information about the value of the item should reduce the prevalence of the winner's curse, while bids should be reduced when there are more bidders. Consistent with theory, KL find that experienced subjects in small groups are less subject to the winner's curse, and the introduction of public information increases the earnings of the winner when there is no winner's curse. However, in contrast with theory, KL find that an increase in the number of bidders *increases* the curse, and an increase in public information reduces the earnings of the winner in this environment.

In his review, Gary Charness begins by emphasizing that the KL paper is path-breaking because it derives a well-defined equilibrium reference point against which the experimental outcomes can be compared. Charness presents the experiment and its results in significant detail, concluding that the results in the KL paper are important because they indicate the winner's curse is a persistent behavioral anomaly.

As Charness presents in some detail, the KL paper has motivated substantial additional research aimed at understanding the winner's curse. It appears the cause of the curse is that bidders focus too much on the fact that a higher bid increases the likelihood of winning, while at the same time they do not focus enough on the likelihood that the willingness to bid higher winning is because one has received a higher private signal of the item's value. Charness gives KL credit for generating interest in how people frame problems like those they confront in the common value auction and, more generally, for helping inspire research in contingent reasoning and hypothetical thinking.

Isaac, R. M., Walker, J. M., 1988. Group size effects in public goods provision: The voluntary contribution mechanism.
Quarterly Journal of Economics 103, 179–199.
(Reviewed by James Andreoni)

Isaac and Walker (1988) consider the question, "How do group size and individual marginal return affect the willingness to voluntarily contribute to the provision of a public good?" Their experiment uses a voluntary contributions mechanism with treatments that vary the group size and the marginal return. They find that group size significantly decreases the willingness to contribute to the public good when the individual marginal return is low but not when it is high. They argue that the marginal per capita return is a key factor determining contributions.

In his review, Jim Andreoni opines that the Isaac and Walker paper is a top paper because it forced the profession to "see an old topic with new eyes." Previous research had led to a near consensus that only small groups can produce coercive mechanisms sufficient to overcome the incentive to free-ride. By showing the marginal individual return from a public-good contribution influences the contribution rate, Isaac and Walker showed that group size is not all that matters.

Andreoni also judges the Isaac and Walker paper important because it raised more questions than it answered, but it did so in a way that "well-articulated a research agenda" on an important topic. If it is not just small-group social norms that can overcome the incentive to free-ride, what other factors influence the willingness people have to contribute to a public good? Andreoni himself has been one of the significant contributors to this research agenda, suggesting one of the factors is "impure altruism": People obtain utility when they contribute, a "warm glow" from knowing they are doing their part in contributing toward a common goal.

In a thank you to Jim Andreoni, Mark Isaac and James Walker add two comments they thought would be useful to young researchers. They discuss how research tends to be messy, and also point out the value of collaboration.

Plott, C., Sunder, S., 1988. Rational expectations and the aggregation of diverse information in laboratory security markets. *Econometrica* 56, 1085–1118. *(Reviewed by Mark Isaac)*

Plott and Sunder (1988) consider the question, "Can an asset market aggregate information of diverse traders with diverse information, so the traders can discover the state of nature from the information pooled by the market?" To examine this question, they create a series of market experiments where subjects have the opportunity to pool information and learn. In doing so, they are able to test the rational expectations hypothesis – that subjects will converge to play that reflects a knowledge of the pooled information, against behavioral alternatives. The prior information alternative is the hypothesis that individuals will ignore the opportunity to pool information and instead use Bayesian updating to update the probabilities of the different states based upon their own individual experiences. They also consider a maxmin alternative.

Plott and Sunder (1988) obtain what they describe as positive and negative results. On the negative side, information was not aggregated as predicted by the rational expectations hypothesis in their non-contingent claim, single-security, experimental markets. On the positive side, they find that markets can aggregate information as predicted by the rational expectations hypothesis in a contingent claim market and in a uniform dividend market. Considering their overall results, they conclude that traders may need some information about the preferences of others in order for markets to aggregate information as the rational expectations hypothesis predicts.

In his review, Mark Isaac provides a good context for the Plott and Sunder (1988) paper, primarily by describing how it emerged from Plott and Sunder (1982). The latter focuses on how markets disseminate information, while the former focuses on how markets aggregate information. Isaac is complementary of the "clever" experimental design, which allows Plott and Sunder to distinguish rational expectations behavior from alternatives. Isaac says the Plott and Sunder papers illustrate that an experimental frame can be useful even when it cannot conclusively test one theory against alternatives. It is not possible to include in an experiment all of the factors relevant to a theory. Nonetheless, such an experiment can provide insight. Isaac identifies a number of other works, motivated by or related to the Plott and Sunder papers, allowing readers interested in learning more about the ability of markets to disseminate and aggregate information to readily explore further.

Kahneman, D., Knetsch, J. L., Thaler, R. H., 1990. Experimental tests of the endowment effect and the Coase theorem. *Journal of Political Economy* **98(6), 1325–1348.**
(Reviewed by John A. List)

Kahneman et al. (1990), hereafter KKT, consider the question, "Is there an endowment effect that creates a preference reference point for a good such that loss aversion will then tend to make the minimum willingness to accept (WTA) greater than the maximum willingness to pay (WTP)?" Their basic experiment involves randomly allocating subjects into two groups, half as potential buyers and half as potential sellers. The potential sellers are endowed with a good. The potential buyers and sellers express their WTP and WTA, respectively. Using these responses, a market price is identified, along with the trades that would occur at the market price. Subjects are incentivized with a randomized payment process. The basic finding is evidence of an endowment effect. The WTA was greater than the WTP, and a KKT treatment aimed at examining the impact of experience indicates experience does not eliminate the endowment effect.

In his review, John List provides excellent summaries of the designs and results of each of the eight experiments reported by KKT. He notes the KKT paper was important in his professional career, motivating him to explore the issue in a variety of ways. List provides theory and results from a number of his own experimental studies aimed at the issue. He concludes that work conducted since KKT's study, including his own, indicates there is much evidence in favor of the endowment effect. However, List also points to evidence that market experience tends to temper the endowment effect, in contrast to KKT's lab experiment finding.

List concludes with a comment on the importance of the KKT paper in terms of stimulating the interaction of theory and empiricism, lab experiments and field experiments. This interaction has helped identify when the endowment effect is more likely to be significant and why. This interactive approach, applied to a wide variety other topics, is a prescription for strengthening the behavioral foundation of economics.

Roth, A. E., Prasnikar, V., Okuno-Fujiwara, M., Zamir, S., 1991. Bargaining and market behavior in Jerusalem, Ljubljana, Pittsburgh, and Tokyo: An experimental study. *American Economic Review* **81(5), 1068–1095.**
(Reviewed by Armin Falk)

Roth et al. (1991), hereafter RPOZ, consider the question, "Do people behave similarly in comparable bargaining and market trading environments, and if not do people in different cultures behave differently?" To examine the question, RPOZ implement sessions where human subjects participate in both bargaining and market experiments. The bargaining experiment is that of Güth et al. (1982). The market experiment involves multiple buyers making bids to a single seller. The seller has the option of accepting the highest buyer bid, in which case the seller and buyer gain from the transaction and all other buyers receive zero. Because cross cultural differences are of interest, RPOZ take care with their experimental design to control for experimenter effects, language effects, and currency effects that might influence decision behavior.

RPOZ find that behavior in the market environment converges to the equilibrium that material self-interest predicts, where buyers' bids cluster near that which provides the single seller with nearly all of the available surplus. However, as per Güth et al. (1982), subjects in the bargaining environment deviate from the pure material self-interest prediction. Also, subject pools from different countries varied systematically. RPOZ conclude that the common outcome for the market environment is the effect of competition, perhaps overriding any individual or cultural differences that might otherwise lead to different outcomes. They also conclude that different cultural expectations about what constitutes a fair or acceptable offer explains the observed differences across cultures in the bargaining environment.

In his review, Armin Falk provides an excellent summary of the RPOZ experiment and results. He compliments RPOZ for demonstrating the usefulness of experimental economics in examining cultural effects. Falk notes that experimental researchers since RPOZ have come to value moving beyond smaller samples and college student subject pools in order to identify specific characteristics that make behavior heterogeneous (i.e., culture, gender, age, other socioeconomic factors). Falk also emphasizes the importance of RPOZ's results for motivating further research aimed at understanding why self-interest predicts market outcomes but not bargaining outcomes. Falk goes into some detail, referencing research since RPOZ, to explain why market competition prevents people from achieving the "fair" outcomes produced by bilateral bargaining. Falk's review illustrates the usefulness of the experimental method in helping us refine our understanding of complex motivational questions. In particular, experimental research since RPOZ has helped us understand when motivators like positive reciprocity can dominate and determine outcomes and when the traditional self-interest is the dominant motivator.

Berg, J., Dickhaut, J., McCabe, K., 1995. Trust, reciprocity, and social history. *Games and Economic Behavior* **10(1), 122–142.** *(Reviewed by Vernon L. Smith)*

Berg et al. (1995), hereafter BDM, ask the question, "Can positive reciprocity support trust and trustworthiness?" To answer this question, BDM design an investment game, also known now as the "trust game." A first mover can trust by transferring some wealth to a second mover. Trust is productive in that the second mover receives three times what the first mover transfers. The transfer is trusting because the second mover can make a "back transfer," but need not. Material self-interest motivates the second mover to not be trustworthy and transfer nothing back, so the Nash Equilibrium prediction is for the first mover to not trust and, thus, transfer nothing. However, BDM find that most first movers send positive amounts and most second movers return positive amounts. BDM suggest positive reciprocity is the motivator that overrides self-interest, facilitating trust and trustworthiness.

In his review, Vernon Smith begins by noting that "few experiments have approached that of BDM in launching such extensive further investigation." Smith reviews BDM's protocol, commenting on its methodological contribution and findings. He reviews works aimed at finding conditions that would reduce the levels of trust and trustworthiness, and works that found results stubbornly robust. After critiquing reciprocity and social preference explanations of BDM's results, Vernon Smith presents evidence that Adam Smith's model of human sociability found in *The Theory of Moral Sentiments* (1759, 1853), which assumes people are self-interested, can explain the results. Self-interested preferences need not preclude actions in the interest of others. Socialization leads us to adopt rules that displace a self-interested action with an other-interested action. The self-interested person recognizes that sacrificing oneself is costly, and socialization teaches us that self-sacrifice is admirable. Admirable self-sacrifice begets gratitude, which is a desire to repay kindness with kindness. That is, from this perspective, positive reciprocity is not the fundamental motivator; rather, it is the result of socialized self-interest.

Nagel, R., 1995. Unraveling in guessing games: An experimental study. *American Economic Review* 85(5), 1313–1326. *(Reviewed by John H. Kagel and Antonio Penta)*

Nagel (1995) asks the question, "How deeply do people reason, and how deeply do people think other people reason?" To address this question, she constructs an experiment where subjects play varying versions of the beauty contest game, also known as the "p-guessing game." The game has a unique Nash Equilibrium associated with each player thinking infinitely deep and believing others will think infinitely deep also. Nagel finds that a particular bounded rationality model explains behavior better than the Nash Equilibrium model. Her bounded-rationality model proposes that players use the mean of a uniform distribution of responses as a baseline expected choice of others, but then adjust that expectation by thinking one or two levels deep. This model predicts that the choices of players will cluster around those associated with thinking one or two levels deep, and this is where Nagel finds clusters of choices. Expecting thinking one or two layers deep also explains repeated plays of the game. That is, people do not seem to expect others to learn to think more than one or two layers deep.

In their review, Kagel and Penta begin by describing the conclusions of Nagel (1995) and then proceed to review the significant research this article has inspired. One subsequent work was a field experiment, with high stakes in some sessions, and the results were comparable to Nagel's lab experiment. A second subsequent experiment used chess players as subjects. The question was whether chess players would think deeper and believe others in the subject pool would also do so, because of their chess training. They did not think deeper, perhaps an indication that others would not. Another work uses Nagel's k-level reasoning to explain auction behavior. These works illustrate how experimental economics can help flesh out economic theory by moving from lab to field, by changing the subject pool, or by changing the experimental context.

Kagel and Penta further emphasize the usefulness of Nagel's framework for understanding how people reason. This has helped scholars understand the importance of the initial response in a learning process and how to think about modeling the reasoning process in a way that can predict behavior across varying environments. Kagel and Penta explain the Endogenous Depth of Reasoning (EDR) model in some detail, a model that recognizes the fact that you should choose based upon how deeply you believe others will reason. This work finds that people do generally consider the beliefs of others when they reason.

Kagel and Penta also note that Nagel's theory has been applied to deliberation and has been examined by neuroscientists. A general finding is that deliberation time and level of thinking increase when the stakes of the decision are higher, though some exploration to the contrary indicates there is still more to learn. The medial prefrontal cortex area of the brain is associated with thinking about other people's thinking. The neuroscience work indicates that subjects who think deeper and have higher IQs experience more activity in this area of the brain when they are playing Nagel's beauty contest game, a sign that deeper thinking has a physiological component.

Fehr, E., Gächter, S., 2000. Cooperation and punishment in public goods experiments. *American Economic Review* 90, 980–994. *(Reviewed by Yan Chen)*

Fehr and Gächter (2000), hereafter FG, consider the question, "Will people incur a personal cost to punish others for non-cooperation, so cooperation is encouraged and free-riding discouraged?" To examine this question, FG conduct a public-good experiment with and without punishment. If subjects are purely selfish and believe the same to be true about others, then free-riding is the dominant strategy in this experiment. Adding punishment does not change matters because no purely selfish subject would pay the personal cost to punish, so that one would expect free-riding to never be punished.

In contrast to the pure self-interest prediction, FG find that human subjects are willing to incur personal costs to punish free-riders, with the punishment being greater when the level of cooperation is further from a cooperative norm. In the punishment condition, contribution rates are high, averaging 50–95% of endowments. Importantly, the FG experimental design precludes reputation building, so they show that the cooperation observed is not an effort to build reputation.

In her review, Yan Chen not only provides a detailed description of the experiment, but she also provides a background story of what motivated the design, obtained from her personal interviews with Fehr and Gächter. Chen emphasizes the innovative inclusion of the peer punishment stage of the experiment, which precludes reputation building.

By asking and answering a series of questions, Chen offers insights obtained from other research about why people may incur a personal cost to punish another and why cooperation develops, contrary to the pure self-interest prediction. One idea is that punishment is an emotional response to the injustice of free-riding. Another is that some people are "conditional cooperators," who will contribute more if they believe others will contribute more but will contribute less if they believe others will contribute less, who punish others because they are averse to disadvantageous inequality. Other research indicates that free-riders are as willing to punish others as conditional cooperators, so the precise motivation for punishing others does not yet seem to be fully understood. What is better understood because of the FG paper, and the many related studies it motivated, is that much more cooperation can occur than might be expected when people have the opportunity to punish others for non-cooperation.

Gneezy, U., Rustichini, A. (2000). A fine is a price. *The Journal of Legal Studies* 29(1), 1–17.
(Reviewed by Alex Imas)

Gneezy and Rustichini (2000), hereafter GR, ask the question, "Will the introduction of a penalty reduce the occurrence of the behavior subject to the penalty as predicted by the deterrence hypothesis?" To examine this question, GR introduce a fine in a field experiment for parents arriving late to pick up their children at school. Contradicting the deterrence hypothesis, GR found that the number of late-coming parents increased significantly in response to the fine. GR explain this paradox by recognizing that the fine serves as an additional provision to an incomplete contract. Prior to the fine, the consequence for late-coming had not been specified. After the fine was implemented, parents may have viewed it as the price that had to be paid for being late, and that price might have been low relative to the guilt or other non-monetary incentives associated with a social norm that might have been keeping the parents from being late. Critically, by the time the fine was removed, people had lost the habit of being timely as a matter of personal responsibility.

In his review, Alex Imas begins by highlighting the importance of the GR paper along with a companion work of theirs (Gneezy and Rustichini, 2000) entitled, "Pay enough or don't pay at all." The best work in behavioral economics, Imas says, "demonstrates how taking psychology seriously is important for thinking about the most basic of economic principles," like the idea that people respond to incentives. Together, these papers show that a fine may not discourage behavior as intended and that pay may not encourage behavior as expected because monetary payments can reduce intrinsic motivations to behave.

Imas proceeds to review other related work that offers a deeper understanding of why monetary payments may change intrinsic motivation. The introduction of pay may send a signal that the activity should not be fun or personally rewarding to pursue, and it may reduce or eliminate the prosocial signal that can be sent by doing the activity. Imas discusses the implications of the work of GR and others for business management, and he concludes by discussing the importance of the work for crafting incentives to accomplish almost any goal (e.g., school performance, weight loss, smoking cessation, regular health checkups, blood donations).

Andreoni, J., Miller, J., 2002. Giving according to GARP: An experimental test of the consistency of preferences for altruism. *Econometrica* 70(2), 737–753.
(Reviewed by Catherine Eckel)

Andreoni and Miller (2002), hereafter AM, consider the question, "Can concerns for altruism exhibited by human subjects in experiments be expressed as a well-behaved preference ordering?" If so, AM contend that altruism is rational as economists normally define rationality, and an economic model assuming fixed preferences and utility maximization can explain altruism. AM consider their question by giving human subjects the opportunity to share a surplus in an experiment, where the cost of sharing and the size of the surplus vary in different treatments. They then use the data and econometric methods to examine whether the revealed preferences fit a well-behaved utility function.

AM find that 98% of their subjects maximize utility for some set of preferences, but the maximization takes different forms. Twenty-five percent of subjects are pure, selfish money maximizers, who don't demonstrate altruism. The remaining 75% are not pure money maximizers but rather exhibit some degree of altruism.

In her review, Catherine Eckel begins by briefly reviewing the experimental design of AM, the results and overall contribution. Then, Eckel's review usefully discusses a variety of the methodological choices made by AM (subject pool, context, payment, and incentives), providing numerous insights into how such choices may impact experimental results. Eckel then reviews the replication and extension studies motivated by AM, providing insight about how the AM approach has facilitated an understanding of charitable giving, social preferences, gender differences, and more. Eckel's review and the AM paper clearly demonstrate the power of the experimental method to complement economic theory in the pursuit of understanding an interesting behavioral choice phenomenon.

Holt, C. A., Laury, S. K., 2002. **Risk aversion and incentive effects.** *American Economic Review* 92(5), 1644–1655. *(Reviewed by Kevin McCabe)*

Holt and Laury (2002), hereafter HL, consider the question, "To what extent does risk aversion exist, to what extent does it depend upon whether incentives are real or hypothetical, and to what extent does it depend upon the size of the stake?" To examine this question, they presented human subjects with a series of lottery choices that allow them to estimate the degree of risk aversion. They implement treatments with real and hypothetical incentives. They implement a low-stakes treatment and a high-stakes treatment. HL find that the average subject is risk averse. They find that behavior under hypothetical incentives is not dramatically different from behavior under real incentives when the stakes are low. However, they find behavior under real incentives does vary with the stakes. In particular, HL find people are considerably more risk averse when the stakes are higher. Overall, HL find that a utility function with increasing relative risk aversion but decreasing absolute risk aversion fits their experimental data relatively well.

Kevin McCabe reviews the HL paper by masterfully mapping it into the "microeconomic systems framework," which is a particular systematic way of explaining observed outcomes. By conceiving of the system in this way, one can methodically examine how changes in the state of the system.

McCabe identifies the HL environment as consisting of a set of lottery choices, a risk-averse decision-maker, and a procedure for playing lotteries that produces a monetary outcome. The institution designed by HL presents a sequence of ordered lottery choices to the decision-maker, and selects one of the decision-maker's chosen lotteries at random, to yield a monetary outcome as determined by the environment. McCabe describes the HL environment and institution in detail. He describes how HL use their data to obtain the HL results in a way that really helps the reader understand this important approach for measuring the degree to which an individual human subject is risk averse.

McCabe the proceeds to review much work inspired by the HL paper. In the process, he exposes the reader to a variety of experimental innovations. Is it possible to obtain results for high stakes without paying out high-stake dollar amounts to human subjects? How does a change in the framing of the lottery pairs change the results? What utility function form best fits the data? What explains the observed heterogeneity in risk preferences? What other methods can a researcher use to elicit risk preferences? McCabe presents research addressing these questions and more.

List, J. A., 2003. Does market experience eliminate market anomalies? *Quarterly Journal of Economics* 118(1), 41–71.
(Reviewed by Matthias Sutter)

List (2003) considers the question, "Does market experience eliminate the endowment effect?" He conducts two field experiments to examine the question, one examining the trading patterns of sports memorabilia and the other examining actual actions at a sports card show. The treatments distinguished very experienced dealers from relatively inexperienced customers. He also conducts some lab experiments that allow subjects to gain experience. He found a significant endowment effect overall. However, he also found that the extent of the endowment effect is inversely related to market experience, with the endowment effect being negligible for the very experienced dealers.

In his review, Matthias Sutter emphasizes both the theoretical and methodological importance of List's paper. On theory, Sutter writes, "Rather than asking whether anomalies and biases in human behavior would require new theories about how markets work, he (List) examines whether markets themselves correct anomalies." On methodology, Sutter notes List's use of two different field settings along with a lab study as an exemplary illustration of how field experiments and lab experiments can complement each other. Sutter emphasizes the importance of research like this for policymakers. Behavioral anomalies often have policy implications, but they are usually complex. Their existence and impacts are often context dependent. Research that varies the context and method of analysis will allow the crafting of better policy by providing a better understanding of how individual behavior maps onto socioeconomic outcomes.

Charness, G., Dufwenberg, M., 2006. Promises and partnership. *Econometrica* 74(6), 1579–1601.
(Reviewed by Urs Fischbacher and Franziska Föllmi-Heusi)

Charness and Dufwenberg (2006), hereafter CD, consider the question, "Will guilt aversion motivate people to keep promises unbacked by material incentives, so that promises and guilt aversion effectively support trust and cooperation?" To examine this question, CD design an experiment where the development of a trusting (one-shot) partnership between two players can develop and yield mutual benefit. However, the first mover has no material reason to trust the second mover. Communication can occur, but it is cheap talk, meaning there is no potential enforcement of any kind. CD do not restrict the form of the messages (apart from anonymity concerns) because they want to see what messages endogenously arise. Their design also measures beliefs, which makes it possible for CD to test whether the desire to meet the expectation of the other (and avert the guilt of not doing so) is motivating trust if it occurs.

CD find players often submit messages they can categorize as promises, and messages of this form increase trust and cooperation. Their experimental evidence suggests that the reason a promise has impact is that it increases the belief in the receiver that the sender will cooperate, increasing the guilt the receiver will experience if he or she does not cooperate.

In their review, Urs Fischbacher and Franziska Föllmi-Heusi, hereafter FFH, provide an exemplary description of CD's experimental framework. In the process, they identify the crucial features of the experiment, explaining why they are either particularly novel or particularly useful. How should you allow an experimental subject to communicate? Why introduce a random component for a second mover in a trust game? How can you effectively elicit first and second order beliefs from subjects playing a game in which the first and second order beliefs matter? FFH provide detailed discussions of CD's experimental framework that provide answers to these questions.

FFH relate the results found by CD to the results of other researchers, providing the reader with a good exposure to related work on promises and social preferences, more generally. FFH note the uniqueness of the CD paper for introducing guilt aversion as a motivator, but also they usefully discuss other ideas scholars have explored, regarding how communication impacts choice behaviors. FFH regard the CD paper as especially influential because it "set the stage for the study of promises," though they also tout the paper as exemplary for its creative experimental design, which allows CD to rule out many possible explanations for the observed cooperative behavior and find support for guilt aversion.

Falk, A., Kosfeld, M., 2006. The hidden costs of control. *American Economic Review* 96(5), 1611–1630.
(Reviewed by Rachel Croson and Laura Razzolini)

Falk and Kosfeld (2006), hereafter FK, consider the question, "Is there a hidden cost to a principal of place a control on an agent that precludes the most opportunistic choices the agent can make?" To consider this, FK design an experiment where the agent chooses the level of a productive effort that is costly to the agent but that increases the principal's payoff. Different treatments allow the principal to set a minimum level of effort for the agent. When principals cannot set the minimum level of effort high, FK find that agent subjects put forth more effort on average when principals set the minimum effort level lower or do not implement any restriction. Verbal feedback from agents indicates that the reason agents provide more effort than pure self-interest predicts is that they view less restriction as a signal of trust, and with positive reciprocity agents respond to this kindness with greater effort. The hidden cost of control, then, is the loss of effort that occurs when control signals distrust and the agent replaces positive reciprocity with negative reciprocity.

In their review, Razzolini and Croson begin by noting the importance of the FK paper in terms of explaining why many contracts (e.g., a marriage contract without a prenuptial agreement) are left incomplete: Making a contract more complete signals distrust, which has negative consequences. We might expect such negative consequences in close personal relationships, but FK show that control can produce negative consequences in an abstract setting where the principal and agent have no pre-existing relationship.

Razzolini and Croson provide an excellent summary of the FK experiment, and focus on the robustness checks FK perform to identify, more carefully, why there is a cost to control. FK run a direct response treatment to see whether their use of the strategy method was causing the results. FK run a treatment where the experimenter abstractly sets the control on the agent, rather than another human subject principal, to confirm that the agents were responding to the intention of the principals rather than to the control itself. FK run a treatment where the opportunity to control is imbedded in an employer-employee gift exchange environment, to confirm the result would arise in a richer environment.

Razzolini and Croson conclude by suggesting an interesting possible extension: to examine what will happen if principal and agent subjects have the opportunity to choose whether to enter or exit a relationship. Provocatively, they ask, "Would you want to work for a firm that locked up its printers?" Or, "Would you want to marry someone who insisted upon a prenuptial agreement?"

Niederle, M., Vesterlund, L., 2007. Do women shy away from competition? Do men compete too much? *Quarterly Journal of Economics* 122(3), 1067–1101.
(Reviewed by Alvin E. Roth and Katie B. Coffman)

Niederle and Vesterlund (2007), hereafter NV, consider the question, "Do men and women of the same ability differ in their selection into a competitive environment?" They construct a real effort experiment (add five two-digit numbers) to examine this question, where men and women play a non-competitive, piece-rate version of the game and a competitive tournament play version. Because their primary interest is in preferences for competition, they seek an experimental design that eliminates other factors that may cause women to be under-represented in competitive jobs (e.g., discrimination, investment in human capital, innate skills, signaling). They find no gender difference in performance under either compensation scheme, but they find that twice as many men as women select the tournament in the next step of the experiment. Considering different alternatives, they arrive at gender differences in overconfidence in own ability as being the primary explanation: Men are substantially more overconfident than women.

In their review, Coffman and Roth review the experiment in some detail. For example, they significantly note NV intentionally conducted sessions in groups of four with two men and two women, never giving any indication that gender was of interest, to reduce experimenter demand concerns. Coffman and Roth focus on the innovative experiment design efforts NV go to in order to control for factors than might influence the results other than competition preferences.

Coffman and Roth then describe the significant subsequent research motivated by NV's study, including replications and field studies. Since 2007, differences in preferences to compete have explained differences in career choices and differences in earnings. In terms of policies designed to close gaps between men and women, this study from NV has motivated much work on institutional design, yielding suggestions like providing more feedback to exceptionally talented women so they know they are more able to compete, or framing job positions as being more cooperative than competitive. Coffman and Roth provide an extensive review of related work on gender differences. They conclude by emphasizing the quality of the NV paper, noting its importance in demonstrating the power of the experimental method for isolating cause and effect and for motivating further research, with significant policy implications.

Chen, Y., Li, S. X., 2009. Group identity and social preferences. *American Economic Review* 99(1), 431–457.
(Reviewed by Marie Claire Villeval)

Chen and Li (2009), hereafter CL, consider the question, "How does group identity affect social preferences and social welfare?" Their experiment induces a group identity in subjects. They compare different ways of inducing group identities to examine how the method of assignment affects social preferences. They use a wide class of games to examine the effects of identity on different types of social preferences. They find categorization alone is sufficient to create group effects. Group problem-solving increases attachment to groups, but does not change decision behavior. More charity and less envy occurs with an in-group match. An in-group match is more likely to be rewarded for good behavior and less likely punished for bad behavior. In-group matching enhances efficiency compared to out-group matching.

In her review, Marie Claire Villeval notes that the work of CL, where subjects are motivated with incentives, provides a robustness check on much of the group identity work that has been done by psychologists, who do not normally incentivize their subjects. CL obtain results consistent with those of psychologists, but they provide a refined understanding. Villeval labels "exemplary" the sequential experimental design CL use, which includes a variety of different games, something instructors can readily use to show students how to identify "the mechanisms triggering the phenomenon under study."

Villeval highlights the CL finding that extra efforts to induce group identity did not generate different behavior from random assignment to groups.

This makes life simpler for those wanting to experiment with group identity, and it reduces the possibility that the extra effort to induce identity introduces a confound. In terms of policy, Villeval highlights a positive and a negative: (1) It may be efficiency-enhancing for an organization to highlight a common culture, but (2) if you want to promote diversity, it might be better not to make a group identity too salient.

Fischbacher, U., Föllmi-Heusi, F., 2013. Lies in disguise— An experimental study on cheating. *Journal of the European Economic Association* 11(3), 525–547. *(Reviewed by Uri Gneezy and Marta Serra-Garcia)*

Fischbacher and Follmi-Heusi (2013), hereafter FFH, ask the question, "Why do people not lie when it is in their material self-interest to do so?" To examine this question, FFH design a novel experiment where subjects roll a die and report the observed number. Neither the experiment administrator nor any other subject is able to observe the die roll, so the subject can easily lie without anyone knowing. However, the degree of lying can be measured by examining how the reported distribution of outcomes compares to that which is expected when one rolls a fair die. FFH use different treatment conditions to examine the effects of different conditions on lying behavior.

FFH find one consistent result regardless of the stakes, consequences, or degree of anonymity: Some subjects lie, some are honest, and some partially lie. FFH conclude that a model of lying aversion, where we assume people trade off the utility obtained from the material gain of lying against the disutility of feeling bad about lying, can explain the behavior of lying and honest subjects. However, partial lying is hard to explain with lying aversion. FFH favor the explanation that people lie partially to disguise their lying in order to maintain a favorable self-image.

In their review, Uri Gneezy and Marta Serra-Garcia, hereafter GSG, emphasize how important the FFH experimental design has become, in such a short time, for examining cheating and lying. The FFH paper is the most recent publication among the top 20 chosen for this book, yet GSG report that there have already been 90 papers published using the FFH method, with over 44,000 human subjects participating. GSG note that the FFH method is useful because it rules out possible retaliation or loss of reputation as reasons for not lying.

GSG review the robustness check treatments FFH perform. They note that the double blind procedure of FFH resulted in no significant difference in behavior from the FFH procedure that was only single blind. However, GSG also report the results of a more recent "mind game," which is meant to address the possibility that the subject might think a researcher using the FFH method could secretly observe the lying. GSG report that cheating in the mind game is higher than in the FFH game and more sensitive to the stakes.

GSG provide further interesting examples of how others have used the FFH framework. Scholars have found evidence that people favor intermediate level lies over small and large lies, indicating there may be a sweet spot for which the benefit of lying is worth the psychological cost. Partial lying increases when no one can observe the lying and when the probability of the highest outcome is lower. Scholars who have used the FFH framework have found the rate of lying can change if the physical environment changes (at home versus the lab) or if the subjects are primed in advance (in a way that might induce a particular culture). Scholars have examined whether the willingness to lie varies by country and how changes in context impact the willingness of men to lie versus women. Scholars have also demonstrated that we can use the FFH lie game to identify who will be more likely to lie, cheat, commit fraud or exhibit other misbehaviors at work, in school, or in the community.

GSG conclude by noting that the FFH paper, like Güth et al. (1982) and Berg et al. (1995), was not published in a "top-5 journal" but, nonetheless, turned out to be a seminal paper that motivated much additional research. GSG use these papers to question the review process. They make the point that papers are regularly rejected at top journals for incompleteness or specific issues, but GSG claim the "usefulness" of the paper (for example for motivating additional research) is perhaps not given enough weight in the review process. Rather than rejecting a paper for not answering all the possible questions, perhaps reviews should give more credit to papers like the FFH paper – ones that raise many interesting questions while answering a few.

We echo these sentiments.

References

Berg, J., Dickhaut, J., McCabe, K., 1995. Trust, reciprocity, and social history. *Games and Economic Behavior* 10(1), 122–142.

Gneezy, U., Rustichini, A., 2000. Pay enough or don't pay at all. *The Quarterly Journal of Economics* 115(3), 791–810.

Güth, W., Schmittberger, R., Schwarze, B., 1982. An experimental analysis of ultimatum bargaining. *Journal of Economic Behavior and Organization* 3(4), 367–388.

Plott, C.R., Sunder, S., 1982. Efficiency of experimental securities markets with insider information: An application of rational expectations models. *Journal of Political Economy* 90, 663–698.

Smith, A. 1759, 1853., *The Theory of Moral Sentiments*. Second Edition. London: Henry G. Bohm.

2

AN EXPERIMENTAL STUDY OF COMPETITIVE MARKET BEHAVIOR (BY VERNON L. SMITH)

Charles A. Holt

The double auction

Vernon Lomax Smith began his economics career as a graduate student at Harvard, where he was first exposed to an economics market experiment run in Chamberlin's class. The students in the class were given buyer or seller roles and corresponding cards with private dollar values or costs that differed from person to person. Trading was generally sequential and decentralized, and the observed transactions quantities tended to be above competitive (supply/demand) predictions. Chamberlin developed an explanation for the higher-than-predicted quantities based on simulations of decentralized structure done by shuffling the deck and dealing small clusters of value and cost cards and calculating the predicted trades for each subgroup. Such simulations would sometimes permit relatively high-cost sellers to sell to high-value buyers (and the reverse), which resulted in price dispersion that elevated transactions quantities above what would be expected in what he termed a "perfect market." His paper ends with a challenge:

> [A]n objection may be made ... that 'no one would have ever thought that if a market were broken up into a series of individual pairs of buyers and sellers, and dealings run through a series of successive contracts through time, there would be any tendency toward the market-clearing price of a perfect market.' But is this not precisely what *has* been thought? It cannot be overstressed that all *actual* markets are, *in fact*, a succession of contracts separated in time .... Perhaps it is the perfect market which is 'strange'; at any rate, the nature of discrepancies between it and reality deserve study.
>
> *(Chamberlin, 1948, p. 108)*

DOI: 10.4324/9781003019121-2

After Smith starting teaching at Purdue, he began running market experiments in class that incorporated three innovations listed in Smith (1962):
market centralization, repetition, and changing structural conditions. He
noted that elements of centralization were prominent in bond, stock, and
commodity markets in which traders can see the standing bid and ask prices
and a ticker tape record of price sequences as they occur. The resulting "oral
double auction" was characterized by sellers undercutting each other's price
offers, with buyers raising other buyers' bids at the same time in a second
auction process. Instead of undercutting an offer or raising a bid, a trader
on either side could accept a bid or offer from the other side, after which
the double auction would resume. Repetition in a series of trading periods
with identical supply and demand conditions permits learning and adjustment that provides an appropriate setting for evaluation of equilibrium theories. Unlike Chamberlin, Smith introduced changes in market conditions
that shifted supply and demand in order to evaluate convergence to new
equilibria. These procedural innovations played a pivotal role in shaping
subsequent work on market experiments. I would also stress that he looked
beyond convergence issues to consider market *efficiency*:

> Indeed, the ability of these experimental markets to ration out
> sub-marginal buyers and sellers will be one measure of the effective-
> ness or competitive market performance of the market.
>
> *(Smith, 1962, p. 114)*

My personal take on the impact of his initial experiment is shaped by my
having to memorize the "five assumptions of perfect competition" when I
took my first economics course in 1967. These assumptions included perfect
information about market conditions and an "infinity" of buyers and sellers. Smith's seminal class experiment violated *all* of the standard perfectness
assumptions, which made the general convergence to a standard predicted
outcome all the more dramatic and important. Smith began by using a cost
and value configuration that was symmetric around the intersection, as
shown in Figure 2.1, a replica of Figure 1 in Smith (1962). Contract prices
are shown on the right side in sequence, with new trading periods separated
by vertical lines. With repeated trading under unchanging structural conditions, Smith observed that prices tended to converge to competitive price
levels. Notice that price variation declines in successive trading periods.

Next Smith implemented variations in supply and demand structures,
and he observed that convergence to the competitive price was generally
not affected by the shapes of supply and demand arrays, although the price
paths toward equilibrium could be strongly influenced by these shapes. The
structure in Figure 2.1 has equal buyer and seller "rents" (surpluses) at the
competitive equilibrium price, as shown by the shaded areas. In contrast,
one extreme case was considered with a flat supply function (sellers had
identical costs up to capacity). In this asymmetric design, the price tended

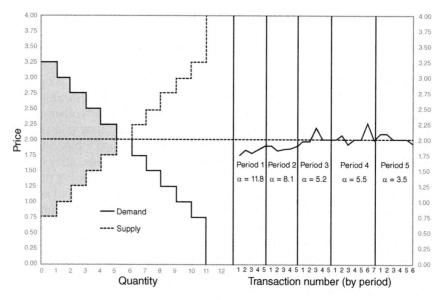

FIGURE 2.1 Symmetric value and cost arrays and contract price sequence (Smith, 1962).

Note: The "α" price variability measures listed for each period are ratios of standard deviation around the theoretical prediction of $2.00, expressed as a percentage of that price.

to stay a little above costs where demand crossed the flat supply function, even after a reduction in demand that increased excess supply at supra-competitive prices. Note that a flat supply function provides sellers with zero rent in equilibrium. This observed deviation from predictions triggered an important methodological conjecture:

> The subjects have shown high motivation to do their best even without monetary payoffs. But our experimental marginal buyers and sellers may be more reluctant to approach their reservations than their counterparts in real markets.
>
> *(Smith, 1962, p. 121)*

This conjecture was later confirmed through a subsequent experiment with financial incentives done with the same market structure (Smith, 1962, footnote 9). The paper is loaded with other thoughtful observations that come from being able to "look inside the box" at individual behavior under stress-test conditions. For example, the extended discussion of price convergence highlights the importance of imbalances in buyer and seller rents, which had a more notable effect on price paths than Walrasian imbalances of demand and supply at current prices.

In total, Smith (1962) provided ten distinct market structures in this seminal paper, each designed to extend or qualify the implications of a prior structure. The general result involved convergence to equilibrium with reductions in variability over time, with the notable exception of "Chart 8," which implemented a change in the market *institution*. In that case, sellers were free to make and undercut others' price offers, as in the double auction, but buyers were not able to call out bids; they could only accept a seller's offer or wait. This resulted in sellers competing with each other, which produced below-equilibrium prices after the initial period. This institutional variation foreshadows much of the subsequent half century of market experimentation with alternative *trading institutions*, beginning with a follow-up experiment that will be considered next.

"Effect of market organization on competitive equilibrium" (Smith, 1964)

When I first began refereeing, many experimental papers were sent to me because the word "auction" in the title reminded editors of my prior work on auction theory. I was immediately struck by the almost exclusive focus on comparisons of different sets of trading rules that distinguish market institutions. I remember noticing the absence of a consideration of the structural elements that were the focus of graduate industrial organization courses at that time, i.e., concentration, capacity constraints, market definition, market power, and potential entry. Only after I started to run experiments myself did I come to realize the sensitivity of market outcomes to the nature of the trading institutions. From a practical perspective, institutional issues come up immediately when one sets up an experiment and begins to craft instructions that mediate subjects' actions. From a policy perspective, institutional design (today we say "mechanism design") is of primary importance to policy makers who need to select the structure of a spectrum or emissions permit auction or a matching market for medical residents or other professionals (Holt and Roth, 2004). Experiments have, at times, been instrumental in guiding such decisions (Holt, 2019, Chapters 21, 28–30). Smith (1964) provided a template for controlled comparisons of alternative market institutions, and, in the process, he developed and refined key aspects of the experimental economics methodology for holding key structural and procedural elements fixed while changing the market institution.

The Smith (1964) experiment was an extension and elaboration of a variation used in the previous paper in which buyers in a double auction were forced into a passive role and were not able to submit bids. In addition to the passive buyer treatment, there was also a reversed setup in which buyers could submit bids in a double auction format, but sellers were passive and not able to post offer prices. Finally, there was a normal double auction with active buyers and sellers that served as a baseline. After discussing the inadequacy of basing hypotheses and analysis on "a posteriori testing and theorizing" in the same experiment, Smith noted that the results of the prior experiment suggest that prices (after the initial period) should be below double auction levels when only sellers can submit offers, and conversely, he conjectured that prices should be above double auction levels when only buyers can submit bids.

Based on prior observations in Smith (1962) that the relative sizes of buyer and seller rents could affect the direction of convergence, this follow-up experiment used the symmetric supply and demand structure analogous to the one in Figure 2.1, with equal buyer and seller surplus rents. This symmetric structure was held constant across trading institution treatment variations. This second paper represents a systematic analysis of a carefully constructed set of treatments with a series of repeated market sequences using different groups of inexperienced human subjects. Smith was careful to find participants in different sections of the same course, which ensured that all subjects would have no prior experience and to generate multiple independent observations of the same phenomena. Subjects were paid in cash, and earnings ($6.50 for 40 minutes in 1963) were comparable to standard payments used today, after adjusting for price increases. The care that went into devising the procedures and written instructions to be read aloud (included in the appendix) established a practice that has since become standard. Finally, there was no debriefing of subjects until after the study was complete. The two papers served different purposes, and it is interesting that Smith (1964) even refers back to the results of the earlier paper as consisting of "pilot experiments."

With multiple independent observations, the second paper pioneered the type of nonparametric data analysis that has come to dominate the experimental economics literature. Smith was influenced by Sidney Siegel's seminal 1956 book, *Nonparametric Statistics for the Behavioral Sciences,* which promoted the use of nonparametric methods for behavioral experiments with sample sizes that are too small for standard large-sample techniques like t tests.[1] One of the tests that Smith used is the Jonckheere test for an ordered alternative hypothesis. This test is natural when treatments differ in terms of intensity, e.g., increasing payoff scales, numbers of competitors, etc. In Smith's case, the predicted order was that prices with sequential seller offers would be below those in a double auction with buyer bids and seller offers, which would be below those with only buyer bids.

The symmetric supply and demand arrays involved buyers and sellers who each had a single unit, so each step in the supply or demand array corresponded to a single buyer or seller. Each group of subjects interacted in five market periods, with no changes from period to period. Each treatment trading sequence was done once with 14 buyers and 14 sellers, and a second time with only 10 buyers and 10 sellers. The markets run with the smaller group had the same equilibrium prediction, since the costs and values that were removed were to the right of the demand-supply intersection. Therefore, in total, there were two (group-size) variations for each of the three trading treatments (seller offers, double auction, and buyer bids), for a total of six separate groups of subjects. With five rounds of trading for each subject group, and about seven units traded in each round, there were hundreds of individual transactions prices. Some of the tests that Smith reports used all of these prices, but today we would be concerned that individual transactions prices for the same group of subjects would not be independent observations and, therefore, an analysis today would be based on average prices for each group. These price averages for the final two trading periods are shown in Table 2.1, where the three columns are the treatments for the different trading institutions, and the two rows correspond to the two groups of subjects (two class sections) in each treatment. The three groups used to generate the averages in the top row had 20 subjects per group, and the three groups in the bottom row had 28 subjects per group. As noted previously, with only 20 subjects, the supply and demand functions were truncated to the right of the equilibrium. This truncation of extra-marginal units that should not trade would have no effect on equilibrium predictions, but of course, there could be behavioral effects.

Although individual contract prices within a five-period market for each group would not be independent observations, the group-level averages in Table 2.1 would be. The Jonckheere test statistic is based on the number of times each price average observation in Table 2.1 is less than a price average to its right. The resulting "binary win count" is 11, which turns out to be significant at $p = 0.05$.[2] Since ordered treatment intensities are common in experimental economics, the Jonckheere test that Smith used in his seminal 1964 paper has wide applicability. Even so, it tends to be under-utilized even today, as compared with workhorse Mann-Whitney tests for unordered treatment effects.[3]

An early active literature developed around extensions of this basic institutional comparison procedure with double auctions (Davis and Holt, 1993, Chapter 3). One strand continued the discussion of markets in which only sellers can submit prices, but with prices posted on a *take-it-or-leave-it basis*, which were called *posted-offer auctions*. While sellers can post prices in this manner without buyer bid responses, as in retail markets, a seller with multiple capacity units might exercise *market power* by raising the price and selling fewer units. Such unilateral price increases could be profitable if the

TABLE 2.1 Average contract price in trading periods 4 and 5 by subject group and trading condition (Smith, 1964)

Group size	Seller offers average	Double auction average	Buyer bids average
20 per group	208	213	217
28 per group	195	209	213
Treatment average	202	211	215

remaining units are sold at a higher price and the foregone sales involved relatively high costs that are close to the competitive equilibrium price. Davis and Holt (1994) document the dramatic effects of creating or destroying this type of market power by mergers or dissolutions in posted-price auctions, and subsequent market power experiments are discussed in Holt (2019, Chapter 21). In contrast, it is surprisingly difficult for sellers with market power to exercise this power in double auctions with active buyer bids (Holt, Langan, and Villamil, 1986),[4] Motivated by the turn-of-century California energy crisis, Rassenti, Smith, and Wilson (2001) consider the effects of deregulating electric utility pricing in an environment with seller market power in which buyers are not permitted to partially withhold purchases when prices spike. The policy implications of this experimental study are summarized in the provocative title: "Turning off the lights: Consumer allowed service interruptions could control market power and decrease prices."

Unhinged outcomes in asset markets

The Nobel committee summary of these early papers notes that "Smith found, much to his surprise, that the prices obtained in the laboratory were very close to their theoretical values, even though subjects lacked the information necessary to calculate the equilibrium price."[5] Importantly, Smith's analysis of the infrequent inclusion of extra-marginal units (with high costs or low values) was the basis for concluding that these markets were remarkably efficient, *even in the presence of small numbers of traders with only private information*. Moreover, the methodological advances (careful specification of market trading rules, meticulously written instructions to be read aloud, use of salient monetary incentives, careful recruiting and delayed debriefing, and the nonparametric analysis of small data sets) set standards for subsequent work that persist even today. Smith richly deserved the Nobel committee's recognition "for having established laboratory experiments as a tool in empirical economic analysis, especially in the study of alternative market mechanisms."[6]

It is useful to interpret the markets in Smith's early papers as pertaining to a good that is produced and consumed immediately at the end of each trading period, i.e., a consumer nondurable. In contrast, many commodities and securities are durable in the sense that they can be resold, e.g., housing or shares of a stock. Smith also pioneered the experimental study of such asset markets, and again there was a surprise, *but it went in the other direction*. Instead of finding that asset markets are surprisingly efficient and aligned with theoretical predictions, Smith observed prices that deviated sharply from fundamental values. Without a baseline, subsequent research consisted of efforts to find conditions that diminish such "unhinged" outcomes.

In its simplest sense, the fundamental value of an asset can be described as the present value of the services or dividends that it provides.

For example, an asset that pays dividends of D dollars and the end of each period in perpetuity would have a present value of D/r, where r is an interest rate representing the opportunity cost of cash that is used to "discount" future payoffs. It is well known that ordinary people tend to have trouble appreciating the power of compound interest over long time horizons, so Smith and his co-authors decided to run short finite-horizon asset markets without any interest rate elements (Smith, Suchanek, and Williams, 1988). The "shares" traded in this experiment would pay a dividend of D after each period, until the experiment ended after period 15, at which point the asset share was worthless. Subjects were endowed with a number of shares and some cash, and these accounts would increase or decrease as a result of trades at prices determined by a double auction run at the beginning of each period. A share that was not bought or sold but was simply held for 15 periods would yield $15D$ in earnings. More to the point, the fundamental value of a share would be D at the beginning of period 15 with one period remaining. Similarly, the value would be $2D$ with two periods remaining, and $15D$ at the start of the initial period, which generates a linearly declining fundamental value.

The initial finite-horizon experiment was intentionally designed to be transparent so as to provide a clear theoretical prediction, with the expectation that prices would track the declining fundamental value and provide a "baseline" from which to investigate factors that might cause deviations from theoretical predictions (Smith and Gjerstad, 2014, p. 22). Instead, prices in many of these laboratory asset markets spiked above the declining value line, generating bubbles that were typically followed by sharp declines. This bubble phenomenon persisted regardless of whether participants were students or professionals, whether dividends were fixed or random, and whether the theoretical predictions were explicitly explained to the subjects.[7] There have been many subsequent experimental studies of asset pricing, and it has been found that the strongest driver behind bubble formation is the presence of the "excess cash" (Caginalp, Porter, and Smith, 2001) that results from cash endowments, incomes, or margin purchases.[8] What often happens is that, as share prices start to rise, momentum traders anticipate further rises, which creates a "positive feedback loop" in which price increases trigger speculation that trigger further speculation, and excess cash permits trading at high prices to continue.[9] When the process slows and prices stop rising, the high prices based on anticipated capital gains cannot be sustained, and a crash follows, which is increasingly likely as the final period approaches. In "boom" periods of increasing prices, elicited price predictions reveal that many subjects extrapolate past increases in an adaptive process.[10] There are, of course, asset market experiments in which bubbles are not observed, but a close examination of those usually reveals a mechanism that drains cash, e.g., if all cash savings are automatically "consumed" and transformed into take-home pay at the end of each period. Taken together, the "good" experimental results in markets for consumer nondurables and the "sometimes ugly" results for asset markets provide much of the basis for our current understanding of market mechanisms.

Notes

1 Siegel was also a pioneer in the use of financial incentives for laboratory tests of economic behavior. For example, he demonstrated that irrational "probability matching" behavior is sharply reduced when small monetary incentives are used (see Figure 7.1 in Holt, 2019).
2 The 208 in the left column is less than all four averages to its right, so the count for it is 4. The 195 is also less than all four numbers to its right. The 213 in the middle column is only less than one number to its right since there is one tie, and the 209 is less than both numbers to its right, so the test statistic is $J = 4 + 4 + 1 + 2 = 11$. With three groups of two observations, the critical value for the Jonckheere test is 11 for $p = 0.05$ (see Table 13.4 in Holt, 2019).
3 Note that Mann-Whitney tests used to evaluate differences between adjacent treatment columns would not work with only four observations. Moreover, the use of multiple tests is not a good practice when a unified test is available.
4 Prices increases above the competitive price prediction were only observed for about half of the subject groups. Another line of inquiry involved seller-only conspiracies to raise prices, e.g., Isaac and Plott (1981).
5 www.nobelprize.org/prizes/economic-sciences/2002/popular-information/
6 www.nobelprize.org/prizes/economic-sciences/2002/popular-information/
7 For a more nuanced survey of these and other results, see Palan (2013) and Section 2.4 of Smith and Gjerstad (2014).
8 The effects of purchasing on margin are considered in King, Smith, and Van Boening (1993); Füllbrunn and Neugebauer (2013); and Coppock, Harper, and Holt (2021).
9 Smith and Gjerstad (2014) take the lessons learned from these experiments and apply them to macroeconomic cycles driven by bubbles and crashes in housing prices. They document how a sharp decline in housing prices generates disruptions in mortgage payments and associated stress on the balance sheets of households and banks. The result is extreme precautionary behavior and deleveraging that tends to nullify the effects of traditional monetary and fiscal stimulus policies.
10 See the "extrapolative" forecasting rules estimated in Haruvy, Lahav, and Noussair (2007) or the "double adaptive" forecasting rule estimated in Holt, Porzio, and Song (2017) and Coppock, Harper, and Holt (2021).

References

Caginalp, G., Porter, D., Smith, V.L., 2001. Financial bubbles: Excess cash, momentum, and incomplete information. *Journal of Psychology and Financial Markets* 2, 80–99.

Chamberlin, E.H. 1948. An experimental imperfect market. *Journal of Political Economy* 56, 95–108.

Coppock, L.A., Harper, D.Q., Holt, C.A., 2021. Capital constraints and asset bubbles: An experimental study. *Journal of Economic Behavior & Organization* 183, 75–88.

Davis, D.D., Holt, C.A., 1993. *Experimental Economics*. Princeton, NJ: Princeton University Press.

Davis, D.D., Holt, C.A., 1994. Market power and mergers in markets with posted prices. *RAND Journal of Economics* 25, 467–487.

Füllbrunn, S., Neugebauer, T., 2013. Deflating bubbles in experimental asset markets: Comparative statics of margin regulations. *Financial Management* 38, 603–630.

Haruvy, E., Lahav, Y., Noussair, C.N., 2007. Traders' expectations in asset markets: experimental evidence. *American Economic Review* 97, 1901–1920.

Holt, C.A., 2019. *Markets, Games and Strategic Behavior: A First Course in Experimental Economics*. Princeton, NJ: Princeton University Press.

Holt, C.A., Langan, L., Anne Villamil, A., 1986. Market power in oral double auctions. *Economic Inquiry* 24, 107–123.

Holt, C.A., Porzio, M., Song, M.Y., 2017. Price bubbles, gender, and expectations in experimental asset markets. *European Economic Review* 100, 72–94.

Holt, C.A., Roth, A.E., 2004. The Nash equilibrium: A perspective. *Proceedings of the National Academy of Sciences USA* 101(12), 3999–4002.

Isaac, R.M., Plott, C.R., 1981. The opportunity for conspiracy in restraint of trade. *Journal of Economic Behavior and Organization* 2, 1–30.

King, R., Smith, V.L., Van Boening, M., 1993. The robustness of bubbles and crashes in experimental stock markets. In: Prigogine, I., Pay, R., Chen, P. (Eds.). *Nonlinear Dynamics and Evolutionary Economics*. Oxford: Oxford University Press, 186–200.

Nobel Prize in Economic Sciences 2002 Popular Information. www.nobelprize.org/prizes/economic-sciences/2002/popular-information/ (accessed October 2020).

Palan, S., 2013. A review of bubbles and crashes in experimental asset markets. *Journal of Economic Surveys* 27, 570–588.

Rassenti, S.J., Smith, V.L., Wilson, B.J., 2001. Turning off the lights: Consumer allowed service interruptions could control market power and decrease prices. *Regulation* 24(3), 70–76.

Siegel, S., 1956. *Nonparametric Statistics for the Behavioral Sciences*. New York: McGraw-Hill.

Smith, V.L., 1962. An experimental study of competitive market behavior. *Journal of Political Economy* 70, 111–137.

Smith, V.L., 1964. The effect of market organization on competitive equilibrium. *Quarterly Journal of Economics* 78, 181–201.

Smith, V.L., Gjerstad, S.D., 2014. *Rethinking Housing Bubbles: The Role of Household and Bank Balance Sheets in Modeling Economic Cycles*. New York, NY: Cambridge University Press.

Smith, V.L., Suchanek, G.L., Williams, A.W., 1988. Bubbles, crashes, and endogenous expectations in experimental spot asset markets. *Econometrica* 56(5), 1119–1151.

3

THE STRATEGY METHOD AS AN INSTRUMENT FOR THE EXPLORATION OF LIMITED RATIONALITY IN OLIGOPOLY GAME BEHAVIOR (STRATEGIEMETHODE ZUR ERFORSCHUNG DES EINGESCHRÄNKT RATIONALEN VERHALTENS IM RAHMEN EINES OLIGOPOLEXPERIMENTES) (BY REINHARD SELTEN)

Claudia Keser and Hartmut Kliemt

The setting

In the late 1950s and early 1960s, Heinz Sauermann and Reinhard Selten conducted a series of experiments to explore boundedly rational decision-making in strategic management games. The results of these applications of experimental methods to oligopoly situations were edited and published by Sauermann and Selten in 1967 as the first volume of *Contributions to Experimental Economics* (CEE) under the German title "Beiträge zur Experimentellen Wirtschaftsforschung."

While Hoggatt (1959), Fouraker and Siegel (1963), Friedman (1963), and Sauermann and Selten (1967b, Chapter 2 in CEE) mainly sought to test generalizations of existing quantity- and price-variation models, Reinhard Selten wanted to go beyond testing such established models (Sauermann and Selten 1967a, Chapter 1 in CEE).

Due to his preceding autodidactic studies in psychology, Selten was weary of testing "as-if" theories of interactive decision making without specifying hypotheses concerning the factual decision processes leading to the observed choices. To gain insights into the cognitive structure of human economic decision-making, Sauermann and Selten (1967b, Chapter 2 in CEE) and Selten (1967a, b, Chapters 3, 4 in CEE) introduced the so-called protocol method. In an analogy to "thinking-aloud" studies, they induced

DOI: 10.4324/9781003019121-3

participants to self-report their deliberations when planning choices in an experimental interaction. In this way, beyond just singling out the planned actions, information concerning the reasons for planning on one action rather than another one could be gathered.

As an initial attempt to go beyond the revealed preference approach of neoclassical economics, the protocol method does not merely infer preferences from empirically observed choice data by ascribing some form of substantive rationality to the choice makers. It considers the decision process from the internal point of view of the decision-maker herself. In other words, it goes beyond considering only pairs of conditions (information sets) and behavioral choices (moves) resulting from deliberative mental processes.

Since the protocols were not sufficient enough to account for quantitative aspects of decision making, in a follow-up study, Selten (1967c, Chapter 5 in CEE) introduced a novel experimental technique he referred to as the "strategy method" (strategiemethode). Since in realistically complex games eliciting individual plans of moves (in the game-theoretic sense) on the basis of an explicit consideration of all information sets would transcend the cognitive capacities of real decision-makers, Selten restricted the multiplicity of possible strategies to alternatives that are actually perceived and deemed relevant by the decision-makers themselves.[1]

Selten's strategy method

The strategy method abstracts much of the qualitative information captured by the protocol method. Rather than inducing participants to list moves in an "information-set-by-information-set" manner, participants are asked to develop a flow chart that procedurally represents their plan of future play based on their past experience with playing the game. The flow chart of the strategy method is procedurally complete in that it provides the planning strategist decision criteria for all contingencies that might arise in any play of the game but does not necessarily list all contingencies in an explicit way.[2]

In the original paper discussed here, Selten's use of flow charts as representations of plans suited his purposes well. Yet, it must not be interpreted as him thinking in terms of committing to a strategy. As the inventor of the concept of subgame perfectness, who put Schelling's (1960) insights into the central role of commitment power in strategic interaction into precise game theoretic terms, Selten was impervious to such temptations.

Selten's original experiment

Selten uses his strategy method in an oligopoly experiment with price variation and investment (as introduced in Selten 1967b, Chapter 4 in CEE). He does not assume a well-defined (Bayesian) game but discusses what later would be referred to as a "game form" of a stylized oligopoly market.

(To avoid terminological clutter, we shall simply use the term "game" here-after.) The market involves three firms producing the same type of commod-ity but at different unit costs. The firms have only qualitative information on demand, which depends not only on the prices but also on previous sales: the higher a firm's price, the lower its sales (i.e., the demand that it faces); customers tend to buy where they used to buy (i.e., demand inertia), but they also tend to switch from firms with higher prices to those with lower prices (i.e., opportunity-taking behavior). Demand increases over time, and there might be some irregularities (i.e., randomness) in demand.

In each period, each firm decides on its price and whether it wants to keep its capacity unchanged or increase/decrease it by one machine. Once all firms have made their decisions, each is informed about its sales and the prices chosen by the other firms. The game is played over 30 game periods.

During the summer term of 1964, 14 advanced economic and social science students of the University of Frankfurt played this business game twice. They were, in a general manner, instructed how to present strategies in flow charts. Then, they were asked to design, in individual homework, a strategy for the game. Formal errors were discussed in several group and individual meetings until all participants had a complete and unambigu-ous strategy. After this the actual demand function was revealed, and the students were offered the opportunity to test-run their individual strategies (relative to a simple strategy provided by Selten) in computer simulations.

The paper does not provide any simulation results but focuses on the analysis of the strategy diagrams. In his own English summary, Selten (pages 262–263 in CEE) states:

> 12 of the 14 participants show a tendency to determine a price in the proximity of the competitors' prices. This tendency serves as a coun-terbalance to the desire to have sales as high as possible. Some strate-gies use profit calculations for price and/or investment decisions. These calculations cannot be called optimizations; they only serve to exclude alternatives which do not meet some aspiration level of profitability.

An important caveat

In his experiment, Selten did not even attempt to induce a well-defined game. Participants develop and adapt means-ends causality perceptions. They plan their moves in the light of feedback information they expect to be provided in the course of repeated market-interaction, represented by the game form. An implemented "strategy can be conceived as a decision pro-cess with environmental situations as 'input' and with decisions as 'output'. Most interesting with regard to the 'output' are the 23 pricing formulas used by the subjects" (CEE, p. 262). Selten adds that "[t]he elementary criteria in a strategy show which features of the environmental situation are consid-ered as relevant" (CEE, p. 262). In short, the strategy concept underlying

Selten's strategy method represents the cognitive processes of strategic planners rather than the results of such processes in terms of functions that map information sets into moves.

Applications of Selten's strategy method

Selten's strategy experiment is an early example of the later strategy tournaments in a variety of contexts. In those tournaments, participants get the opportunity to gain experience in playing a specific game and then design strategies (flow charts of computer programs), which will be matched with each other on a computer. Such strategy tournaments have been conducted, for instance, in repeated prisoner's dilemma games (Axelrod, 1984), dynamic and repeated oligopoly games (Keser, 1992; Selten et al., 1997), two-person bargaining with incomplete information (Kuon, 1994), common-pool-resource games (Keser and Gardner, 1999), public-good games (Keser, 2000), and (one-shot) two player-(3×3)-games with random payoffs (Selten et al., 2003).

All these applications deviate, to some extent, from Selten's original intentions. To the extent that players are informed that the success of a strategy is measured by how well (in terms of its individual payoff) it performs on average in interactions with other strategies, there is an experimental demand effect concerning competitive behavior. To the extent that strategies can be chosen as fixed programs, this implicit introduction of commitment power propels the simulations into the field of "evolutionary" game analysis.

Variants of the strategy method

Numerous experimental studies use a variant of the strategy method without calling it by this name. For example, the clearing-house (also known as call-market) method (e.g., Plott and Smith, 1978), when experimentally testing theories of competitive markets, relies on the strategy method by asking trader participants for their positive or negative excess demand for all (experimentally) possible prices. Güth, Schmittberger, and Schwarze (1982), another top influential paper discussed in this volume, used a variant of the strategy method: it elicited response strategies in the ultimatum game by asking the responders for their acceptance thresholds. Furthermore, in one of the treatments, it introduced a "strategy vector method." To examine the consistency of demands in ultimatum bargaining, participants were required to simultaneously indicate both their demand as proposer and their minimal acceptable offer as responder. Asking for the strategy vector allowed the authors to investigate to what extent participants behave in a consistent way in that the sum of their demands as proposer and responder equals the amount to be allocated.

About a decade later, explicitly referring to Selten's (1967c) strategy method and their own intention to derive a theory of boundedly rational behavior, Mitzkewitz and Nagel (1993) applied a simple variant of the strategy method in an experiment with incomplete information: in each of eight interaction rounds with perfect-stranger matching, participants were asked to submit state-contingent strategies (based on 6 possible pie sizes for proposers and 13 possible offers to responders).

A more recent debate in experimental economics, highlighted in a survey by Brandts and Charness (2011), is on the behavioral relevance of choice elicitation in sequential-game playing via the traditional play method (participants decide on their moves only when they have to be chosen), the strategy method (as a simple variant of Selten's method), or the strategy vector method (each participant decides for all player roles). This discussion is less influenced by Selten's early discussion of the "strategiemethode" as an information-representation and information-collection device for empirical research. It speaks more to the conceptual discussion over whether or not the "normal-form" representation of games expresses all that matters strategically (e.g., von Neumann and Morgenstern, 1944; Kohlberg and Mertens, 1985). And it is still contested whether two games are strategically equivalent if and only if they have the same normal-form representation.

Selten (1975) and Harsanyi and Selten (1988) demonstrate how to guarantee sequential rationality via suitable equilibrium refinement and equilibrium selection criteria. Despite the as-if approach in game theory (Weibull, 1994) – which aspires to represent, in terms of evolutionary adaptation and selection, all considerations that can be made concerning strategies as plans – Selten would have argued that the real causal process matters even if results of one account of interaction can be represented "as if" brought about by another. As far as empirics are concerned, Selten would have added that, in his eyes, theories of pure rationality were non-empirical enterprises, which he – explicitly combining rationality with theology – referred to non-pejoratively as "rationology" (Selten, 1999). This should be borne in mind, when discussing the strategy method as a device primarily meant to serve purposes of empirical research.

The impact of the paper

Though this paper by Selten is often cited as an early precursor of asking for strategic plans rather than moves in experiments on sequential decision-making, in the strategic management literature it is hardly ever mentioned, despite the fact that Selten intended to explore bounded rationality in strategic sales planning. We view Selten's paper as a milestone for the data-guided development of bounded-rationality theory combining path dependence with forward-looking, consequentialist decision-making.

The paper has been truly innovative as a contribution to boundedly rational decision adaptation, if without explicitly eliciting aspiration adaptation (e.g., Sauermann and Selten, 1962) or aspiration formation and satisficing more generally (Simon, 1955).

Its focus on bounded rationality should be borne in mind when referring to it.

Notes

1 Eliciting response strategies in the ultimatum game, for instance, would require responders to decide between acceptance and rejection for all possible offers, which become more numerous when the smallest money unit becomes smaller.
2 In the case of response strategies of ultimatum responders, one may, for instance, impose monotonicity by only eliciting acceptance thresholds.

References

Axelrod, R., 1984. *The Evolution of Cooperation*. New York, NY: Basic.

Brandts J., Charness, G., 2011. The strategy versus the direct response method: A first survey of experimental comparisons. *Experimental Economics* 14, 375–398.

Fouraker, L.E., Siegel, S., 1963. *Bargaining Behavior*. New York, NY: McGraw-Hill.

Friedmann, J.W., 1963. Individual behavior in oligopolistic markets: An experimental study. *Yale Economic Essays* 3(2), 359–417.

Güth, W., Schmittberger, R., Schwarze, B., 1982. An experimental analysis of ultimatum bargaining. *Journal of Economic Behavior and Organization* 3, 367–388.

Harsanyi, J.C., Selten, R., 1988. *A General Theory of Equilibrium Selection in Games*. Cambridge, MA: MIT Press.

Hoggatt, A.C., 1959. An experimental business game. *Behavioral Science* 4, 192–203.

Keser, C., 1992. *Experimental Duopoly Markets with Demand Inertia*. Berlin: Springer Verlag.

Keser, C., 2000. Strategically planned behavior in public good experiments. CIRANO Scientific Series 2000s-35.

Keser, C. Gardner, R., 1999. Strategic behavior of experienced subjects in a common pool resource game. *International Journal of Game Theory* 28, 241–252.

Kohlberg, E., Mertens J.F., 1985. On the strategic stability of equilibria. *Econometrica* 54, 1003–1037.

Kuon, B., 1994. *Two-Person Bargaining Experiments with Incomplete Information*. Berlin: Springer Verlag.

Mitzkewitz, M., Nagel, R., 1993. Experimental results on ultimatum games with incomplete information. *International Journal of Game Theory* 22, 171–198.

Plott, C.R., Smith, V. L., 1978. An experimental investigation of two exchange institutions. *Review of Economic Studies* 45, 133–153.

Sauermann, H., Selten, R., 1962. Anspruchsanpassungstheorie der Unternehmung. *Zeitschrift für die gesamte Staatswissenschaft* 118, 577–597.

Sauermann, H., Selten R., 1967a. Zur Entwicklung der experimentellen Wirtschaftsforschung. In: Sauermann, H. (Ed.). *Beiträge zur experimentellen Wirtschaftsforschung*, Vol. I. Tübingen: J.C.B. Mohr (Paul Siebeck), 1–8.

Sauermann, H., Selten R., 1967b. Ein Oligopolexperiment. In: Sauermann, H. (Ed.). *Beiträge zur experimentellen Wirtschaftsforschung*, Vol. I. Tübingen: J.C.B. Mohr (Paul Siebeck), 9–59.

Schelling, T. C., 1960. *The Strategy of Conflict*. New York, NY: Oxford University Press.

Selten R., 1967a. Investitionsverhalten im Oligopolexperiment. In: Sauermann, H. (Ed.). *Beiträge zur experimentellen Wirtschaftsforschung*, Vol. I. Tübingen: J.C.B. Mohr (Paul Siebeck), 60–102.

Selten, R., 1967b. Ein Oligopolexperiment mit Preisvariation und Investition. In: Sauermann, H. (Ed.). *Beiträge zur experimentellen Wirtschaftsforschung*, Vol. I. Tübingen: J.C.B. Mohr (Paul Siebeck), 103–135.

Selten, R., 1967c. Die Strategiemethode zur Erforschung des eingeschränkt rationalen Verhaltens im Rahmen eines Oligopolexperiments. In: Sauermann, H. (Ed.). *Beiträge zur experimentellen Wirtschaftsforschung*, Vol. I. Tübingen: J.C.B. Mohr (Paul Siebeck), 103–168.

Selten, R., 1975. Reexamination of the perfectness concept of equilibrium points in extensive games. *International Journal of Game Theory* 4, 25–55.

Selten, R., 1999. Response to Shepsle and Laitin. In: Alt, J., Levi, M., Ostrom, E. (Eds.). *Competition and Cooperation: Conversations with Nobelists about Economics and Political Science.* New York: Russel Sage Foundation, 303–308.

Selten, R., Abbink, K., Buchta, J., Sadrieh, K., 2003. How to play (3 × 3)-games: A strategy method experiment. *Games and Economic Behavior* 45, 19–37.

Selten, R., Mitzkewitz, M., Uhlich, G., 1997. Duopoly strategies programmed by experienced players. *Econometrica* 65, 517–555.

Simon, H.A., 1955. A behavioral model of rational choice. *Quarterly Journal of Economics* 69, 99–118.

Von Neumann, J., Morgenstern, O., 1944. *Theory of Games and Economic Behavior.* Princeton, NJ: Princeton University Press.

Weibull, J.W., 1994. The 'as-if' approach to game theory: Three positive results and four obstacles. *European Economic Review* 38, 868–881.

4

AN EXPERIMENTAL ANALYSIS OF ULTIMATUM BARGAINING (BY WERNER GÜTH, ROLF SCHMITTBERGER, AND BERND SCHWARZE)

Brit Grosskopf and Rosemarie Nagel

Introduction

The ultimatum game (UG), as we know it today, has its origin in a paper by Werner Güth, Rolf Schmittberger, and Bernd Schwarze (hereafter GSS) in 1982. Its game structure, behavioral outcomes, and theoretical solutions are among the most fundamental building blocks of behavioral economics. After heated debates and controversies between theorists and experimenters about interpretations of the differences between the observed behavior and game-theoretical logic, it has become one of the most important experimental paradigms for studying social behavior across disciplines and geographical spheres.

Because of the UG and its many replications and follow-up studies, we now have a much better understanding about human motivation in simple social settings and the limits of actual human rationality. It is one of the most productive examples of integration across disciplines, widely known outside economics, cited more than 5,500 times. It is a challenge to write a review of the ultimatum game, as introduced by Werner Güth and two of his students, given the many survey papers that already exist on the subject. There is a special issue of the *Journal of Economic Behavior and Organization*, where the paper was originally published (see Van Damme et al., 2014), a special column in the *Journal of Economic Perspectives* by Thaler (1988), a chapter on bargaining in the first *Handbook of Experimental Economics* (Kagel and Roth, 1995) with the UG as a central theme, as well as a review paper by Werner himself (Güth and Kocher, 2014). These previous surveys and laudations underscore why this paper belongs in this volume.

Here, our main endeavor in appraising GSS is to uncover the rich set of original (design) ideas and discuss the reasons for the survival or disappearance of those ideas in the light of today's experimental economics

DOI: 10.4324/9781003019121-4

standards. We conclude with a list of sample highlights of the abundant follow-up literature.

The birth of the ultimatum game

The paper by GSS bears similarities to Columbus' discovery of the Americas, as quoted in Roth and Sotomayor (1990, p. 170).

> Columbus is viewed as the discoverer of America, even though every school child knows that the Americas were inhabited when he arrived and that he was not even the first to have made a round trip, having been preceded by Vikings and perhaps by others. What is important about Columbus' discovery of America is not that it was the first, but that it was the last. After Columbus, America was never lost again.

Similarly, some authors had conducted bargaining games with an "ultimatum aspect" before GSS (notably Fouraker and Siegel, 1963). Stahl (1972) and Rubinstein (1982) laid the theoretical foundation for structured multi- or an infinite bargaining procedure. However, the designs were more complicated and different from what we refer to today as the ultimatum game.

As proposed by GSS, the ultimatum game could not be simpler, and yet it remains psychologically complex. Two players are allotted a sum of money, a "pie." The first player, also called the Proposer, offers some portion of the money to the second player, called the Responder. If the Responder accepts the offer, she obtains the offer, and the Proposer receives the rest. If the Responder rejects, both players get nothing. Theoretically, one of the predictions of the game can be found by backward induction. Any positive amount offered to the Responder is better than nothing, which is the alternative when rejecting. Proposers know this and, therefore, should offer a penny (or the smallest unit of currency available) that is accepted by the rational Responders, resulting in the so-called subgame perfect equilibrium (Selten, 1975).

However, there are also other equilibria. Any offer can be an equilibrium strategy, given a corresponding minimum acceptance level of the Responder, smaller than the pie size. There can be no rejections in equilibrium. GSS (and a lot of the subsequent literature) do not discuss these equilibria. Because of the multiplicity of equilibria, the ultimatum game turns into a complicated coordination game. If the game-theoretical concept of rationality accepting everything is not considered, the simple equal split typically comes to mind; yet, game theoretically, a Proposer would like to offer just the minimum acceptable offer. Thus, the debate has induced a tension about full rationality versus social preferences or correct beliefs of acceptance levels on the Proposer side.

The above describes the UG as we know it today. However, GSS go into great detail in describing bargaining games more generally (see also Thaler, 1988). They then define the character of an ultimatum bargaining game – a bargaining game with a final stage of one player having a binary choice (e.g., accepting or rejecting a previous offer). This final stage can be reached after many offers, rejections, and counteroffers. A bargaining game with several possibilities for the last player's final choice is bargaining with ultimatum aspects.

GSS were interested in implementing the simplest form of all UGs, with only two decision stages and two possible choices at the last stage. Ever since, the literature has uniquely defined this setup as the ultimatum game, and most neoclassically trained undergraduate students will have heard of the UG. Less known is that the original paper included another more complicated two-stage "ultimatum bargaining game" and more design features. Writing this review gave us the wonderful opportunity to go back to the original article, enjoy all the insights it offers, and contemplate how some of its attributes reappeared decades later while others were lost.

The original design and today's implementations

GSS conducted three (repeated) sessions, which they called "experiments," with the same subjects. In the first two experiments, two different types of UGs were played, with different design features in each one. The first type contains "Easy Games," which is the UG as described above.

The second type, played after the Easy Games within one session, was referred to as "Complicated Games." In these games, the Proposer had to decide on allocating a bundle of chips with different known values for each player. In particular, there were five black chips and nine white chips. For Player 1, each chip's value was equal to 2 DM (Deutsche Mark), independent of the chip color. In contrast, Player 2's value for black chips was 2 DM whereas her payoff for white chips was only 1 DM. Player 1 offers to Player 2 two different bundles of white and black chips, with the sums of the chips equaling the original endowment of chips. Player 2 chooses one of the bundles – having a binary choice, as in the original UG, and similar to "divide and choose" games (Steinhaus, 1948; Güth, 1979). Unlike in the UG, the method of divide and choose yields an envy-free and Pareto Optimal (PO) allocation, the unique subgame perfect equilibrium (SPE), five black and no white chips for Player 1, and nine white but no black chips for Player 2. This equilibrium is also more salient or easily available, as the equilibrium combination is equal to the initial chip distribution five black vs. nine white, which a Proposer might evaluate first. On the one side, as in the SPE UG, there is a higher payoff for Player 1 with a difference of nine points in both games. But on the other side, unlike in the UG, the other equilibrium allocations are not PO but can yield more equal payoffs across bundles.

In a second session (replication) one week later, the same subjects, matched randomly, repeated the "Easy Games" with minor differences in pie sizes, and the "Complicated Games" with ten times higher stakes, creating "inexperienced" and "experienced" choices. In the third repetition, only the Easy Game was conducted. Therein, all subjects made decisions for both roles, Player 1 and Player 2 using strategy-vector method (see also Keser and Kliemt in this volume). While the choice of Player 1 was as before, Player 2 had to specify the minimum acceptance threshold for a fixed, known pie size. As a subject specifies the choices in both roles, the game is played in normal form. Thus, Player 1 chooses a possible offer, and Player 2 chooses a possible acceptance level.

Other design features are also worth mentioning. Participants were graduate students in economics at the University of Cologne. Experimental sessions were conducted in the fall of 1978 (after pilot sessions in the summer of 1978). Participants were not explicitly recruited to the experiment but attended Werner Güth's class for course credit. Yet, they were paid in DM according to the outcome of their decisions. Upon entering the classroom used as the "laboratory," and seated far apart without visual barriers between them, they were matched anonymously with another participant in the experiment. Instructions were given to them orally for the subsequent "pen and paper" experiments. The "pie size" could vary between pairs.

Comparing design features now and then

In the following, we highlight features of the GSS experiments still common and those that have not survived, for varied but specific reasons.

Selection of subject participants

Student level. Graduate students (of economics) are rarely used as subjects today, as one typically would like to have subjects not trained in the Game Theory. GSS noted that most of their subjects did not have training in Game Theory in 1978, typical at the time in Germany. Today, most lab experiments use undergraduates (not necessarily students in economics though), who are available in greater numbers. Furthermore, most undergraduate economics students have some Game Theory training, but do not necessarily have knowledge of experimental economics.

Friendship. Given that the students were within the same class, GSS discuss the role of friendship affecting their choices. Yet, the matching was done anonymously. Since most experiments in the last 30 years have been done via the computer, the effects of such "friendship" aspects have been mostly removed. The advent of new technology (i.e., face recognition) and the understanding of mimics through machine learning have now facilitated a "controlled" return to the "human face" of strategic interaction (e.g., Eckel and Petrie, 2011).

Experimental procedures

Experimental currency units. The pie was denominated in actual money units (i.e., DM). While this was common in the 1990s, we typically use points or experimental currency units these days, which are converted into the country's currency at the end of the experiment. This procedure ensures easier comparisons across labs/countries that facilitate replication (see also the discussion in Roth et al., 1991, and List, this volume).

Instructions. Instructions were given orally. Written instructions are included in the original paper, which was not standard at the time (at least in Germany). For replication purposes, it is standard today that instructions are written and read the same way across sessions.

Use of computers. The experiment was conducted with "pen and pencil." Nowadays, computers are commonly used to facilitate timely and anonymous interactions. However, given the simplicity of the UG, computers are unnecessary. This is important for experiments in remote parts of the world that use subjects pools not even using money as a medium of exchange, or young children and elderly, who are less computer savvy. Development economists, anthropologists, and other behavioral scientists have increasingly used such implementations to establish a link between fairness issues and the main treatment questions (see Henrich et al., 2004, and for a review, see Cardenas and Carpenter, 2008).

Repetition. The experiment was repeated with a week in between. Such call-back experiments have rarely been done. They have reappeared to consider stability and consistency of behavior over a longer time horizon (see, for example, Bosch and Silvestre, 1999, studying risk attitudes). With the introduction of computer laboratories in the mid-1980s, repeating the same game with the same subjects either under random or fixed matching became a standard procedure in experimental economics for formulating parsimonious models of bounded rationality and learning.

Within-subject comparison. Using different games with the same subjects within the same session (within-subject comparison) is done less often in lab settings than in field studies. Ideally, one needs to understand whether order effects call for sessions with different game sequences. This way, economizing on the number of subjects through within-subject comparison is offset. Yet, studies about players' consistency of behavioral rules across different games call for more within-subject comparison (see, for example, Georganas et al., 2015, on the questions of level k consistency).

Between subject comparison. Comparing similar games with different parameters and the same game-theoretic solutions played by different subjects has always been a common practice. Often, off-equilibrium properties determine behavioral differences between games (see a discussion of this in the "Results" section of this chapter).

Information asymmetries. Players bargained over chips with different values in the Complicated Games. Such asymmetries, especially information asymmetries about the other players' chip values, have also been conducted in other bargaining settings (e.g., Nydegger and Owen, 1975; Roth and Malouf, 1982; Roth and Murnighan, 1982).

Stake size. Experimental economists have long been criticized for using low payoffs in experiments, typically no more than the equivalent of a few dollars. In the second session within the Complicated Game, GSS introduced large pies of 28 DM (see also literature below).

Ex-post changes. The paper introduces a third experiment as an afterthought, after the results of the first two sessions were analyzed. Such exploratory ex-post additions to the experimental protocol are limited nowadays if the procedure requires preregistrations. Therefore, the researcher must prespecify the entire design and possible hypotheses for later publication (Munafò et al., 2017; Nosek et al., 2018). This procedure is still rare for purely lab-based experiments. Some researchers argue that experimental economics seems to suffer less from p-hacking – selective reporting of statistically significant results – than other applied fields in economics (e.g., Coffman and Niederle, 2015; Camerer et al., 2016; Maniadis et al., 2017). Still, journals increasingly require it for field experiments or RCTs, and in other social and natural sciences, registered reports are common practice.

Use of the strategy method

In a first step (GSS experiments 1 and 2), the subject plays the UG in the spontaneous way. In a second step, after gaining enough experience with the game and the behavior of other subjects, she has to develop a complete strategy. GSS asked responders to submit a threshold, a minimum acceptance level, thus imposing a monotonic response strategy method for the Easy Games. This creates a choice for all possible decision nodes reachable via all possible offers by the Proposer. It has the flavor of Selten's (1967) two-stage "strategy method," where the first experience of the game involves single offers and responses, and then a final experience that provides a complete strategy (perhaps even a computer program provided by the student subject). This method is still rarely applied nowadays (see Keser and Kliemt, this volume).

Given the nature of playing in both positions in the third session, the authors were able to study (in)consistencies of behavior within the same subject. The procedure is called strategy-vector choices for distinguishing behavioral types within the same subject (e.g., Fischbacher, Gächter, and Fehr, 2001). This procedure is useful but rarely conducted in experimental economics. With this method, the researcher can classify participants by types. GSS (1982) find three types in their UG:

1. Conflict: As Proposer, one offers less than demanding as Responder (e.g., via acceptance thresholds);
2. Semi-dimensional: As Proposer, one offers exactly what one minimally demands as Responder;
3. Anti-conflict: As Proposer, one offers more than demanding as Responder.

By using the strategy (vector) method, GSS also introduced the design feature of playing the UG, which is an extensive form game, in a reduced normal form. The SPE, of course, turns into a Nash Equilibrium. However, behaviorally and also game theoretically, there should be no difference between both presentations. Mitzkewitz and Nagel (1993) implemented the normal form for UGs with incomplete information and Nagel and Tang (1998) the reduced normal form for the Centipede Game more formally.

Reporting pilot study results

GSS report pilot study results. It would be recommendable if this norm were kept up nowadays as online material, especially with discussions about design features that worked and which ones were discarded.

However, the richness of the design is also a burden, considering more recent demands of calculations of effect sizes and multiple hypothesis testing. There are two different games (easy and complicated) with similar pie sizes. There is spontaneous play in the first "period." In the second period, in the Easy Games, there are seven pie sizes for different pairs, and in the Complicated Games ten times higher payoffs than in the first period. In the third period, all play in both player positions, knowing that they are paid according to their demands via random role assignment. Given the variations of parameters from one period to the next and few subjects in some setups, it was difficult to judge the reasons for changes beyond checking the robustness of qualitative findings. Nevertheless, the main results and intuitions of behavioral differences from game-theoretic solutions were replicated in the many experiments that followed.

Nowadays, most experimental papers have no more than a few treatments with enough data. Yet, original papers such as Kalisch et al. (1954) on characteristic function games or Smith, Suchanek, and Williams (1988) on bubbles, provide a similar richness of treatments while appearing to be pilot studies with few replications. It is unlikely that nowadays a paper without any statistical tests would be published on these grounds. Yet, on the positive side, there is value in figures (drawn by hand) and tables represent individual data points, rather than just averages with variances as the typical descriptive statistics.

Results of the original paper

The authors obtain decisions from 21 pairs for the "Easy" and "Complicated" games. All individual data is presented in different tables and figures. There were two rejections from inexperienced and six from experienced players in the "Easy Games." GSS stipulate that the greater frequency of conflict was caused by experienced players increasing their average demand. Surprisingly, from today's perspective, the authors provide no statistical tests on whether these differences are significant. The authors conducted a correlation analysis to see how the Proposer's demand depends on the pie size but do hint at the scarcity of data in some cases.

Whereas only one experienced Proposer demanded 4.99 of a pie out of five in the "Easy Games," 35% of the inexperienced proposers selected the SPE allocation in the "Complicated Games." This percentage increases to 53% for experienced subjects who also faced larger payoffs. GSS argue that the deviation from optimal behavior (SPE) in the "Easy Games" is not the difficulty of finding it, but its social unacceptability and unfairness. We like to add that in the Complicated Games the SPE allocation of nine white chips for the Proposer and five black chips for the Responder is more easily available than the more equal payoff bundles, which need to be consciously constructed. Rubinstein (2007) confirms that the response time for 50–50 proposal is much lower than the SPE offer in UGs.

The comparison of the results obtained in "Easy Games" versus "Complicated Games" is similar to the comparison Harrison and Hirshleifer (1989) make between behavior in the UG and the Best Shot game. Prasnikar and Roth (1992) discuss the idea that the "Best Shot" games, with the same perfect equilibrium predictions as the UG, give Player 1 very different incentives off the equilibrium path. Offering positive amounts in the UG has different implications than in the best shot game. In the UG, offers in the 40–50% range result in higher payoffs than lower offers. If Player 1 provides a positive quantity in the Best Shot game, Player 2 free-rides (and, thus, Player 1 earns very little). Contrarily, if Player 1 free-rides according to the perfect equilibrium path, he will earn much more than Player 2. Furthermore, all outcomes in the Easy Games (UG) are PO – not so for those in the Complicated Games. Many later experiments have made similar observations that unequal splits, being the unique maximal payoff-sum, are typically accepted.

The results from the strategy-vector method treatment reveal three intrapersonal types mentioned above: Only 41% of proposers (semi-dimensional) were "best responding" to their own minimal thresholds. Almost half (46%, anti-conflict) stated acceptance thresholds lower than their own offers, maybe due to tolerance of other than their own behavior. Only a minority (13%, conflict) offered less than their acceptance levels.

The general findings from UGs, replicated in the following almost 40 years, typically average about 30–40% of the total pie, with a 50–50 split being the mode. Offers of less than 20% are frequently rejected. Theorists and experimenters agree that selfish behavior is, to a large extent, unacceptable in such two-person situations, which leads to social preference theories about fairness or strategic behavior of higher offers, to avoid rejections of greedy proposals. In the following, we provide a list of follow-up papers, so as to highlight the impact of the original source.

A hit list of subsequent work

While this review is no attempt to present a full summary of the literature spanning almost 40 years after the seminal GSS publication, we would still like to sketch how the literature has developed since.

Variations in experimental procedure

Alternating offer games. One of the first variations to study the tension between the large amount of (near) equal split offers and the SPE are presented through the alternating offer games, in which both players can make several counter-proposals after rejecting an offer. Different outside options are possible, along with new proposals. Typically the pie size shrinks (see Rubinstein 1982). The results show that subjects consider only one or two stages of such alternating rounds, thus only coming closer to the SPE of two-stage games (Bolton, 1991).

Dictator games. Dictator Games (e.g., Kahneman, Knetsch, and Thaler, 1986) are the most extreme simplification of the UG, with the second player having no say at all. More zero offers were observed, revealing that the fear of rejection is a strong motive in making higher offers in the UG. A small spike at equal split remained. This was also observed in the Yes-No games where proposers suggest how to share a given positive monetary amount and responders decide without knowing the proposal (Güth and Kirchkamp, 2012).

Anonymity. Anonymity, double-blind – not only against the subject but also against the experimenters (Forsythe, Horowitz, Savin, and Sefton, 1994; Hoffman, McCabe, and Smith, 1994; Bolton and Zwick, 1995) – increased zero offers in dictator games, but less so in UGs. Güth and Otsubo (2020) explore a 100-round Yes-No game with random strangers. The dynamics of play differ fundamentally from the quick convergence to equal sharing for ultimatum games. There is neither convergence to equal sharing nor to equilibrium play, but persistent heterogeneity in offers and (non)acceptance.

Entitlement. Determining who is entitled to be the Proposer, based on real effort tasks, increases accepted payoff differences (e.g., Hoffman, McCabe, Shachat, and Smith 1994; Demiral and Mollerstrom 2018). GSS mention this design implementation that they had already started at the time of publication with auctioning off the player positions (Güth and Tietz, 1985, 1986).

Incomplete information. Unknown pie size to the Responder (e.g., Mitzkewitz and Nagel, 1993; Rapoport and Sundali, 1996) or to the Proposer (Nagel and Harstad, 2004) increases (sequential) equilibrium play (with unfair offers) and acceptance over time. This is more strongly observed with responder competition (Grosskopf, 2003).

Strategy method. The strategy method in the game-theoretic interpretation for simple games was introduced by Mitzkewitz and Nagel (1993), without the spontaneous play stage as required by Selten (1967). Each Proposer put forth a demand (offer) for multiple pie sizes (to be determined by the roll of a six-sided die). Each Responder had to state an acceptance or rejection for each possible proposal without knowing the pie size. An advantage of this method is a richer data set than would have been obtained with spontaneous play alone. Brandts and Charness (2011) survey the literature on spontaneous play versus the strategy method for simple games. In most such games, there is not much difference between the two different methods.

Causal attribution. Blount (1995) shows that playing against a bingo cage generated offers reduces rejection levels, especially for low offers as compared to human offers. This indicates causal attribution.

Stakes. Higher stakes do not seem to alter the choices of proposers but tend to increase the acceptances of responders (see Roth, Prasnikar, Okuno-Fujiwara, and Zamir, 1991; Hoffman, McCabe, and Smith, 1996, and the chapter by List, this volume).

Neuroeconomics and psychological techniques

FMRI studies. FMRI studies (see Sanfey et al., 2003, and for a review, see Gabay et al., 2014) show that there is a high correlation between insula activity (responsible for disgust and anger) and the rejection of small offers, while this is not the case for accepted small offers. Cognitive areas like the lPFC (conflict resolution) do not show these discrepancies for accepted versus rejected small offers. A correlation of genetics rejection rates by Wallace et al. (2007) is shown in twin studies. As a side remark, Sanfey et al. computerize Proposer behavior without telling the subjects. In economics, this kind of deception is frowned upon and can lead to exclusion for publication in economics journals.

Chemical influences. Crockett et al. (2008) show that enhancing serotonin makes subjects less likely to reject unfair offers as it increases their aversion to harming the other side financially. Men who received extra doses of testosterone the night before are more generous as proposers but more likely to turn down low offers as responders (Burnham, 2007). Takagishi et al. (2009) find that responders who rejected unfair offers showed an increased level of the enzyme Salivary Alpha-Amylase. This indicates that rejection of the unfair offers is a reflection of emotional arousal associated with adrenergic activations. There is also evidence that subjects induced to be in an unpleasant mood rejected unfair offers more often than subjects induced to be in a pleasant mood (Harlé et al., 2012; Chung et al., 2016).

Response time. Measuring response time (RT) in ultimatum and other games, Rubinstein (2007) reveals that equal split offers are intuitively easy to perceive and thus require less RT, while small offers need more RT. Another reason for this difference is that low offers are more likely to be rejected and, therefore, careful reasoning is more taxing. Crosetto and Güth (2020) find that responders who mainly accept (reject) low offers, take more time when they ponder the opposite action. The authors attribute this finding to heterogeneity in self-priming.

Variations in the subject pool

Cultural influences. Studies in different countries or societies (e.g., Roth et al., 1991; Henrich et al., 2004; Ensminger and Henrich, 2014) show that offer and rejection rates vary, due to cultural differences. Notably, anthropologists have picked up the UG to study and compare behavior in small-scale societies that differ along many dimensions but most notably in terms of their market integration (see also the chapter by List in this volume).

Güth, Schmidt, and Sutter (2007) show cultural heterogeneity within the same society in UG experiments run with readers of a large German weekly newspaper. Avatars, from different second life environments, have also appeared, and people seem to be more cooperative in virtual reality than in the usual lab experiments (see Innocenti, 2017, for a survey).

Mental development, capability, and health. The observed behavior of children is similar to that of adults, and models of behavior work about as well for children as they do for adults (Murnighan and Saxon, 1998). The rejection of unfair offers is not uniquely human. Even monkeys reject unequal compensation (Brosnan and de Waal, 2003). Individuals with autism offer closer to the SPE than the non-autistic student population (Sally and Hill, 2006; Wang et al., 2019). Compared with healthy subjects, the rejection rates of most unfair offers in the UG were significantly higher under low-offer-size conditions among heroin addicts. In contrast, the most unfair offers were more likely to be accepted by heroin addicts in the high-offer-size condition than by healthy subjects (Hou et al., 2016).

Behavioral theories on fairness and learning

Inequity aversion. Models of inequity aversion formulate disadvantageous inequity aversion as the "willingness to sacrifice potential gain to block another individual from receiving a superior reward" in their social preference model and incorporate the notion of relative payoffs (Fehr and Schmidt, 1999; Bolton and Ockenfels, 2000). Models of reciprocity assume that one's altruistic act may evolve from the anticipation of future reciprocal altruistic behavior from others (Bolton, 1991; Rabin, 1993; Levine 1998; Dufwenberg and Kirchsteiger, 2004). Models of altruism represent an agent's concern about others' wellbeing. A person exhibits altruistic preferences if their utility increases with others' payoff (e.g., Andreoni, 1989). A belief-based model is formulated by Mitzkewitz and Nagel (1993), not requiring consistency of beliefs. Given the usage of the strategy method, they classify behavior of proposers by two anticipation strategies based on expected fairness and resistance to visible unfairness, and two equal split strategies, all of which are attempts to avoid rejections and the (sequential) equilibrium strategies.

Learning. Learning over time in ultimatum games does not drive behavior to the subgame perfect equilibrium. Roth and Erev (1995) introduced a reinforcement (RE) model showing that behavior remains near the equal split distribution. Avrahami et al. (2013) find similar fast convergence in 100-round UG experiments with random stranger re-matching. In the analog market game, the RE model simulates convergence to the unique unfair offer. Similarly, Grosskopf (2003) shows that with responder competition, a reinforcement model a la Roth and Erev (1995) also converges to the SPE. Mitzkewitz and Nagel (1993) apply the learning direction theory (Selten and Stoecker, 1986) for behavior in UG with incomplete information, which leads a significant proportion of subjects to the sequential equilibrium.

Concluding appraisal

Albert Einstein's quote, "Everything should be made as simple as possible, but no simpler," suits the UG as introduced by GSS. Through the lens of empirical economics, the observed and replicated behavior in the beautifully simple UG has given rise to a series of even simpler games, such as the dictator game and the mini UG, and some more complicated ones such as the trust game, gift exchange (the two latter introduced into labor economics), and public good games with punishment. Behavioral regularities observed in these games have helped us obtain a much more robust understanding of the psychological aspects involved in decision-making and have even sparked social preference theories, as indicated above. While Werner himself still refers to them as attempts of the "neoclassical repair shop" to rationalize behavior, altruism, reciprocity, and inequity aversion are with us to stay.

Described above as the "Easy Game," the UG has survived in its original form with many new variations. When one thinks of the GSS paper these days, the "Complicated Games" are forgotten. Yet, many other variations appeared later, often without a reference to the GSS source. However, GSS might not have been the original inventors either, unbeknown to themselves, just as Columbus was not the first to discover America.

Thank you, Werner and his co-authors, for giving us the lens through which to look at the complex world of human decision-making and the tools to embark on the demanding job of explaining the robust "irregularities" of human social behavior. For sure, more exciting research discoveries are left to the young generation. Still, we are closer to a complete understanding because of the article by Werner and his co-authors published in the *Journal of Economic Behavior and Organization* in 1982.

References

Andreoni, J., 1989. Giving with impure altruism: Applications to charity and ricardian equivalence. *Journal of Political Economy* 97(6), 1447–1458.

Avrahami, J., Güth, W., Hertwig, R., Kareev, Y., Otsubo, H., 2013. Learning (not) to yield: An experimental study of evolving ultimatum game behavior. *Journal of Behavioral and Experimental Economics* 47(C), 47–54.

Blount, S., 1995. When social outcomes aren't fair: The effect of causal attributions on preference. *Organizational Behavior and Human Decision Process* 63(2), 131–144.

Bolton, G.E., 1991. A cooperative model of bargaining: Theory and evidence. *American Economic Review* 81(5), 1096–1136.

Bolton, G.E., Ockenfels, A., 2000. ERC: A theory of equity, reciprocity, and competition. *American Economic Review* 90(1), 166–193.

Bolton, G., Zwick, R., 1995. Anonymity versus punishment in ultimatum bargaining. *Games and Economic Behavior* 10(1), 95–121.

Bosch, A., Silvestre, J., 1999. Does risk aversion or attraction depend on income? An experiment. *Economics Letters* 65, 265–273.

Brandts, J., Charness, G., 2011. The strategy versus the direct-response method: A first survey of experimental comparisons. *Experimental Economics* 14, 375–398.

Brosnan, S., de Waal, F., 2003. Monkeys reject unequal pay. *Nature* 425, 297–299.

Burnham, T.C., 2007. High-testosterone men reject low ultimatum game offers. *Proceedings of the Royal Academy: Biological Sciences* 274(1623), 2327–2330.

Camerer, C.F., Dreber, A., Forsell, E., Ho, T.H., Huber, J., Johannesson, M., Kirchler, M., Almenberg, J., Altmejd, A., Chan, T., Heikensten, E., Holzmeister, F., Imai, T. Isaksson, S., Nave, G., Pfeiffer, T., Razen, M., Wu, H., 2016. Evaluating replicability of laboratory experiments in economics. *Science* 351(6280), 1433–1436. doi:10.1126/science.aaf0918.

Cardenas, J.C., Carpenter, J., 2008. Behavioural development economics: Lessons from field labs in the developing world. *Journal of Development Studies* 44, 311–338.

Chung, H., Lee, E.J., Jung, Y.J., 2016. Music-induced mood biases decision strategies during the ultimatum game. *Frontiers of Psychology* 7(453). doi:10.3389/fpsyg.2016.00453

Coffman, C.L., Niederle, M., 2015. Pre-analysis plans have limited upside, especially where replications are feasible. *Journal of Economic Perspectives* 29(3), 81–98.

Crockett, M.J., Clark, L., Tabibnia, G., Lieberman, M.D., Robbins, T.W., 2008. Serotonin modulates behavioral reactions to unfairness. *Science* 320(5884), 1739.

Crosetto, P., Güth, W., 2020. What are you calling intuitive? Subject heterogeneity as a driver of response times in an impunity game. Working Papers 2020–09, Grenoble Applied Economics Laboratory (GAEL).

Demiral, E., Mollerstrom, J., 2018. The entitlement effect in the ultimatum game: Does it even exist? *Journal of Economic Behavior and Organization* 175. doi:10.1016/j.jebo.2018.08.022

Dufwenberg, M., Kirchsteiger, G., 2004. A theory of sequential reciprocity. *Games and Economic Behavior* 47(2), 268–298.

Eckel, C., Petrie, R., 2011. Face value. *American Economic Review* 101(4), 1497–1513.

Ensminger, J., Henrich, J., 2014. *Experimenting with Social Norms: Fairness and Punishment in Cross-Cultural Perspective*. New York, NY: Russell Sage Foundation.

Fehr, E., Schmidt, K.M., 1999. A theory of fairness, competition, and cooperation. *The Quarterly Journal of Economics* 114, 817–868.

Fischbacher, U., Gächter, S., Fehr, E., 2001. Are people conditionally cooperative? Evidence from a public goods experiment. *Economics Letters* 71(3), 397–404.

Forsythe, R., Horowitz, J., Savin, N.E., Sefton, M., 1994. Fairness in simple bargaining experiments. *Games and Economic Behavior* 6(3), 347–369.

Fouraker, L.E., Siegel, S., 1963. *Bargaining Behavior.* New York: McGraw-Hill.

Gabay, A.S., Radua, J., Kempton, M.J., Mehta, M.A., 2014. The ultimatum game and the brain: A meta-analysis of neuroimaging studies. *Neuroscience and Biobehavioural Reviews* 47, 549–558.

Georganas, S., Healy, P.J., Weber, R.A., 2015. On the persistence of strategic sophistication. *Journal of Economic Theory* 159, 369–400.

Grosskopf, B., 2003. Reinforcement and directional learning in the ultimatum game with responder competition. *Experimental Economics* 6(2), 141–158.

Güth, W., 1979. Kriterien für die Konstruktion fairer Aufteilungsspiele. In: Albers, W., Bamberg, G., Seiten, R. (Eds.). *Entscheidungen in kleinen Gruppen. Mathematical Systems in Economics* 45, 57–89.

Güth, W., Kirchkamp, O., 2012. Will you accept without knowing what? The Yes-No game in the newspaper and in the lab. *Experimental Economics* 15(4), 656–666.

Güth, W., Kocher, M., 2014. More than thirty years of ultimatum bargaining experiments: Motives, variations, and a survey of the recent literature. *Journal of Economic Behavior and Organization* 108, 396–409.

Güth, W., Otsubo, H., 2020. Trust in generosity: An experiment of the repeated Yes-No game. *Evolutionary and Institutional Economics Review*. doi:10.1007/s40844-020-00170-5

Güth, W.R., Schmidt, C., Sutter, M., 2007. Bargaining outside the lab: A newspaper experiment of a three-person ultimatum game. *Economic Journal* 117(518), 449–469.

Güth, W.R., Schmittberger, B. Schwarze, 1982. An experimental analysis of ultimatum bargaining. *Journal of Economic Behavior & Organization* 3(4), 367–388.

Güth, W.R., Tietz, P., 1985. Strategic power versus distributive justice: An experimental analysis of ultimatum bargaining. In: Brandstätter, H., Kirchler, E. (Eds.). *Economic Psychology Proceedings of the 10th IAREP Annual Colloquium*. Linz: International Association for Research in Economic Psychology, 129–137.

Güth, W.R., Tietz, P., 1986. Auctioning ultimatum bargaining positions: How to act if rational decisions are unacceptable? In: Scholz, R.W. (Ed.). *Current Issues in West German Decision Research*. Frankfurt: P. Lang Publisher, 173–185.

Harlé, K.M., Chang, L.J., van't Wout, M., Sanfey, A.G., 2012. The neural mechanisms of affect infusion in social economic decision-making: A mediating role of the anterior insula. *Neuroimage* 61(1), 32–40. doi:10.1016/j.neuroimage

Harrison, G.W., Hirshleifer, J., 1989. An experimental evaluation of weakest link/Best shot models of public goods. *Journal of Political Economy* 97(1), 201–225.

Henrich, J., R., Boyd, R., Bowles, S., Camerer, C., Fehr, E., Gintis, H., 2004. *Foundations of Human Sociality: Economic Experiments and Ethnographic Evidence from Fifteen Small-Scale Societies*. Oxford: Oxford University Press.

Hoffman, E., McCabe, K., Shachat, K., Smith, V., 1994. Preferences, property rights, and anonymity in bargaining games. *Games and Economic Behavior* 7(3), 346–380.

Hoffman, E., McCabe, K.A., Smith, V.L., 1996. On expectations and the monetary stakes in ultimatum games. *International Journal of Game Theory* 25, 289–301.

Hou, Yu, Zhao, L., Yao, Q., Ding, L., 2016. Altered economic decision-making in abstinent heroin addicts: Evidence from the ultimatum game. *Neuroscience Letters*, 148–154. *doi*: 10.1016/j.neulet.2016.06.002

Innocenti, A., 2017. Virtual reality experiments in economics. *Journal of Behavioral and Experimental Economics* 69(C), 71–77.

Kagel, J.H., Roth, A.E., 1995. *The Handbook of Experimental Economics*. Princeton, NJ: Princeton University Press.

Kahneman, D., Knetsch, J., Thaler, R., 1986. Fairness as a constraint on profit seeking: Entitlements in the market. *The American Economic Review* 76(4), 728–741.

Kalisch, G.K., Milnor, J.W., Nash, J.F., Nering, E.D., 1954. Some experimental n-person games. In: Thrall, R.M., Coombs, C.H., Davis, R.L. (Eds.). *Decision Processes*. New York, NY: Wiley, 301–327.

Levine, D.K., 1998. Modeling altruism and spitefulness in experiments. *Review of Economic Dynamics* 1(3), 593–622.

Maniadis, Z., Tufano, F., List, J.A., 2017. To replicate or not to replicate? Exploring reproducibility in economics through the lens of a model and a pilot study. *The Economic Journal* 127(605), F209–F235.

Mitzkewitz, M., Nagel, R., 1993. Experimental results on ultimatum games with incomplete information. *International Journal of Game Theory* 22(2), 171–198.

Munafò, M.R., Nosek, B.A., Bishop, D.V., Button, K.S., Chambers, C.D., du Sert, N.P., Simonsohn, U., Wagenmakers, E.J., Ware, J.J., Ioannidis, J.P., 2017. A manifesto for reproducible science. *Nature Human Behaviour* 1 (2017), Article 0021. www.nature.com/articles/s41562-016-0021.

Murnighan, J.K., Saxon, M.S., 1998. Ultimatum bargaining by children and adults. *Journal of Economic Psychology* 19(4), 415–445.

Nagel, R., Harstad, R., 2004. Ultimatum games with incomplete information on the side of the proposer: An experimental study. *Cuadernos de Economía* 27(75), 37–74.

Nagel, R., Tang, F.F., 1998. An experimental study on the centipede game in normal form: An investigation on learning. *Journal of Mathematical Psychology* 42S(2), 256–384.

Nosek, B.A., Ebersole, C.R., DeHaven, A.C., Mellor, D.T., 2018. The preregistration revolution. *Proceedings of the National Academy of Sciences* 115(11), 2600–2606.

Nydegger, R., Owen, G., 1975. Two person bargaining: An experimental test of the Nash axioms. *International Journal of Game Theory* 3, 239–249.

Prasnikar, V., Roth, A., 1992. Considerations of fairness and strategy: Experimental data from sequential games. *Quarterly Journal of Economics* 107(3), 865–888.

Rabin, M., 1993. Incorporating fairness into game theory and economics. *The American Economic Review* 83, 1281–1302.

Rapoport, A., Sundali, J., 1996. Ultimatums in two person bargaining with one sided uncertainty: Offer games. *International Journal of Game Theory* 25, 475–494.

Roth, A.E., Erev, I., 1995. Learning in extensive-form games: Experimental data and simple dynamic models in the intermediate term. *Games and Economic Behavior* 8(1), 164–212.

Roth, A.E., Malouf, M.W.K., 1982. Scale changes and shared information in bargaining: An experimental study. *Mathematical Social Sciences* 3(2), 157–177,

Roth, A.E., Murnighan, J.K., 1982. The role of information in bargaining: An experimental study. *Econometrica* 50(5), 1123–1142.

Roth, A.E., Prasnikar, V., Okuno-Fujiwara, M., Zamir, S., 1991. Bargaining and market behavior in Jerusalem, Ljubljana, Pittsburgh, and Tokyo: An experimental study. *American Economic Review* 81(5), 1068–1095.

Roth, A.E., Sotomayor, M., 1990. *Two Sided Matching*. Cambridge: Cambridge University Press.

Rubinstein, A., 1982. Perfect equilibrium in a bargaining model. *Econometrica* 50, 97–109.

Rubinstein, A., 2007. Instinctive and cognitive reasoning: A study of response time. *The Economic Journal* 117, 1243–1259.

Sally, D., Hill, E., 2006. The development of interpersonal strategy: Autism, theory-of-mind, cooperation and fairness. *Journal of Economic Psychology* 27(1), 73–97.

Sanfey, A.G., Rilling, J.K., Aronson, J.A., Nystrom, L.E., Cohen, J.D., 2003. The neural basis of economic decision-making in the ultimatum game. *Science* 300(5626), 1755–1758. doi:10.1126/science.1082976

Selten, R., 1967. Die Strategiemethode zur Erforschung des eingeschränkt rationalen Verhaltens im Rahmen eines Oligopolexperiments. In: Sauermann, H. (Ed.). *Beiträge zur experimentellen Wirtschaftsforschung*, Vol. I. Tübingen: J.C.B. Mohr (Paul Siebeck), 103–168.

Selten, R., 1975. Reexamination of the perfectness concept for equilibrium points in extensive games. *International Journal of Game Theory* 4, 25–55.

Selten, R., Stoecker, R., 1986. End behavior in sequences of finite prisoner's dilemma supergames: A learning theory approach. *Journal of Economic Behavior & Organization* 7(1), 47–70.

Smith, V.L., Suchanek, G.L., Williams, A.W., 1988. Bubbles, crashes, and endogenous expectations in experimental spot asset markets. *Econometrica* 56(5), 1119–1151.

Stahl, I., 1972. *Bargaining Theory*. Stockholm: Economic Research Institute.

Steinhaus, H., 1948. The problem of fair division. *Econometrica* 16, 101–104.

Takagishi, H., Fujii, T., Kameshima, S., Koizumi, M., Takahashi, T., 2009. Salivary alpha-amylase levels and rejection of unfair offers in the ultimatum game. *Neuro Endocrinology Letters* 30(5), 643–646.

Thaler, R.H., 1988. The ultimatum game. *Journal of Economic Perspectives* 2(4), 195–206.

Van Damme, E.V., Binmore, K.G., Roth, A.E., Samuelson, L., Winter, E., Bolton, A.E., Ockenfels, A., Dufwenberg, M., Kirchsteiger, G., Gneezy, U., Kocher, M., Sutter, M., Sanfey, A.G., Kliemt, H., Selten, R., Nagle, R., Azar, O., 2014. How Werner Güth's ultimatum game shaped our understanding of social behavior. *Journal of Economic Behavior and Organization* 108(C), 292–318.

Wallace, B., Cesarini, D., Lichtenstein, P., Johannesson, M., 2007. Heritability of ultimatum game responder behavior. *Proceedings of the National Academy of Sciences* 104(40), 15631–15634.

Wang, Y., Xiao, Y., Li, Y., Chu, K., Feng, M., Li, C., Qiu, N., Weng, J., Ke, X., 2019. Exploring the relationship between fairness and 'brain types' in children with high-functioning autism spectrum disorder. *Progress in Neuro-Psychopharmacology and Biological Psychiatry* 88, 151–158.

5

THE WINNER'S CURSE AND PUBLIC INFORMATION IN COMMON-VALUE AUCTIONS (BY JOHN H. KAGEL AND DAN LEVIN)

Gary Charness

Introduction

Kagel and Levin (1986, hereafter "KL") is a path-breaking paper on a phenomenon called the "Winner's Curse" (hereafter "WC"), in which the winner of an auction is unhappy with the outcome on account of earning negative or below-normal profits. In the words of the authors: "You win, you lose money, and you curse." Capen, Clapp, and Campbell (1971; hereafter "CCC"), three petroleum engineers, were the first to identify this phenomenon, involving bidding for federal offshore oil leases. But economists largely dismissed this result as CCC had no equilibrium against which to judge the earnings reported. In addition, any earnings must account for the risk inherent in bidding and the number of competing bidders, neither of which was provided as part of CCC's claim (and which are virtually impossible to obtain). In KL, players received well-defined signals from a commonly known distribution, with the number of competing bidders' common information as well. Thus, this experiment was the first to study the WC with a well-defined reference point against which to compare outcomes. To my knowledge, this is the first work with an explicit closed-form solution for the common-value auction.[1] Many subsequent researchers have used the model, and its solution, commonly referred to as the KL model.

The KL model established a range of possible values for the item – say, between $50 and $500 from a uniform distribution – along with each bidder being provided their own private signal for the true value drawn from a uniform distribution of $\pm \varepsilon$ of the true value. In this way each bidder had their own private signal as to the lowest possible value for the item, along with its maximum possible value. In addition, they provided bidders with a starting capital balance against which any losses would be subtracted, or gains would be added to, with the ending balance paid in cash.[2] These cash

DOI: 10.4324/9781003019121-5

balances were large enough for bidders to commit one gross bidding error, learn from their mistake, and still have a large enough balance to actively bid in later auctions. In the case of bankruptcies, subjects were no longer permitted to bid. They used a variety of tactics to try and keep the number of bidders fixed in each session, but these were not always successful. They employed a first-price, sealed-bid-auction procedure, using subjects who all had prior experience in a series of first- or second-price, common-value auctions, and had not gone bankrupt in their inexperienced subject sessions. To enhance learning, after each auction period bids were listed from highest to lowest along with the corresponding signal values and the winner's earnings. And there were several dry runs before playing for cash. They employed both undergraduate students and MBA students. In short, efforts were made to help subjects avoid the worst effects of the WC.[3]

As Table 5.1 shows average earnings (profits) in the sealed-bid auctions, along with several reference points – average profits under the Risk Neutral Nash Equilibrium (RNNE), average actual profits as a percentage of the RNNE, and the percent of auctions won by the high signal holder. There are positive average profits with smaller numbers of bidders (three to four), clearly closer to the RNNE predictions than the zero/negative profit levels of the WC: average of $4.68 per auction period, about 65% of the RNNE model's prediction. However, in auctions involving larger numbers of bidders (six to seven), average profits were actually −$0.88, which, while clearly greater than predicted with strategic discounting alone, were well below the

TABLE 5.1 Profits and bidding: Kagel and Levin (1986), Table 3

No. of bidders	ε	Average profits with strategic discounting (standard error of mean)	Average actual profits (t-statistics)[a]	Average profits under RNNE[b] (standard error of mean)	Profits as a percentage of the RNNE prediction
3–4	12	−1.24 (.69)	2.60 (1.74)	4.52 (1.44)	57.5
	18	−.24 (1.03)	3.98 (3.71)[c]	7.20 (1.05)	55.4
	24/30	.60 (1.94)	6.75 (3.33)[c]	11.22 (2.06)	60.2
6–7	12	−3.68 (.54)	−1.86 (−2.21)[d]	3.46 (.56)	−53.8
	18	−8.51 (.52)	−.95 (−1.00)	3.19 (.51)	−29.8
	24/30	−12.31 (.89)	.60 (.51)	7.12 (.94)	8.4

a Tests null hypothesis that mean is different from 0.0.
b Based on sample of signal values drawn.
c Significant at 1% level, 2-tailed t-test.
d Significant at 5% level, 2 tailed t-test.

RNNE prediction of $4.68 per auction. Comparing small and large group auctions, actual profits decreased substantially more than profit opportunities as measured by the RNNE.

KL also investigated two of the comparative static predictions of the model: (1) the effects of increasing numbers of bidders on individual subject bids and (2) the impact of public information (the lowest signal value drawn; x_L) on bids and earnings. With respect to increasing numbers of bidders, the model predicts lower bids, conditional on the signal value drawn. However, actual results showed just the opposite, with bids increasing with increased numbers of bidders (N). With respect to the impact of public information about the lowest signal value, in auctions with six to seven bidders, on average public information *reduced* seller revenue by $1.79 per auction, compared to a predicted *increase* of $1.78 per auction. Table 5.2 shows a within-auction series analysis of auctions with six to seven bidders. This shows that, conditional on a WC with private information, 69% of the time seller revenue *decreased* with public information. In contrast, conditional on no WC with private information, 67% of the time seller revenue *increased* with the release of public information. These differences are significant at the 5% level (two-tailed test of proportions, $Z = 1.97$) despite the small number of observations.[4]

KL relate their experimental results for public information to empirical estimates of rates of return from bidding in offshore lease auctions in the Gulf of Mexico (Meade, Moseidjord, and Sorensen, 1984). For oil leases, there is a distinction between wildcat leases, where bidders only have imprecise sonic readings as to the oil in the ground, and drainage leases that abut wildcat leases where oil is found, for which there is far more precise information as a result of drilling in the neighboring wildcat lease. Meade et al. report higher rates of return on drainage leases compared to wildcat leases for *both* neighbors and non-neighbors. While the higher rates of return on drainage leases for neighbors can be explained by insider information, the higher rates of return for non-neighbors as well remains puzzling within the context of Nash equilibrium bidding theory. These higher rates of return on

TABLE 5.2 Effects of winner's curse: Kagel and Levin (1986), Table 6

	Number of periods in auction[a]		
	Large numbers (6–7)		*Small numbers*[b] *(3–4)*
Change in seller's revenues	*Winner's curse*	*No winner's curse*	*No winner's curse*
Increase	6	12	29
Decrease	11	5	10

a Auction market periods where RNNE predicted an increase in seller's revenues. Winner's curse defined in terms of high bid in private information market in excess of.

b Winner's Curse present in three auction periods.

drainage leases for both neighbors and non-neighbors is similar the effect of public information in the presence of a WC on for wildcat lease.

Mead et al. offer two possible explanations for the higher rates of return on drainage leases: (i) The lower rates of return on wildcat leases reflects the option value of having better information in bidding on drainage leases and/or (ii) the insider information scared non-neighbors into bidding lower on drainage leases so that when they won, they too achieved higher rates of return than on wildcat leases. KL argued that their explanation (public information in conjunction with a WC on wildcat leases) had the virtues of parsimony and consistency with the experimental results reported with respect to the impact of public information in the presence of a WC. While this is far from settling the correct explanation for the higher rates of return for both neighbors and non-neighbors on the drainage leases, it does provide a striking parallel between the experimental and field data, going some way in responding to one of the standard criticisms of experimental research – but is this how agents behave these outside the lab, in the "real" world.

Few economists were fond of such disequilibrium phenomena at the time KL was published, as the presumption was that such oddities would go away with time. But the WC is difficult to eliminate, particularly since one sometimes makes positive earnings in such auctions. I use the "Acquire-a-Company Game" (Bazerman and Samuelson, 1983), a simplified one-bidder task with adverse selection, to illustrate this point: "You can bid for a firm with a value between 0 and 100. The firm knows its current value, but you do not. Your bid is accepted if and only if the bid is at least as large as the current value. If it accepted, the business is worth 50% more in your hands. If it is not accepted, no money changes hands. What is your bid?"

The optimal bid in this design is zero since any positive bid only wins when it is no greater than the seller's value for the item, resulting in negative average earnings for the bidder. However, this rarely happens – bids often range between 50 and 75. No experiment has ever eliminated the WC in this simple task (and not for lack of trying).

Herein lies the central issue of the WC: People fail to reason (or think hypothetically), conditional on winning. In this case, winning means that the firm is currently worth no more than your bid. Thus, the range of values given acceptance of any bid x is 0 to x, rather than 0–100 as in the unconditional case. So, the expected value upon acceptance is $x/2$ (not 50), with bidders losing $x/4$ on average.[5]

The same principle applies to more standard common-value auctions, for which Wilson (1977) developed the RNNE solution. One must condition one's bid on the consideration that one (in principle) had the highest signal of all the bidders. Since winning is the only event that maters (in this model), a bidder, at the time of bidding, needs to form his or her bid, conditioned on (later) winning the auction. Thus, winning implies that rivals submitted lower bids, reflecting lower estimates (i.e., the "adverse selection"), and the bid must account for it at present. This critical issue is now at the heart of a great deal of research on reasoning and information processing in economics and the social sciences.

Advances in experimental methodology

KL shows that a clever experimental design can overcome problems that might seem insurmountable. First, there is the problem of people making negative profits over the course of a session. Several tactics were used to deal with this issue: only experienced bidders participated, each person received an additional endowment, and sometimes more subjects were present than the number of requisite bidders and a rotation scheme was used. Each subject that went bankrupt would have to leave, so having extra subjects ensured the experiment could continue.

As noted earlier, the concern of bankruptcy stems from the fact that it is not generally feasible to make subjects pay for losses out of pocket so a subject with a negative balance would have an incentive to gamble to reach positive territory.[6] This would obviously distort the bidding. Contemporary practices (evolved to some extent to deal with issues of cumulative earnings over the course of a session) now permit the experimenter to pay for one or more periods random-selected at the end, thereby sidestepping this concern (since subjects don't know their balances when bidding).[7]

Summary

This paper considers bidding in first-price auctions with a common value and private signals. The number of bidders in the auctions is varied, as is the public information provided to the bidders. Experienced bidders who have done relatively well (not gone bankrupt) in a previous auction experiment with the same (or similar) setup are given private signals about an item with a common value; each signal gives a range in which the common value must be. Participants then bid for the item in a first-price, sealed-bid auction.[8]

In equilibrium, the winning bidder should earn positive profits. However, KL showed that though experienced bidders in auctions with three to four bidders overcame losses (avoided losses), they fell right back into the WC when the number of bidders was increased. Overall, there is some evidence of learning with experience. However, what learning there is, appears to be of the "hot stove" variety, as bidders learn to bid less, but seems to have no understanding of why they *need* to bid less. Thus, they systematically lose again following a simple increase in the number of bidders. That is, they fail to realize that the underlying adverse-selection effect is exacerbated with more bidders, instead responding only to the competitive effect of bidding against more other bidders.

Charness, Levin, and Schmeidler (2019) also find this effect of group size with second-price, common-value auctions (SPA). Their within-subject design with four- and eight-person groups shows that people tend to bid *higher* in the larger groups, in contrast to the theoretical prediction for SPA. Note that there is no competitive effect in SPA, so that one's bid should be unambiguously lower with more bidders. Here people are shown ten sheets of paper with ten rows for each sheet. Each row gives three numbers as entries and these three numbers are combined in an undisclosed manner to get a fourth number, which is shown. People make their guesses of the actual number and are rewarded for accuracy. They then bid for this value simultaneously in eight-person (and sometimes four-person) auctions. While the average guess was always reasonably close to the actual number, there was a considerable WC (particularly with the eight-person groups).

KL was the first to show that providing public information when there is a strong WC reduces seller revenue. This is in contrast to the prediction in Milgrom and Weber (1982) that it would increase seller revenue. Kagel, Harstad, and Levin (1987) confirmed that the failure resulted from the winner's curse. They conducted a first-price, sealed-bid auction with affiliated private values – essentially the same design as in KL but with private values. Now when the lowest signal value drawn was publicly announced, it reliably *increased* seller revenue, regardless of the number of active bidders.

In summary, KL showed conclusively that the WC is "alive and well" in common-value auctions, even with experienced bidders. The article states (p. 917): "The winner's curse is a disequilibrium phenomenon that will correct itself given sufficient time and the right kind of information feedback." But the WC has proven devilishly difficult to dispel, with many laboratory attempts failing. Firms have earned large consulting fees by teaching the art of bidding in oil-leasing auctions.[9] Even in what is arguably the simplest case (the Acquire-a-Company Game with only two possible values for the firm, 0 or 99), positive bids are made at least 40% of the time (Charness and Levin, 2009).

In general, the issue is one of failure to perform contingent reasoning. This can be taught but seems to be quite unintuitive. People bid more in an eight-person auction than in a four-person auction more than twice as often as the reverse (259 versus 119) in the common-value auctions in Charness, Levin, and Schmeidler (2019), suggesting that the intuition behind RNNE discounting is typically not present. But even when people learn to condition in one setting, the ability to reason in a contingent manner in one specific setting may very well not transfer to other settings. Again, one must be able to update priors correctly for future events. While the WC should not be present in equilibrium, getting to that equilibrium is certainly not easy. KL provide clear and solid laboratory evidence that even people with experience in auctions fall prey to the WC.

Novelty and contribution

There are a number of reasons this article is considered to be a top-20 experimental paper. First, the phenomenon studied is of major financial concern, since bidding and auctions are nearly omnipresent in our contemporary economic society. This was one of the earliest works to consider an important (and controversial) real-world issue and to successfully and elegantly model and re-create it in the laboratory. In doing so, this article demonstrated the value of the experimental approach in distilling the essence of the environment and yielding convincing results. Not only do people suffer from the WC, the comparative statics of the theory fail as well: Subjects bid more aggressively with more bidders, rather than less as the theory predicts under their design; furthermore, public information reduces, rather than increases revenue in the presence of this excessive bidding.

A key issue is how well people think, or what is often termed "rationality." KL delves into this issue, making note of two opposing forces with respect to bidding. Indeed, they find that people grasp the strategic aspect of bidding (higher bids are more likely to be chosen) but don't seem to have absorbed the idea that winning may well mean that one has received the highest signal (p. 917): "Experienced bidders show sensitivity to strategic considerations underlying common value auctions, but not to item valuation considerations." This point had not been made clearly in any previous empirical study. In other words, while people realize that higher bids are more likely to win, they are typically unaware of the adverse-selection problem inherent with multiple bidders. This is also seen in the "one-person adverse-selection" environment in Charness and Levin (2009).

If even experienced bidders fall prey to the WC, this issue must not be easy to grasp. While KL suggest that this will correct itself given sufficient time and the right kind of information (feedback), it is not actually clear that this will be corrected at all quickly; in addition, insights gleaned in one environment may not transfer very well into a different one. Since KL was published, other models under which disequilibrium can be persistent have been developed. For example, Eyster and Rabin (2005) show that a "cursed equilibrium" can exist and Rabin and Schrag (1999) show that the confirmation bias can persist even with an unlimited amount of information. KL was one of the very first laboratory studies to show a persistent disequilibrium phenomenon in an environment involving serious financial consequences in the field; really this is one of the early behavioral papers that consider deviations from rationality in an arena largely devoid of social preferences. This article helped further research on behavioral biases in decision-making in economic contexts.

In fact, it may not be too much of a stretch to claim that this pioneered a whole new area of research about how people think. Hypothetical and contingent reasoning have become more and more important for understanding behavior; it does seem that there is something inherently difficult about strategic interactions. This type of strategic thinking is potentially present in any environment where people make decisions based on private information that is relevant to other people; a recent bounded rationality theoretical and experimental body of literature has offered different ways to model the mistake.

Subsequent work

KL has inspired a great deal of additional research, much of it theoretical. Jehiel (2005) puts forth the notion of analogy-based expectation equilibrium, whereby people use simplified representations to learn about their environment; people only try to learn the average behavior in every class. In his solution concept, players choose the best responses to their analogy-based expectations at every node, and expectations correctly represent the average behavior in every class. Jehiel and Koessler (2008) apply the model to a variety of well-known games such as the electronic mail game (Rubinstein, 1989) and signaling games (Crawford and Sobel, 1982), and show how analogy grouping may give rise to betting in betting games used to illustrate the no-trade theorem.

Eyster and Rabin (2005) introduce the cursed equilibrium, in which bidders correctly predict and best respond to the distribution of the other bids, but do not perceive correctly how these other bids depend on signals. This model, describing steady states of a cognitively constrained learning process, permits flexible levels of value adjustment, depending on the degree of "cursedness." Crawford and Iriberri (2007) propose a model concerned with initial responses in incomplete-information games using "level-k" thinking, where each player's behavior is drawn from a common distribution of "types" that vary in their degree of sophistication. There are completely naïve and nonstrategic players, denoted as $L0$ types. Level-k type players, where $k = 1,2,...$, best respond to their beliefs that all other players are of types k-1 and so are less sophisticated.

On the experimental side, Casari, Ham, and Kagel (2007) consider demographic and ability effects on one's propensity to fall prey to the WC, providing insights into how people adjust their bids to avoid the WC and also offering methodological insights. They find that inexperienced women are much more affected by the WC than men (controlling for SAT/ACT scores and college major), but that this difference narrows over time. The primary effect is more the result of people with below-median scores doing poorly rather than those with high scores doing well. Interestingly, economics and business majors seemed to be highly overconfident and bid higher than other majors. The experimental design enables the authors to identify strong selection effects that cannot be identified with standard econometric techniques, pointing out that careful experimental design can be very useful too.

Charness and Levin (2009) use a robot as the seller in the Acquire-a-Company Game, thereby eliminating the claim that people don't take into account the cognition of the other player. In fact, the experimental evidence presented in that paper flies in the face of the theories presented in the elegant papers mentioned in the preceding paragraph since there is no other person's cognition at issue. In the baseline condition, there are 100 cards on the screen, with integer values ranging from 0 to 99. Each subject chose a bid and then selected a face-down card, which represented the value. A bid was accepted if and only if it was not less than the number on the card. Very few people bid zero. A two-value treatment was also run, where 50 of the cards had value 0 and the other 50 had value 99. While the authors had expected this would be easy, in fact the WC was still quite pervasive; although few people bid anywhere between 0 and 99, showing a degree of rationality, bids of 99 were the most common.[10]

Ivanov, Peck, and Levin (2009) test an investment game in which subjects privately observe their cost of investing in addition to a signal correlated with the common investment return. They consider whether subjects draw inferences, in hindsight, and use foresight to delay profitable investment and learn from market activity. The combination of hindsight and foresight can be seen as insight. In contrast to Nash, cursed equilibrium, and level-k predictions, behavior hardly changes across their experimental treatments. They offer an explanation in terms of boundedly rational rules of thumb, based on insights about the game; this organizes the data substantially better than quantal-response equilibrium. Interestingly, they estimate that about 25–30% of subjects are "self-contained" (do not draw inferences from the decisions of others), 10% are "myopic" (drawing inferences in hindsight from the other past decisions), and 60–65% have "foresight" (investing when profitable unless valuable information might be learned by waiting).

A series of papers involving Esponda, Vespa, and co-authors consider issues involving hypothetical thinking and adverse selection. Esponda (2008) considers environments with naïve agents, who do not account for the informational content of other players' actions in adverse-selection settings. He applies his framework to particular adverse-selection environments and shows that contrary to the existing literature, the adverse-selection problem is exacerbated when naïve players fail to account for selection. Esponda and Vespa (2014) conduct a clever voting experiment to distinguish between hypothetical thinking and information extraction. Not only do more than half of the participants behave non-optimally, the critical issue is "these mistakes are driven by difficulty in extracting information from hypothetical, but not from actual, events." Esponda and Vespa (2018) study a specific aspect of contingent thinking (the Sure-Thing Principle) and show that it potentially underlies many of the classic anomalies in decision and game theory. The experimental results indicate that failure of this type of contingent thinking can explain some of the most common anomalies found in the laboratory. Martinez-Marquina, Niederle, and Vespa (2019) introduce uncertainty into a contingent-reasoning setting, finding that "a lack of certainty hampers payoff maximization and ... accounts for much of the difficulties with contingent reasoning."

Conclusion

The WC has been observed in auctions of book-publication rights, in bidding for free agents in baseball, and in corporate takeover bidding. It turns out to be quite difficult to learn to avoid the WC. The results in KL have led to important literature on the common inability to perform contingent reasoning or hypothetical thinking. In other words, one must account for the meaning of future events (contingencies).

KL took a real-world puzzle with major financial consequences and created a convincing demonstration of this phenomenon in the laboratory. In doing so, they provide strong evidence of behavioral effects in an auction environment. Here errors in individual judgment lead to quite different outcomes than predicted by the equilibrium. "Bidders in common value auctions ... are sensitive to the strategic opportunities inherent in the auction process. However, when strategic considerations and adverse-selection forces resulting from uncertainty about the value of the item conflict, behavior fails to conform, in important ways, with the requirements of Nash equilibrium bidding strategies." Perhaps more importantly, the insights provided by the WC regarding the failure of contingent reasoning have generated new fields of interest that consider, in more depth, the source of the problems with hypothetical thinking and perhaps possible methods to ameliorate this in the field.

Notes

1 Bazerman and Samuelson (1983) reported a WC experiment with MBA students where, for example, subjects bid on a jar of paper clips each worth, say, five cents. However, this confounds errors in guessing at the number of clips in the jar with bidding more than the value of the jar. In KL, bidders had well-defined signals as to the value. There is also an additional element of uncertainty in that even if one somehow can know this number, one has no idea about the perception of others. It is a bit odd to talk about the WC *per se* without a standard Bayesian model with priors and common knowledge of the information structure.

2 IRB rules, as well as reputational effects, would typically prohibit researchers from demanding that subjects cover any losses out of pocket.

3 A subject could, in principle, use the information provided to calculate the expected value conditional on the signal and bid below this. However, I am told that one of the reviewers of the paper, a well-known auction theorist, noted that the amount of this discount is surprisingly large: $x_i - \varepsilon (N - 1)/N + 1$ where N is the number of bidders in the auction.

4 These results were obtained using the dual-market technique: Subjects first bid in an auction with only private information, followed by bidding with the same signal values in auctions with public information, with the payoffs determined randomly between the two in each auction period. Cox, Dinkin, and Smith (1999) identified an error in the proposed Nash Equilibrium with public information in KL. Campbell, Kagel, and Levin (1999) solved for the correct benchmark against which to evaluate the experimental outcomes in KL, showing that the correct benchmark predicts higher revenues in each and every auction period than those of the bidding profile in KL. Thus, the correct benchmark strengthens KL's conclusion that (i) in markets with three to four bidders and no WC, public information reliably increases seller revenue and (ii) in markets with six to seven bidders where the WC reemerged, public information reduced seller revenue, contrary to the theory.

5 This holds for values distributed uniformly, which is the case in these experiments.

6 Even subjects with small positive balances could be affected, since they have limited liability. They can win big but can lose little. This is similar to what happened in the S&L crisis with lending institutions.

7 See Charness, Gneezy, and Halladay (2016) for a detailed discussion. There are theoretical arguments in the literature (see Azrieli, Chambers, and Healy, 2018), but the theory does not appear to be a settled issue.

8 Thus, the range of the signal was 43–207.

9 In fact, I was once asked about going to Venezuela to do exactly this, but the deal fell through.

10 A treatment with integer values between 20 and 119 was also conducted so that the optimal (theoretical) solution, which is 40 and, thus, not on the boundary. That was done as a control for the concern that since one could not bid below 0 (below 20 here). So here bidding higher in fact reflects that all errors are sided upwards and, thus, do not necessarily reflect non-contingent bidding. There was also abundant evidence of the WC in this setting.

References

Azrieli, Y., Chambers, C., and Healy, P.J., 2018. Incentives in experiments: A theoretical analysis. *Journal of Political Economy* 126(4), 1472–1503.

Bazerman, M., Samuelson, W., 1983. I won the auction but don't want the prize. *Journal of Conflict Resolution* 27(4), 618–634.

Campbell, C.M., John H. Kagel, J.H., Levin, D., 1999. The Winner's Curse and Public Information in Common Value Auctions: Reply. *American Economic Review* 89(1). 1, 325–334.

Capen, E.C., Clapp, R.V., Campbell, W.M., 1971. Competitive bidding in high-risk situations. *Journal of Petroleum Technology* 23, 641–653.

Casari, M., Ham, J., Kagel, J.H., 2007. Selection bias, demographic effects, and ability effects in common-value auction experiments. *American Economic Review* 97, 1278–1304.

Charness, G., Gneezy, U., Halladay, B., 2016. Experimental methods: Pay one or pay all. *Journal of Economic Behavior and Organization* 131, 141–150.

Charness, G., Levin, D., 2009. The origin of the winner's curse: A laboratory study. *American Economic Journal: Microeconomics* 1, 207–236.

Charness, G., Levin, D., Schmeidler, D., 2019. An experimental study of estimation and bidding in common-value auctions with public information. *Journal of Economic Theory* 179(C), 73–98.

Cox, J.C., Dinkin, S.H., Smith, V.L., 1999. The Winner's Curse and Public Information in Common Value Auctions: Comment. *American Economic Review* 89(1), 319–324.

Crawford, V.P., Iriberri, N., 2007. Level-k Auctions: Can a nonequilibrium model of strategic thinking explain the winner's curse and overbidding in private-value auctions? *Econometrica* 75, 1721–1770.

Crawford, V.P., Sobel, J., 1982. Strategic information transmission. *Econometrica* 50, 1431–1451.

Esponda, I., 2008. Behavioral equilibrium in economies with adverse selection. *American Economic Review* 98, 1269–1291.

Esponda, I., Vespa, E., 2014. Hypothetical thinking and information extraction in the laboratory. *American Economic Journal: Microeconomics* 6, 180–202.

Esponda, I., Vespa, E., 2018. Endogenous sample selection and partial naivete: A laboratory study. *Quantitative Economics* 9, 183–216.

Eyster, E., Rabin, M., 2005. Cursed equilibrium. Econometrica 73, 1623–1672.

Ivanov, A., Levin, D., Peck, J., 2009. Hindsight, Foresight, and Insight: An Experimental Study of a Small-Market Investment Game with Common and Private Values. *American Economic Review* 99(4), 1484–1507.

Jehiel, P., 2005. Analogy-based expectation Equilibrium. Journal of Economic Theory 123, 81–104.

Jehiel, P., Koessler, F., 2008. Revisiting games of incomplete information with analogy-based expectations. *Games and Economic Behavior* 62, 533–557.

Kagel, J.H., Harstad, R., Levin, D., 1987. Information impact and allocation rules in auctions with affiliated private values: A laboratory study. *Econometrica* 55(6), 1275–1304.

Kagel, J.H., Levin, D., 1986. The winner's curse and public information in common value auctions. *American Economic Review* 76, 894–920.

Martinez-Marquina, A., Niederle, M., Emanuel Vespa, E., 2019. Failure in contingent reasoning: The role of uncertainty. *American Economic Review* 10, 3437–3474.

Meade, W.J., Moseidjord, A., Sorensen, P.E., 1984. Competitive bidding under asymmetrical information: Behavior and performance in Gulf of Mexico drainage lease sales, 1959–1969. *Review of Economics and Statistics* 66, 505–508.

Milgrom, P.R., Weber, R.J., 1982. A theory of auctions and competitive bidding. *Econometrica* 50, 1089–1122.

Rabin, M., Schrag, J.L., 1999. First impressions matter: A model of confirmatory bias. *Quarterly Journal of Economics* 114, 37–82.

Rubinstein, A., 1989. The electronic mail game: Strategic behavior under 'almost common knowledge. *American Economic Review* 79, 385–391.

Wilson, R., 1977. A bidding model of perfect competition. *Review of Economic Studies* 44, 511–518.

6

GROUP-SIZE EFFECTS IN PUBLIC GOODS PROVISION: THE VOLUNTARY CONTRIBUTIONS MECHANISM (BY R. MARK ISAAC AND JAMES M. WALKER)

James Andreoni

Introduction

One thing that makes Isaac and Walker's paper a top one is that it forces the profession to see an old topic with new eyes. I first saw the Isaac and Walker "group size" paper when, in 1986, I was visiting the University of Arizona as candidate for an assistant professor's position. I had just finished my job talk on the crowding out of public goods and the warm-glow of giving. Mark Isaac was taking me to coffee and was carrying a mysterious document under his arm. I could tell he had something of great urgency to speak with me about. When we and our coffees settled in a shady spot, and I removed my woolen suit jacket, Mark placed the document in front of me and, in about 15 minutes, explained his experimental design, described the conclusions, and asked me how I planned to use experiments to strengthen the ideas in the first two chapters of my thesis. Indeed, Chapter 3 of my dissertation was an experimental paper that built on ideas generated in part from the mysterious document passed to me by Mark at that interview.[1]

The times

In 1988, the literature on privately provided public goods was beginning to heat up. Before the mid-1980s, there was a strong consensus that the topic of the private provision of public goods was largely solved, and the conclusion was, essentially, that it was all measurement error. Or perhaps the topic was better suited for sociology or psychology than economics. As Mancur Olson argued in his treatise (1965), echoing the earlier conclusions of Samuelson (1954), free-riding incentives are so strong as to preclude any significant value to private provision of public goods. The only exception, importantly,

DOI: 10.4324/9781003019121-6

is very small groups, such as the family, a club, or an office, which can bring unique powers of coercion that are not available in large groups. As Olson put it,

> [U]nless the number of individuals in a group is quite small, or unless there is coercion or some other special device to make individuals act in their common interest, rational, self-interested individuals will not act to achieve their common or group interests.

The value of "coercion," which I interpret as the enforcement of social norms, is most easily employed in small groups where there can be both swift retribution and a long memory. "The larger a group is," Olson continues,

> the farther it will fall short of providing an optimal supply of any collective good, and the less likely that it will act to obtain even a minimal amount of such a good. In short, the larger the group, the less it will further its common interests.

In the meantime, new papers were emerging that inverted Olson's claim. Increasing group size should increase giving.[2] Importantly, testing which prediction is correct requires a random assignment of potential donors to different group sizes to provide public goods in otherwise identical environments, a feat that can likely only be accomplished through a controlled experiment.

What Olson failed to acknowledge was that charitable giving in the U.S. has been at 1.7–2.1% of GDP since it was first measured in the early 1960s. Money spent on charitable giving exceeds that spent on essentials like electricity – in clear contradiction of both Olson's and Samuelson's conjectures that its role in the economy is trivial. Yet it was not until the mid-1980s that economics as a profession began to take seriously that free riding may not be the right model of giving.

Besides seeing the old facade of free riding crumble on the theoretical side, we also were witnessing something of a building boom of new ideas for how to reconstruct an understanding of the private provision of public goods and prosocial behavior. What this branch of public economics needed was a unified way of testing our ideas that would make our studies easy to compare and our progress simple to track. This organizing device was cemented on the day in February 1988 that the new issue of the *Quarterly Journal of Economics* hit newsstands.

A second element of the times surrounding Isaac and Walker's publication was an opening up of Game Theory to allow for deviations from common knowledge of rationality in repeated games.[3] In the now famous "Gang of Four" paper, David Kreps, Paul Milgrom, John Roberts, and Robert Wilson (1982) showed that mutual cooperation can be sustained in a finitely repeated prisoners' dilemma game if there is a belief held by some players that a small fraction of other players could in fact not be rational. Such a situation would give rational players an incentive to behave as if they themselves were not rational. Instead of employing the subgame perfect strategy derived by backward induction (that is, always defect), rational players instead adopt a strategy of cooperating until some period, call it t_i^*, such the rational agent i will cooperate until period t_i^*, or until her opponent defects, then defect ever after.[4] Given the similarity between public goods and a multi-person prisoner's dilemma, it is natural to look at the strategic reputation building as a serious alternative to Olson's intuitive notion of coercion in small groups.

The main hypothesis

Isaac and Walker (IW) began by restating Olson's hypothesis more formally as resting in the technology of public goods. IW observed that public goods in the real world might be characterized by some degree of congestion.[5] For instance, as more people consume California's highways at any one time, each driver experiences less utility from consuming those highways. Visiting the San Diego Zoo is far more pleasurable when fewer other people are already there. Law enforcement and fire protection are more likely to help in an emergency at my house if the number of trucks and personnel is high relative to the number of calls. A public good that can be congested in this way can be called an "impure public good." The degree of congestion in inversely proportional to the number of individuals consuming the good. If g_i is individual i's contribution to a public good and n is the number of consumers, then we can define a congestible public good as the function $G^c = \frac{1}{n^\rho} \sum_{i=1}^n g_i$, where ρ, $0 \le \rho \le 1$, indicates the degree of congestion. If $\rho = 0$ then $\frac{\partial G^c}{\partial g} = 1$, and the good is a pure public good. At the other extreme, $\rho = 1$, then $\frac{\partial G^c}{\partial g} = \frac{1}{n}$ and we say the public good is completely congestible.

Another way to interpret this formulation is that more congestible public goods are more expensive to provide – to get one more unit of a congestible public good the person needs to contribute $g(\alpha, n) = n^\rho g$. For a given ρ, the higher n, the more a person needs to contribute to get a desired increase in the public good.[6]

IW's hypothesis is that the general intuition that public goods are harder to provide in large groups stems from the fact that these public goods are congestible. That is, as you increase n, you must also increase the cost of providing the good. Congestion means that we may not observe an effect of the cost of a unit of g for a given group size, and we may not observe a pure effect of increasing the group size n, while keeping the cost constant, but an increase in group size combined with an increase in cost due to congestion could validate the common intuition.

Isaac and Walker's experimental design

The first decision to make when designing an experiment is what payoff function to employ. IW adopted the linear payoff scheme introduced by Marwell and Ames (1981). IW called this the voluntary contributions mechanism, or VCM. Payoffs are described by the linear function

$$\pi_i = w_i - g_i + \alpha \sum_j g_j \tag{6.1}$$

$$= w_i - g_i + \frac{\beta}{n} \sum_j g_j \tag{6.2}$$

where w_i is subject i's endowment of tokens, g_i is i's contribution to the public good, $G = \sum_1^n g_j$, and $\alpha = \beta / n$. IW referred to α as the *marginal per capita return* or MPCR. To make this a proper public goods game we require $0 \le \alpha \le 1$, and $n\alpha = \beta > 1$. The first condition implies that $\frac{\partial \pi_i}{\partial g_i} = -1 + \alpha < 0$, so choosing $g_i = 0$ (that is, free riding) is a dominant strategy Nash Equilibrium for all subjects. The second condition guarantees us that $\frac{\partial \sum \pi_i}{\partial g_i} = -1 + n\alpha = -1 + \beta > 1$. This implies that $g_i = w_i$ for all i is a symmetric Pareto efficient allocation.

Separating α from equation (6.1) into the two components of $\frac{\beta}{n}$ in equation (6.2) provides an interesting way to test free riding. First, if we assume that the subjects' only interest is in making money, then giving them a well-defined payoff function should "induce" a utility function on them. This methodological approach was common at the time of IW's publication. Economists were yet to seriously use experiments as tools for subjects to reveal their true utility functions. Induced value theory was tested nicely by IW simply by employing different values of β and n, such that $\alpha = \frac{\beta_1}{n_1} = \frac{\beta_2}{n_2}$, but $\beta_1 > \beta_2$ and $n_1 > n_2$. If subjects are adopting the payoff function as their objective function, then such subjects would be free riders regardless of the values of β and n. If subjects fail to free ride and, moreover, if they respond to changes in β and n in systematic ways, this suggests that the payoff function did not induce preferences but rather was subsumed into true preferences. Recognizing subjects' "homemade preferences" was an important step in experimental economics.

IW selected n to be four (small group) or ten (large group) and chose α low (L) at 0.3 or high (H) at 0.75, for a classic 2×2 design. IW had 6 sets of 4 subjects, and 6 sets of 10 subjects participate in their study, for a total of 84 subjects. However, each subject in a set of four participated in two ten-period repeated public goods games, one of which was 4L and the other was 4H, *with the same set of four subjects for each of the 20 games played.* The order of L and H conditions was balanced across the six sets. A similar

TABLE 6.1 Parameters of the experimental design

Condition	n	α	β	w	Payoff function, π	$NE\,\pi$	$PE\,\pi$
4L	4	0.30	1.2	62	$\pi_{4L} = 62 - g + 0.30G_{4L}$	62	75
4H	4	0.75	3.0	25	$\pi_{4H} = 25 - g + 0.75G_{4H}$	25	75
10L	10	0.30	3.0	25	$\pi_{10L} = 25 - g + 0.30G_{10L}$	25	75
10H	10	0.75	7.5	10	$\pi_{10H} = 10 - g + 0.75G_{10H}$	10	75

process was followed for the ten-person groups, including using the same ten subjects for all 20 decision rounds. The parameters of IW's design are shown in Table 6.1.

The fact that the same group of four or ten subjects were in all 20 rounds complicates independence across rounds or even across ten-period games. Thus, subjects were more accurately described as in a single 20-period repeated game. This allows IW a clean statistical test if they treat the session as the unit of observation and use the final group choices in the 20th round of a session as a single observation. We are left to assume that all the subjects had equal opportunity to learn the game in those 20 rounds. Whether they chose to adopt the dominant strategy in this final round would then be a matter of taste.

Isaac and Walker's results

The primary results of IW can be illustrated in one graph with four points. This is shown in Figure 6.1. Here our measure of generosity is the percent of token contributed to the public good in the final round of the 20-round session. Nearly identical results also follow from the percent of subjects free riding ($g = 0$) in the final round of play.

Look first at the two highest points in the figure, corresponding to 4H and 10H. These two points show a small *negative* effect of group size on giving, conditional on a high α. Next consider the two lowest points 4L and 10L. These two show a small *positive* effect of group size given a low α. Thus, in looking for a pure group-size effect, the data are mixed as to whether it is negative, as hypothesized, or positive. The bottom line is that pure group-size effect, positive or negative, is not present in the data.

Next, look at the two left-most points, 4H and 4L, which shows the pure MPCR effect given a small group. Likewise, the two right-most points, 10H and 10L, show the pure MPCR effect conditional on a large group. Both effects are positive and significant.[7]

What about the interaction effect? If public goods in life are mostly subject to congestion, then large and small groups should have the same β, but the large group should have a lower α. If the negative effect of a lower α dominates any positive effect of n that might exist (although it did not exist in IW's data), then the total effect would be a decrease in giving. This

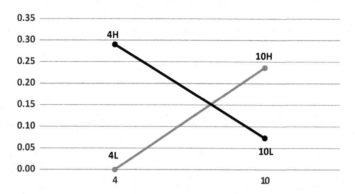

FIGURE 6.1 Percent of endowment given.

decrease can easily be seen in the black line in Figure 6.1. The effect is highly significant.

Other theories

IW discuss two other aspects of decision-making as possible explanations. One is the strategic reputation building of Kreps, Milgorm, Roberts, and Wilson (1982). This model is very subtle, suggesting that one would expect that after only two ten-period interactions we would be surprised to see the tell-tale signs of this kind of equilibrium, that is, high cooperation at the start of the super-game, with a point of sudden precipitation of giving and a quick convergence to free riding. Rather giving in all groups seems best characterized by gradual "decay" toward lower average giving as the game proceeds.

Despite the tepid reception of this theory from IW, a vibrant literature emerged from it and is vital today. Most studies center on finitely repeated prisoners' dilemma games, with some considering as many as 20 10-period games (Andreoni and Miller, 1993). For a review and meta-analysis, see Embrey, Fréchette, and Yuksel (2018). Within the public goods domain, Andreoni (1988b) tested the reputation-building hypothesis by comparing subjects in a finitely repeated game (partners matching) to those in a repeated single-shot game (strangers matching). Surprisingly, the finding was contrary to the hypothesis – strangers contributed more than partners. This was challenged in a replication by Croson (1996) and was further addressed in a series of papers by Palfrey and Prisbrey (1996, 1997). They argued through their experiments that strangers matching added more variance to the data. In a review of the literature on this question, Andreoni and Croson (2008) found about one-third of the studies agreed with the original finding, one-third showed no difference, and one-third favored Croson's finding. They concluded that Palfrey and Prisbrey's explanation was the most convincing.

The second theory IW consider is that subjects are still trying to understand the incentives and are not displaying well-developed preferences in the experiment. This is a general hypothesis and they did not include manipulations to test this explicitly. To explore this question, we must first ask what kind of learning we are looking for. Suppose subjects who are playing a finitely repeated game are asked after round 10 to stay for another ten-period game? One thing learning suggests is that a surprise restart is strategically meaningless, and all the information about opponents' preferences should be used to update (presumably revise down) expectations for future cooperation. When introducing a surprise restart, Andreoni (1988) found the subjects in the strangers matching condition were, indeed, largely unaffected, but those in the partners' matching condition presented a pattern of play nearly identical to the first ten rounds. This lifted hopes that perhaps subjects were beginning to learn the logic of reputation building.

Discussion

A curious aspect of the early literature on public goods is that theories were not presented to explain why subjects would choose a g that was not a corner solution. A natural suggestion is that subjects cared not just for the money they could earn in the experiment, but they also cared about the distribution of payoffs of others. Typically, subjects in public goods experiment are only told the total giving $G = \sum g_i$ and not the individual amounts, g_i. Still, this is enough to calculate the average earning of the other players.

As before, let π_i be the payoff of individual i, and π_o be the average earnings of the others. Suppose there are $m = n - 1$ other subjects in the group, then it would be natural to assume subjects have utility

$$u_i = u_i\left(\pi_i, m^b \pi_o\right)$$

where $b = 1$ means the subject cares about the total payoff of others, $b = 0$ means the subject cares only for the average payoff, while $b \in (0,1)$ is consistent with a behavioral model where the subject cares about total payoffs but with diminished sensitivity to additional group members.

One can now use this definition of preferences in an experiment much like the one of IW in order to estimate the value of b. The result is an estimate of $b = 0.68$, which can be interpreted as saying that the average subject would be indifferent to giving an amount x to one person or giving an amount $x / m^{0.68}$ to m people.[8]

Why this is a great paper

There are four reasons this is a great paper.

Reason 1: well-defined and important question

At the time the IW paper was first drafted, we had no clear alternative models that would suggest to us why individuals in a linear public goods game would choose anything besides $g = 0$, no matter the group size. Olson's loosely reasoned description of normative giving was one of the few hypotheses leading the literature to a toe-hold of a new model. IW presented a clever new alternative model to address an enduring question.

Reason 2: left more questions than answers

This paper is about more than just group-size effects in linear public goods games. The fact that the main result is inconsistent with any hypothesis on public goods, including Nash Equilibrium free riding, shows that deeper questions are at stake here. It is a siren song to all budding young economists looking for a puzzle to explain. I consider myself fortunate to have been among those catching this wave.

Reason 3: provocative alternative hypotheses

IW go on to cast doubt both on ideas of learning and strategic reputation building. Strategic reputation building leads to sharp changes in behavior. Instead, the IW data has a lot of underlying variance, and average behavior tends rather slowly toward the dominant strategy. This does not directly rule out either hypothesis, however. Strategic reputation building is a complicated notion, and it could take several passes at playing super-games of finitely repeated public goods, and this has been shown to be the case.

Reason 4: a well-articulated research agenda

IW could have written this paper rather narrowly focused on the question on group size. Instead the paper was written expansively, opening experimental economics to a plethora of new, deep, and challenging questions, many of which remain active areas of research to this day, including both strategic reputation building and learning in games. This paper by IW showed the potential for experiments to inform us on topics of great interest. Their paper spelled out a whole agenda for future research, leading many to take up their challenge.

Conclusion

Did the paper by IW present a flawlessly designed experiment that provided conclusive evidence and unifying insight on a fraught and contested area of the literature? No. The paper is not without its flaws. But alongside those methodological issues (which, frankly, we all learned from at the time) was an open and honest discussion of these shortcomings, and an imaginative and expansive articulation of the possibilities of experimental economics. To me, the greatest gift of this paper was the invitation to innovate and to tackle difficult and important questions.

A thank you to James Andreoni from R. Mark Isaac and James M. Walker

We would like to thank Jim Andreoni for a kind and constructive overview of our paper. It is particularly special to us coming from someone with such an illustrious career researching public goods provision.

We also thought this would be a nice opportunity to provide a couple of comments aimed at younger researchers who, we hope, are taking the opportunity provided by this volume to "walk down the memory lane" of these articles.

First, as Jim has ably pointed out, the advance of knowledge is messy. One problem with "preregistered" research, for example, is that it assumes that all the questions in the domain in the inquiry are known and well formulated in advance. That is not, in fact the case, and was certainly not the case when we began our work on public goods. In advance, we hadn't a clue as to why this "thing" that we now call the MPCR would prove to be empirically meaningful, nor how subtle and complex was the question of asking, "When does a large group have a harder time providing a public good than a small group?" The 1988 paper included here is actually the second paper in a series, designed to be focused on the question of group size after we realized that there was something interesting going on with these concepts with our first paper – Isaac, Walker, and Thomas (1984).

As Jim correctly states, even a very good experimental paper should actually not be considered as "settling" anything. New questions are generated, and new boundaries to be explored. As Jim points out, we started working just as the "Gang of Four" papers on reputation in finite games provided a new approach to equilibria (e.g., Kreps, Milgorm, Roberts, and Wilson, 1982). The literature on "social preferences" evolved somewhat later, in part as a response to early work on public goods, not only ours but also other papers such as Isaac, McCue, and Plott (1985) and Jim's paper on crowding out (Andreoni, 1993).

Likewise, as Bob and Leo famously explained in *What About Bob?*, babysteps matter. Running initial simple experiments can lead to building the confidence to explore more focused questions. We don't think we would have ever jumped into this paper without having conducted the research for the first paper. Likewise, experimental technologies change and open up new possibilities. For example, in our 1994 paper with Arlie Williams (Isaac, Walker, and Williams, 1994), using both synchronous and calibrated asynchronous experimentation, we were able to push the boundaries of the "pure numbers" effect to 40 and even 100. In the process, we reproduced the MPCR effect and demonstrated areas of the parameter space where the MPCR effect weakened because contributions were high in all conditions. Importantly, we also reproduced the MPCR effect with a very small MPCR and a very large group size of 40, where contributions were found to decay rapidly.

And, as Jim also points out, even well-designed (for their time) experiments are set in a given world of statistical knowledge and tools; experiments should raise questions about the robustness of statistical analysis. This statistical skepticism leads to new debates and approaches, with the result that those who come later can look at similar questions with more statistical heft (of course, this is not unique to laboratory experimental work, by any stretch of the imagination).

Secondly, separately from the specifics of public goods, we hope that younger readers will get a sense of the excitement that can come from a really meaningful collaboration with colleagues. The opportunity of thinking back on this research reminded the two of us of the hours spent in Jimmy's office in front of the white board working out what the MPCR implied for the design, or reading through Olson and Buchanan to try to figure out what *they* meant by a "larger" group. Enjoy, appreciate, and value your time with your collaborators.

Notes

1 The answer to that question is no, I did not get a job offer from Arizona. I accepted the offer from University of Wisconsin, where I worked from 1986 until January 2006 when I joined the faculty at UC San Diego. I conduct research on public goods to this day.
2 Bergstrom, Blume, and Varian (1985) and Andreoni (1988a) predicted the opposite in models of pure altruism. Private giving would rise with group size although asymptotically, meaning the average size of gifts got smaller as n increased. Andreoni (1989, 1990) also predicts (via a normal goods assumption) a positive relation.
3 Game Theory had not yet embraced evolutionary game theory or the related models of learning, although these two advances were surely ushered in by experimental findings, and by this experiment on public goods. See Miller and Andreoni (1991) on using nascent evolutionary game theory to study the results of Isaac and Walker.
4 Notice, no one in this model needs to be irrational, but there only needs to be sufficient (potentially incorrect) belief that some fraction of the players could be irrational.
5 There is a long literature on congestion in public goods, starting with Bergstrom and Goodman (1973). See also Chamberlin (1974).
6 Think of the extreme cases and this point becomes obvious.
7 Mann-Whitney U-test, $z = 2.48$ ($p \leq 0.006$).
8 See Andreoni (2007). Take the example of giving \$20 to one person or \$2 each to ten people. Because of the diminished sensitivity, $\$2 < \$20/10^{0.68} = \$4.78$, the person would prefer giving \$20 to one person to giving \$2 each to ten people.

References

Andreoni, J., 1988a. Privately provided public goods in a large economy: The limits of altruism. *Journal of Public Economics* 35(1), 57–73.

Andreoni, J., 1988b. Why free ride? Strategies and learning in public goods experiments. *Journal of Public Economics* 37(3), 291–304.

Andreoni, J., 1989. Giving with impure altruism: Applications to charity and Ricardian equivalence. *Journal of Political Economy* 97(6), 1447–1458.

Andreoni, J., 1990. Impure altruism and donations to public goods: A theory of warm-glow giving. *The Economic Journal* 100(401), 464–477.

Andreoni, J., 1993. An experimental test of the public-goods crowding-out hypothesis. *The American Economic Review* 83, 1317–1327.

Andreoni, J., 2007. Giving gifts to groups: How altruism depends on the number of recipients. *Journal of Public Economics* 91(9), 1731–1749.

Andreoni, J., Croson, R., 2008. Partners versus strangers: Random rematching in public goods experiments. In: Plott, C.R., Smitt, V.L. (Eds.). *Handbook of Experimental Economics Results*, Vol. 1. Amsterdam: North-Holland, 776–783.

Andreoni, J., Miller, J.H., 1993. Rational cooperation in the finitely repeated prisoner's dilemma: Experimental evidence. *The Economic Journal* 103(418), 570–585.

Bergstrom, T.C., Blume, L.E., Varian, H.R., 1985. On the private provision of public goods. *Journal of Public Economics* 29, 25–49.

Bergstrom, T.C., Goodman, R.P., 1973. Private demands for public goods. *The American Economic Review* 63(3), 280–296.

Chamberlin, J., 1974. Provision of collective goods as a function of group size. *American Political Science Review* 68(2), 707–716.

Croson, R., 1996. Partners and strangers revisited. *Economics Letters* 53, 25–32.

Embrey, M., Fréchette, G.R., Yuksel, S., 2018. Cooperation in the finitely repeated prisoner's dilemma. *The Quarterly Journal of Economics* 133(1), 509–551.

Isaac, R., McCue, K., Plott, C., 1985. Public goods provision in an experimental environment. *Journal of Public Economics* 26, 51–74.

Isaac, R., Walker, J., Thomas, S., 1984. Divergent evidence on free riding: An experimental examination of possible explanations. *Public Choice* 43, 113–149.

Isaac, R., Walker, J., Williams, A., 1994. Group size and the voluntary provision of public goods: Experimental evidence utilizing large groups. *Journal of Public Economics* 54, 1–36.

Kreps, D.M., Milgrom, P., Roberts, J., Wilson, R., 1982. Rational cooperation in the finitely repeated prisoners' dilemma. *Journal of Economic Theory* 27(2), 245–252.

Marwell, G., Ames, R.E., 1981. Economists free ride, does anyone else. *Journal of Public Economics* 15(3), 295–310.

Miller, J.H., Andreoni, J., 1991. Can evolutionary dynamics explain free riding in experiments? *Economics Letters* 36(1), 9–15.

Olson, M., 1965. *The Logic of Collective Action: Public Goods and the Theory of Groups.* Cambridge, MA: Harvard University Press.

Palfrey, T.R., Prisbrey, J.E., 1996. Altruism, reputation and noise in linear public goods experiments. *Journal of Public Economics* 61, 409–428.

Palfrey, T.R., Prisbrey, J.E., 1997. Anomalous behavior in public goods experiments: How much and why? *The American Economic Review* 87(5), 829–846.

Samuelson, P.A., 1954. The pure theory of public expenditure. *The Review of Economics and Statistics*, 387–389.

7

RATIONAL EXPECTATIONS AND THE AGGREGATION OF DIVERSE INFORMATION IN LABORATORY SECURITY MARKETS (BY CHARLES R. PLOTT AND SHYAM SUNDER)

Mark Isaac

Introduction

The inclusion of this paper in this volume of foundationally important papers is a testament to its influence throughout the profession, but this is no surprise. The paper has almost 600 citations on Google Scholar. It has inspired significant further research. I am honored to be given the opportunity to review this paper. To segue into my admiration for this paper (hereafter "P&S88"), I want to start with my equal admiration of a previous paper, "Efficiency of Experimental Security Markets With Insider Information: An Application of Rational Expectations Models" by Charles R. Plott and Shyam Sunder (1982) (hereafter "P&S82"). The two papers taken together (not to mention their numerous extensions) constitute an arc of a classic research program.

In fact, I teach my undergraduate experimental economics course around a set of topics anchored by one or more "classic" papers. The final course assignment is a hypothetical research grant proposal. Through this final project, I introduce research that is more modern. I try to cover 10–12 classic papers, and P&S82 is one of them. I have also found it to be one of the most popular, even though it is in many ways one of the most difficult for non-specialist undergraduates. (P&S82 itself has almost 700 citations on Google Scholar.) Often in the course of classroom conversations or discussion about final projects, we move from the stronger evidence for rational expectations in P&S82 to the weaker evidence of P&S88 and the problem of information aggregation. This likewise grabs the students' attention. Allow me to take a similar short walk through the background of this research, stopping and considering P&S82, and finally arriving at a discussion of P&S88.

DOI: 10.4324/9781003019121-7

Information dissemination (Plott and Sunder [1982])

In the P&S82 sessions, subjects are endowed with shares of a good that lasts only one trading period but that has "asset-like" properties in that subjects are not constrained to one side of the market or the other but are generalized traders who can make profits in two different ways: holding onto the shares for a dividend payable at the end of the period, or trading the shares for capital gains. Dividends payable to holding the shares depend upon a randomly determined state of nature (X or Y, or in the final session, X, Y, or Z) and are different for each of three different classes of individuals. Although subjects know the ex-ante probabilities of the states, in most periods the realization of the actual state is unknown to the subjects. Finally, in many of the periods in which the state realization is not common knowledge, a subset of the traders (typically one or two – out of three or four – of each type) is provided with private information on the true state. (In the first session, the "insiders" were instead provided only with "clues.") All traders were generally aware of the possible existence of some "insider traders," but they did not know the identity of the insiders, because everyone received an envelope of some kind (these were hand-run sessions). From Table 1 in P&S82, it appears that in most "insider trading" periods, it was not common knowledge how many insiders there were, but it was common knowledge what an insider, if one existed, would know.

These are market experiments, and the authors use a hand-run (pencil and paper) version of the double auction as the trading mechanism. With the exception of the change in the information conditions – which the next section will elaborate – it appears that essentially the same double auction trading mechanism was used for both P&S82 and P&S 88. Each subject (trader) was provided with an endowment of both working capital and shares in the relevant securities. Short sales were not permitted. A complete set of sample instructions is included as an Appendix to P&S82. These instructions demonstrate how subjects were trained with the double auction trading mechanism, the rules of the market, and the determination of the underlying random state. (Plott and Sunder used an actual bingo cage in the presence of the traders to determine the state of nature.)

Plott and Sunder conducted this research in the days in which funding for experimental economics was limited, and the number of sessions (five) was lower than we would expect today, with greater funding opportunities available. Because of these limitations, the authors had to make every period of every session meaningful for their eventual analysis. The key outcome of the many design choices that Plott and Sunder had to make was the existence, across the five sessions, of 17 periods in which their operationalization of two pricing models ("rational expectations" versus "prior information") diverged.

In 13 of those 17 periods, the rational expectations model (see, for example, Grunberg and Modigliani [1954], Muth [1961], Fama [1970], and

Lucas [1972]) described the price data better than the prior information model. The two models likewise made different predictions about the holdings of the assets at the end of the period in many of the periods, even in periods in which the price predictions of the two models were the same. Again, the rational expectations model tended to be more accurate on average.

Finally, one notes that Plott and Sunder are able to eliminate two more "extreme" types of models. One of these is a beauty-contest type of prediction in which almost anything can be an asset-market equilibrium. This is clearly not supported by the data, as the prices appear to be driven significantly by either the prior information or the rational expectations equilibria (obviously, given the discussion above, more by the latter). The data are likewise inconsistent with a "crystal ball" version of rational expectations.

At first glance, P&S82 might seem like an odd choice to include in a relatively short list of papers for undergraduates. The experimental design is not "going where no one has gone before" in the same sense as Vernon Smith's (1962) first published experimental paper (on the double auction) or the paper from Fiorina and Plott (1978) on majority rule voting experiments. It is not the first paper to advance beyond the restriction of market participants being preset as either "buyers" or "sellers" (becoming, instead "traders"). That goes back to, at least, Miller, Plott, and Smith (1977). It is not the first paper to examine rational expectations models in experimental asset markets. Forsythe, Palfrey, and Plott (1982) appeared just a few months earlier.[1] Indeed, in P&S82, the assets do not carry over from period to period, and so become "asset-like" only because they can be re-traded in real time during a single period, allowing for the possibility of intra-period capital gains. It was only several years later when the bubbles and crashes in Smith, Suchanek, and Williams (1988) took asset-market research by storm that we observed a design in which a researcher could say, "Here, indeed, is a design in which deviations from rational expectations are robustly observed."

Instead, I teach P&S82 to introductory undergraduates because it is so bold, because it is built around a clever experimental design, and because the theory separation is important but is relatively easy for undergraduates to handle. Furthermore, both P&S82 and P&S88 hit a sweet spot in the guidance of theory on experiments, a sweet spot that I believe that we are seeing less and less of in experimental papers today. Indeed, other papers had begun the tough process of moving from instantaneous consumption goods to asset goods. However, Plott and Sunder were not content to build incrementally on that work. Instead, while still working in general in the world of questions of rational expectations and asset markets, they pivoted to the role of information in forming (or not) trader expectations in an asset market. In doing so, they were addressing questions that ranged from the deeply theoretical (basic debates about the performance of asset markets) to applied (models of the profitability of insider trading).

While it must be emphasized that P&S82 is not a policy "wind tunnel" experiment in the same sense that Hong and Plott (1982) staked out at about the same time, the "early, simple" experiment model is also at play. The authors state, "Our goal is to determine the appropriateness of various models for predicting the behavior of very simple markets with the hope that the understanding gained will be useful in ascertaining features of models which will have successful application to more complex markets." This statement of purpose is followed by a footnote: "We cannot claim to have tested any of the models found in the literature. All models are accompanied by technical assumptions and qualifications which are not present in the simple models we created. These markets may be used to test these models only if such assumptions are placed in an 'as if' category and are not to be taken literally."

In my opinion, the methodological field of play as described in this footnote is one reason why both this paper and P&S88 are so important. Smith (1982), in his methodological treatise on experimental microeconomics, described three initial categories of experiments: "nomo-theoretical," "nomo-empirical," and "heuristic." I have noticed a tendency among experimental economists, most likely myself included, to shift slightly to the dichotomy of "theory-testing" and "heuristic" experiments. Thinking about this paper has made me realize that this simple dichotomy is a mistake.

Once we say a research program is "theory-testing" as opposed to "heuristic" it is as though we are asking to be enrobed in a set of rules about what it means to have a research design that is appropriately grounded and informed by theory. Even Plott and Sunder state, as above, that they "cannot claim to have tested" their reference models because their design could not capture every significant assumption needed for a pure theory-testing exercise. But if we view Smith's architecture not so much as a trichotomy as much as a continuum, it is clear that both P&S82 and P&S88 are, in their essence, pieces of research that are intensely interested in and guided by theories of information transmission in asset markets. This is critical to understanding the importance of the research.

Another marker of a great paper is that it inspires further study. This is most definitely the case for P&S82. For example, Jeff Banks (1985) created a design in which it was harder to follow specific people known to be insiders by rotating who was an insider. Copeland and Friedman (1987) changed the process of the arrival of the "insider" information. Camerer and Weigelt (1991) looked for information "mirages" when traders were uncertain about the presence of insiders. Another of my personal favorites is Sunder (1992), "Markets for Information: Experimental Evidence," in *Econometrica*. Sunder gives a dramatic proof of concept of the Grossman-Stiglitz paradox (1980), comparing markets with a fixed supply of insider traders (where traders must bid on the right to be one of the insiders) as opposed to markets in which there is a fixed price to be an insider (and the number of traders is exogenous). With a fixed supply of insider traders, the demand curve to be an insider shifts back across periods. With a fixed price, the number of traders is unstable. The Sunder paper makes us realize that we have to consider not only the markets for securities and the information in the market but likewise the market that produces the information.

Ultimately, this stream of research brings us to P&S88, and the expansion of inquiry to the aggregation of information in markets, not merely the questions of information dissemination.

Plott and Sunder 1988 and the question of information aggregation

Four of the five sessions in P&S82 had only two states (X and Y). Session 5 was different in having three states (X, Y, and Z), but it was still the case that if the true state was Z, the insider traders knew that it was Z. However, it is only a small step from this configuration to one in which if the true state is Z, some informed traders know that it is "Not X" and others know that is "Not Y." The information that the true state is Z is "in the market," but it has to be aggregated for the rational expectations family of models to work. Recall that it is not merely the transmission of information but foremost its aggregation among dispersed individuals that was critical to the foundational issues proposed by Hayek (1945). This provides the segue to the economic environment of P&S88.

In P&S88, the issue is not the transmission of information from some informed traders to the rest of the market of uninformed traders. Rather, the issue is that different traders have diverse imperfect signals of the true state. Thus, "Series A" in P&S88 (Sessions 1, 2, 3, 6, 10, 11, and parts of 4 and 5) are the closest to making these simple but crucial changes from Session 5 in P&S82.

Plott and Sunder used essentially the same double auction trading mechanism and state-determination process here as in P&S82. The main wrinkle in the experimental design was the necessity for easily and confidentially distributing the, for example, "Not X; Not Y" information. This was accomplished in two steps. First, before the experiment began, a group randomization process divided the traders into two separate groups (different in each period). Second, during the experiment, the bingo cage determined the realized state (as in P&S82), and then the experimenters used a pre-prepared "clue sheet" announcement to quickly transmit the individualized "not" information to the traders. The details of these additions to the market process are contained in the Appendix to P&S88.

Given the robust tendency for the data in P&S82 to be well explained by the rational expectations model, the authors state that they had similar expectations about Series A. It is hard to put oneself back in time, but I would concur that I would have thought that this information aggregation problem in Series A was "close" to the information dissemination problem of Experiment 5 in P&S82, and that I would have expected successful information aggregation. However, in fact, these expectations were not supported. The data in Series A demonstrate a strong tendency for private information models to out-perform rational expectations information aggregation models in organizing the data, and this conclusion is supported across several criteria, including prices and efficiencies.

At this point, Plott and Sunder introduced two alternate treatments. In Series B, there were complete contingent claims markets (three markets for securities payable upon state X, Y, or Z being the true state, respectively). In Series C, heterogeneity of dividends across trader classes was replaced with identical dividend distributions across all traders. Both of these design changes yielded data much more reflective of successful information aggregation. Thus, with "Series B" and "Series C" this paper becomes the pioneer in demonstrating the possibility for conditions for aggregation of diverse information in a market.

The price dynamics for the contingent claims markets in Series B are particularly fascinating. Consider, for example, the first three periods of Session 4 in Figure 4 (p. 1097). These are all "Z" periods. Notice how quickly the prices of the X and Y securities fall toward zero, as the price of the Z security approaches the rational expectations price.

After the presentation of the results, the authors demonstrate their concern for interacting data and theory by considering the implications of their results for models of price dynamics, including a tâtonnement model of Jordan (1982) and a time path model for specifically informed traders in the contingent claims market. They also analyze the possibilities of profitable trades by mechanical filters and find, somewhat surprisingly, that a fair game conclusion is a necessary but not sufficient condition for the achievement of rational expectations prices ("Markets in Series A are fair games but these markets are not near RE equilibrium" [p. 1114]).

Unfortunately, there are not enough session replications to examine the independent effects of the treatment changes within series type. For example, Series A has some subjects in sessions with two trader types and eight total traders (Sessions 1, 2, and 3) and others in sessions with three trader types and 12 total traders (Sessions 4 [last]; 5 [last], 6, 10, and 11). Likewise, some Series A sessions used inexperienced subjects (Sessions 1, 3, 4 [last]) while the others had experienced subjects (Sessions 2, 5 [last], 6, 10, and 11). However, short of a formal statistical analysis, one thing that is striking is that the dog that doesn't bark – namely, the lack of an obvious effect of experience in moving outcomes noticeably toward the rational expectations predictions. More broadly, these subtle but potentially important differences within Series A increase our confidence that the failure of these markets to aggregate information is not due to some narrow "sweet spot."

Likewise, while the small sample size doesn't allow us to conclude that Series B or Series C (or similar) conditions are always going to yield similar results, Series B and Series C do give us a proof of concept that markets can both aggregate and disseminate private information in a way that supports market outcomes broadly consistent with rational expectations models. Taken together, the failure of aggregation in Series A, together with the success in Series B and C, demonstrate that there are boundaries to the ability of markets to aggregate information successfully, thus making the totality of these results path-breaking in guiding where we need to look to find those boundaries (again see Smith [1982]). For example, Chen and Plott (2008) report an ambitious extension with ten, rather than three, states (and, thus, ten contingent claims markets), stochastic rather than deterministic clues distributed to the traders, and a continuous computerized trading mechanism with over 60 subjects. In one session, the resulting market for the contingent claims aggregates successfully in six of seven periods, but fails in one.[2]

For later researchers, the design changes in Series B and Series C were important guideposts. For example, Forsythe and Lundholm (1990) demonstrate that, in an analog to P&S88's Design A, adding the joint conditions of more intensive experience and more common knowledge can significantly improve the predictive ability of the rational expectations model. Lundholm (1991) and O'Brien and Srivastava (1991) pursued even more complex conditions to establish boundaries. In the mid 1990s, asset research may have turned more to the "bubbles and crashes" issue, but that doesn't mean that the questions of dissemination and aggregation were settled.[3] Just recently, Choo, Kaplan, and Zultan (2019) report on an important extension of the contingent claims design (P&S88 Series B) where there is a more complex (and, hence, difficult for rational expectations) mapping of states onto the markets for the assets. Furthermore, the issues of information aggregation in markets, especially with contingent claims, added important DNA to the new (in the early 1990s, at least) and quickly evolving literature on prediction and wisdom-of-the-crowds markets (see Deck and Porter [2013] for a survey). In addition, price-formation questions focusing on trader decisions specifically in the double auction were certainly an influence on the papers in the Friedman and Rust volume (1992) on complexity in markets. This volume contained an early version of what became Gode and Sunder's (1993) classic paper on zero-intelligence traders, which itself has over 1,900 Google Scholar citations.

That 32 years after its publication this paper continues to inspire important new research about both the core topic of information aggregation in asset markets as well as new streams of research is a testament to the fact that this paper truly deserves the honor of being called a "pioneer." I am certain that it will continue to inspire future researchers for years to come.[4]

Notes

1 Here is a bit more chronology. When I was a graduate student at Caltech (1976–1980), Miller, Plott, and Smith (1977) had just been published. I recall Bob, Charlie, and Tom working on what would become Forsythe, Palfrey, and Plott (1982). In personal correspondence commenting on an earlier draft of this introduction, both Shyam and Charlie recalled that they interacted in 1980 at the University of Chicago, which was home to much theoretical and (especially)

archival empirical work on asset pricing models, particularly models that we would think of as rational expectations, fully efficient markets, etc. The two of them realized that controlled laboratory experiments had the potential to add a great deal to this line of inquiry.

2 I often describe to my students the search for these boundaries as being akin to looking for the boundaries of an oil field. Note that the productive part of the research program is the equivalent of looking substantively for the presence or absence of oil; looking for that physical boundary of "no oil" is not the same thing as trying to find a way to fail in looking for oil that might be there.

3 Sunder himself (1995) authored a definitive survey of the laboratory assert market literature as it stood in the mid 1990s. Plott (2000) offers an updated look through approximately 1999.

4 I would like to acknowledge the very helpful feedback of the editors Gary Charness and Mark Pingle. In addition, Charles Plott and Shyam Sunder were most generous with their time in conveying comments on my preliminary ideas and drafts. As always, I am alone responsible for any errors or omissions.

References

Banks, J.S., 1985. Price-conveyed information vs. observed insider behavior: A note on rational expectations convergence. *Journal of Political Economy* 93, 807–815.

Camerer, C.F., Weigelt, K.W., 1991. Information mirages in experimental asset markets. *Journal of Business* 64(4), 463–493.

Chen, K.Y., Plott, C.R., 2008. Markets and information aggregation mechanisms. In Plott, C.R. and Smith, V.L. (Eds.). *Handbook of Experimental Economics Results*, Vol. 1. Amsterdam: North-Holland, 344–352.

Choo, L., Kaplan, T.R., Zultan, R., 2019. Information aggregation in Arrow-Debreu markets: An experiment. *Experimental Economics* 22, 635–652.

Copeland, T.E., Friedman, D., 1987. The effect of sequential information arrival on asset prices: An experimental study. *Journal of Finance* 42, 763–797.

Deck, C., Porter, D., 2013. Prediction markets in the laboratory. *Journal of Economic Surveys* 27, 589–603.

Fama, E.F., 1970. Efficient capital markets: A review of theory and empirical work. *Journal of Finance* 25, 383–417.

Fiorina, M.P, Plott, C.R., 1978. Committee decisions under majority rule: An experimental study. *American Political Science Review* 72, 575–598.

Forsythe, R., Lundholm, R., 1990. Information aggregation in an experimental market. *Econometrica* 58, 309–347.

Forsythe, R., Palfrey, T.R., Plott, C.R., 1982. Asset valuation in an experimental market. *Econometrica* 50, 537–567.

Friedman, D., Rust, J. (Eds.), 1992. *The Double Auction Market: Institutions, Theory, and Evidence* (Santa Fe Studies in the Sciences of Complexity, Vol. 14). Boulder, CO: Westview Press.

Gode, D.K., Sunder, S., 1993. Allocative efficiency of markets with zero-intelligence traders: Market as a partial substitute for individual rationality. *Journal of Political Economy* 101, 119–137.

Grossman, S.J., Stiglitz, J.E., 1980. On the impossibility of informationally efficient markets. *American Economic Review* 70, 393–408.

Grunberg, E., Modigliani, F., 1954. The predictability of social events. *Journal of Political Economy* 62, 465–478.

Hayek, F.A. 1945. The use of knowledge in society. *The American Economic Review* 35, 519–530.

Hong, J.T., Plott, C.R., 1982. Rate filing policies for inland water transportation: An experimental approach. *The Bell Journal of Economics* 13, 1–19.

Jordan, J., 1982. A dynamic model of expectations equilibrium. *Journal of Economic Theory* 28, 235–254.

Lucas, R.E., 1972. Expectations and the neutrality of money. *Journal of Economic Theory* 4(2), 103–124.

Lundholm, R., 1991. What affects the efficiency of the market? Some answers from the laboratory. *The Accounting Review* 66, 486–515.

Miller, R.M., Plott, C.R., Smith, V.L., 1977. Intertemporal competitive equilibrium: An empirical study of speculation. *Quarterly Journal of Economics* 91, 599–624.

Muth, J.F., 1961. Rational expectations and the theory of price movements. *Econometrica* 29, 315–335.

O'Brien, J.W., Srivastava, S., 1991. Dynamic stock markets with multiple assets: An experimental analysis. *Journal of Finance* 46, 1811–1838.

Plott, C.R., 2000. Markets as information gathering tools. *Southern Economic Journal* 67, 2–15.

Plott, C.R., Sunder, S., 1982. Efficiency of experimental securities markets with insider information: An application of rational expectations models. *Journal of Political Economy* 90, 663–698.

Plott, C.R., Sunder, S., 1988. Rational expectations and the aggregation of diverse information in laboratory security markets. *Econometrica* 56, 1085–1118.

Smith, V.L., 1962. An experimental study of competitive market behavior. *Journal of Political Economy* 70, 111–137.

Smith, V.L., 1982. Microeconomic systems as an experimental science. *American Economic Review* 72 (5), 923–955.

Smith, V.L., Suchanek, G.L., Williams, A.W., 1988. Bubbles, crashes, and endogenous expectations in experimental spot asset markets. *Econometrica* 56(5), 1119–1151.

Sunder, S., 1992. Market for information: Experimental evidence. *Econometrica* 60, 667–695.

Sunder, S., 1995. Experimental asset markets: A survey. In Kagel, J.H. Roth, A.E. (Eds.) *The Handbook of Experimental Economics*. Princeton, NJ: Princeton University Press, 445–500.

8

EXPERIMENTAL TESTS OF THE ENDOWMENT EFFECT AND THE COASE THEOREM (BY DANIEL KAHNEMAN, JACK L. KNETSCH, RICHARD H. THALER)

John A. List[1]

Introduction

Stated preference surveys were first proposed by Ciriacy-Wantrup (1947), and have served an important role ever since in generating total values of non-market goods and services (see Bishop et al., 2017). Yet, one anomaly that began to surface in the early 1970s was that willingness to accept (WTA) and willingness to pay (WTP) measures of value for a commodity were systematically different. For example, Hammack and Brown (1974) found that hunters questioned about possible destruction of a duck habitat stated that they would be willing to pay an average of $247 to prevent the loss but demanded a compensation of $1,044 to accept the destruction. Similarly, Rowe et al. (1980) found that WTA values were from 5 to over 16 times higher than WTP values in their survey. These are not cherry-picked examples, as the review of Cummings et al. (1986) shows.

In these stated preference examples, the basic independence assumption naturally leads to the prediction that with small income effects and many available substitutes, the WTA and WTP measures of value should be roughly equivalent. When such data patterns began to surface, scholars wondered if a key tenet of neoclassical theory – that preferences are independent of the consumer's current entitlements – was being violated.

As one might guess, the initial reaction of many economists was to argue that these early results were a survey artifact and that WTA estimates were unreliable and should not be treated seriously. This is because whether preferences are defined over consumption levels or changes in consumption has serious implications for the discipline of economics. In a normative sense, the basic independence assumption (that preferences are orthogonal to current entitlements), which is used in most theoretical and applied economic models to assess the operation of markets, is directly refuted. In a

DOI: 10.4324/9781003019121-8

positive sense, the disparity has considerable relevance. For example, such preferences call into question commonly held interpretations of indifference curves, make cost-benefit analyses illegitimate, change the procedure necessary to resolve damage disputes, and prompt a reconsideration of several of our other deep intuitions, such as the invariance result of Coase, which relies on Hicksian equivalent surplus and Hicksian compensating surplus to be roughly equivalent.

What was needed to help resolve the dispute was an empirical assessment of whether this systematic occurrence of stated values represented real preferences or was indeed an artifact. Relatedly, are these stated values best described by a neoclassical model or do we need to scrap that model and use an entirely new economic paradigm?

Onto the scene step Daniel Kahneman, Jack Knetsch, and Richard Thaler. Danny and Dick need no introductions. They are Nobel Prize winners (Danny in 2002 and Dick in 2017) as pioneers of the behavioral economic approach, and rightfully so. To my eye, Jack Knetsch is one of the unsung heroes of the behavioral economics movement, one of the most under-appreciated and under-rated economists of the 1980s and 1990s. He was not only a coauthor of the seminal work on the endowment effect that I discuss here but he also contributed to several other stellar contributions in the 1980s and 1990s (see, e.g., Knetsch and Sinden, 1984; Kahneman et al., 1986a, b; Knetsch, 1986; Kahneman et al., 1991).

From a historical perspective, the Big Bang for modern behavioral economics was a theoretical paper on preferences over gambles written by Kahneman and Tversky (1979), but the Kahneman et al. (1990; KKT hereafter) work defined and struck a deep empirical chord. This is because KKT reported broad experimental evidence of an *endowment effect*, which was earlier coined by Thaler to denote that people offer to sell a good in their possession at a substantially higher level than they will pay for the identical good not in their possession. Indeed, KKT assert two important conjectures that have had an important influence on the profession: (1) they forward eight experimental demonstrations that they argue shows evidence of the endowment effect and (2) they argue that their evidence shows the endowment effect is a fundamental characteristic of preferences that will not be eliminated by market experience.

To make my review a "one stop" shop, the next section provides a "workmanlike" look at the KKT study, which they present as eight different experiments. With this in hand, the "KKT experiment 1" section provides a theoretical exploration showing certain imperfections in their work that might temper one's enthusiasm for a strong interpretation of their data. I then proceed to explore briefly some work catalyzed from their study that shows, from the aggregate evidence, that one can make both arguments in concert with the original KKT conclusions and some that are at odds with KKT. I hope that this approach not only places KKT in proper perspective but also provides some relief to those scholars making solid incremental advances in a world that seemingly demands every single issue to be tackled in one study. Impatient or well-read scholars familiar with the original KKT work might wish to jump directly to the "KKT experiment 1" section.

KKT experimental particulars

In this section, I provide an overview of the various experiments in the original KKT study and the results forwarded by their analysis. I do not return to their data and perform a replication, rather I take as given their results.

KKT Experiment 1

Description

In Experiment 1, 44 students in an advanced undergraduate law and economics class at Cornell University faced 11 different markets. The first three markets were conducted for induced-value tokens. Sellers (or buyers) were told that they were owners of a token (or that they had the opportunity to buy a token), the value it had for them and that the tokens had different values for different individuals. They subsequently were asked to indicate whether they would sell (or buy) the token at that price or keep the token and cash it in for the sum of money indicated (or not buy the token at that price).

Forms with a distribution of values and prices ranging from $0.25 to $8.75 in increments of $0.50 were prepared for both buyers and sellers. Not all the forms were distributed, as such the induced supply and demand curves were not always symmetric. Subjects alternated between the buyer and seller role in the three successive markets and were assigned a different individual redemption value in each trial. After each market period, the experimenters collected the forms from all participants, and immediately calculated and announced the market-clearing price, the number of trades, and the presence or absence of excess demand or supply at the market-clearing price. Three buyers and three sellers were selected at random after each of the induced markets and were paid according to the preferences stated on their forms and the market-clearing price for that period.

After the three induced-value markets, subjects in alternating seats were given Cornell coffee mugs, which sell for $6.00 each at the bookstore. The experimenter then informed subjects that four markets for mugs would be conducted using the same procedures as the previous induced market, with two exceptions. First, one of the four market trials would be selected at random and only the trades made on this market would be executed. Second, in the binding market trial, all trades would be implemented, unlike the subset implemented in the induced-value markets. The initial assignment of buyer and seller roles was maintained for all four trading periods. The clearing price and the number of trades were announced after each period. After the fourth period, the market that "counted" was indicated and transactions were executed immediately. All sellers who had indicated that they would give up their mugs for a sum at the market-clearing price exchanged their mugs for cash, and successful buyers paid this same price and received their mugs. This design was used to permit learning to take place over successive trials and yet make each trial consequential in expectations.

The same procedure was then followed for four more successive markets using boxed ballpoint pens with a visible bookstore price tag of $3.98, which were distributed to the subjects who had been buyers in the mug markets. Subjects completed a form similar to that which was used for the induced-value tokens; they were asked to indicate, for a list of prices, whether they preferred to sell (or buy) the object and receive the price listed or keep the object and take it home (or not buy the object at that price).

Results

The markets for induced-value tokens and consumption goods yielded different results. In the induced-value markets, as the authors anticipated, the median buying and selling prices were identical. The ratio of actual to predicted volume (V/V*) was 1.0, aggregating over the three periods. In contrast, the median selling prices in the mug and pen markets were more than twice the median buying prices. The V/V* ratio was only 0.20 for mugs and 0.41 for pens. The observed volume did not increase over successive periods in either the mug or the pen markets, providing no indication that subjects could learn to adopt equal buying and selling prices.

KKT Experiments 2–4

Descriptions

Experiment 2 was conducted with an undergraduate microeconomics class with 38 students. The procedure was identical to that of Experiment 1, except that the second consumption good was a pair of folding binoculars in a cardboard frame, available at the bookstore for $4.00.

Experiments 3 and 4 were conducted in Simon Fraser University undergraduate economics classes and, in these treatments, subjects were asked to provide minimum selling prices or maximum buying prices rather than answering the series of yes or no questions used in Experiments 1 and 2. The induced-value markets were conducted with no monetary payoffs and were followed by four markets for pens in Experiment 3 and five markets for mugs in Experiment 4. In Experiment 3, subjects were told that the first three markets for pens would be used for practice, so only the fourth and final market would be binding. In experiment 4, one of five markets was selected at random to count, as in Experiments 1 and 2.

Results

All three experiments yield insights consonant with Experiment 1. Summing over the induced-value markets in all four experiments produced a V/V* index of 0.91. This performance was achieved even though the participants did not have the benefit of experience with the trading rules, there were limited monetary incentives in Experiments 1 and 2, and there were no monetary incentives in Experiments 3 and 4. In the markets for consumption goods, in which all participants faced monetary incentives and experience with the market rules gained from the induced-value markets, V/V* averaged 0.31, and median selling prices were more than double the corresponding buying prices.

KKT Experiment 5

Description

Experiment 5 was carried out similarly to the first four experiments, except that subjects were told that the executed market price would be selected at random. This change was made because readers of early drafts of the paper suggested that because of the manner in which market prices were determined, subjects might have felt that they had an incentive to misstate their true values to influence the price.

This fifth experiment was conducted in a series of six tutorial groups of a business statistics class at Simon Fraser University with 59 students. The use of small groups was used to ensure that complete understanding of the instructions, and the exercises were conducted per the course of a single day to minimize opportunities for communication between participants. Each group was divided equally: half of the subjects were designated as sellers by random selection, and the other half became buyers.

Results

Empirical results of this experiment were nearly identical to the earlier ones in which the actual exchanges were based on the market-clearing price. In the mugs market, the results again showed a large and significant endowment effect. The V/V* index was 0.41.

KKT Experiments 6 and 7

Descriptions

Experiments 6 and 7 were conducted to assess the weight of reluctance to buy and reluctance to sell in the under-trading of a good such as the ones used in the earlier experiments.

Subjects in Experiment 6 were 77 Simon Fraser students, randomly assigned to three groups. Members of one group, designated sellers, were given a coffee mug and were asked to indicate whether they would sell the mug at a series of prices ranging from $0.00 to $9.25. A group of buyers indicated whether they were willing to buy a mug at each of these prices. Finally, choosers were asked to choose, for each of the possible prices, between a mug and cash.

Experiment 7 was carried out with 117 students at the University of British Columbia. It used an identical design, except that price tags were left on the mugs.

Results

Experiment 6

The results again reveal substantial under-trading, the V/V* ratio was 0.24. The close similarity of results for buyers and choosers indicates that there was relatively reluctance to pay for the mug.

Experiment 7

Results were consistent with those in Experiment 6. The V/V* ratio was 0.05.

Experiment 8

Description

The last experiment was a bilateral bargaining variant to test if the individual who is assigned the property right to a good will be more likely to retain it because the marginal rate of substitution between one good and another is affected by the endowment.

Subjects were 35 pairs of students in seven small tutorials at Simon Fraser University. The students were enrolled in either a beginning economics course or an English class. Each student was randomly paired with another in the same tutorial group, with care taken to ensure that students entering the tutorial together were not assigned as a pair. A game of Nim, a simple game easily explained, was played by each pair of participants. The winners of the game were each given a 400 g Swiss chocolate bar and were told it was theirs to keep. An induced-value bargaining session was then conducted. The member of each pair who did not win the Nim game, and therefore did not receive the chocolate bar, was given a ticket and an instruction sheet that indicated that the ticket was worth $3.00 because it could be redeemed for that sum.

Ticket owners were also told that they could sell the ticket to their partner if mutually agreeable terms could be reached. The partners (the chocolate bar owners) received instructions indicating that they could receive $5.00 for the ticket if they could successfully buy it from the owner. Thus, there was a $2.00 surplus available to any pair completing a trade. The pairs were then given an unlimited amount of time to bargain. Subjects were told that both credit and change were available from the experimenter.

Results

Of the 35 pairs of participants in the induced-value experiment, 29 agreed to an exchange (V/V* = 0.83). Alternatively, there were only seven trades in the chocolate bar treatment (V/V* = 0.40).

Taken together, KKT interpret data from their eight experiments as follows (p. 1335):

> As shown in tables 2–4, subjects showed almost no under-trading even in their first trial in an induced-value market. Evidently neither bargaining habits nor any transaction costs impede trading in money tokens. On the other hand, there is no indication that participants in the markets for goods learned to make valuations independent of their entitlements. The discrepant evaluations of buyers and sellers remained stable over four, and in one case five, successive markets for the same good and did not change systematically over repeated markets for successive goods.

And, later in the study they conclude by noting that (pp. 1342–1344):

> The evidence presented in this paper supports what may be called an instant endowment effect: the value that an individual assigns to such objects as mugs, pens, binoculars, and chocolate bars appears to increase substantially as soon as that individual is given the object.
> [...]
> The results of the experimental demonstrations of the endowment effect have direct implications for economic theory and economic predictions. Contrary to the assumptions of standard economic theory that preferences are independent of entitlements, the evidence presented here indicates that people's preferences depend on their reference positions. Consequently, preference orderings are not defined independently of endowments: good A may be preferred to B when A is part of an original endowment, but the reverse may be true when initial reference positions are changed. Indifference curves will have a kink at the endowment or reference point.

And, KKT conclude their epilogue with the following passage (p. 1346):

> To conclude, the evidence reported here offers no support for the contention that observations of loss aversion and the consequential

evaluation disparities are artifacts; nor should they be interpreted as mistakes likely to be eliminated by experience, training, or "market discipline." Instead, the findings support an alternative view of endowment effects and loss aversion as fundamental characteristics of preferences.

A theoretical exploration of KKT

KKT's cleverness and thorough design should be applauded. As mentioned previously, they assert their evidence leads to two important conjectures that have had an important influence on the profession: (1) they forward eight experimental demonstrations that they argue shows evidence of the endowment effect and (2) they argue that their evidence shows that the endowment effect is a fundamental characteristic of preferences that will not be eliminated by market experience.

Clearly this is a seminal piece of scholarship, and the market has shown it to be such. Moreover, for me personally this work represents my inauguration into the field of experimental and behavioral economics. Yet, this is a review piece and I owe it to the reader to ask if the evidence presented by KKT is airtight on these two conjectures. This section focuses on whether, from their data, they can conclusively claim that the observed behavior is in line with prospect theory rather than neoclassical theory. Rather than focus on nitpicks of their various designs in terms of incentive compatibility, flat-payoff issues, hypothetical bias, multiple-price lists, multiple hypothesis testing, whether open form bargaining models of their type are even solved theoretically, etc., I will focus on a simple neoclassical economic argument.

As I describe more patiently in List (2004a), which I draw on heavily in this section, considering the major theoretical predictions of neoclassical and endowment theory side by side allows us to compare predictions in experiments like those of KKT. Assume that an individual derives utility, $u = u(g, x)$, from consuming two goods, X and G, where X could be viewed as a composite commodity, quantities of which could be measured in money units, and G is a particular consumption good such as mugs, candy bars, or binoculars.

In Figure 8.1, I assume perfect substitution exists between X and G. In this case, neoclassical theory predicts WTA = WTP: minimum WTA (or Hicksian equivalent surplus) of $x_1 - x_0$ is equivalent to maximum WTP (or Hicksian compensating surplus) of $x_0 - x_2$.

If one relaxes the strict substitutability assumption and assumes quasi-concave utility functions, these linear indifference curves become strictly convex to the origin, as presented in Figure 8.2. In this case, there are well-known results from the literature that demonstrate the WTA/WTP disparity depends on the "price flexibility of income": the elasticity of the marginal valuation of g with respect to x. Indeed, the "price flexibility of income" is analytically equivalent to the ratio of the ordinary income elasticity of

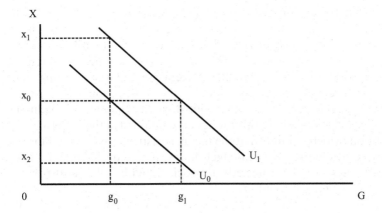

FIGURE 8.1 Linear indifference curves and WTA/WTP.

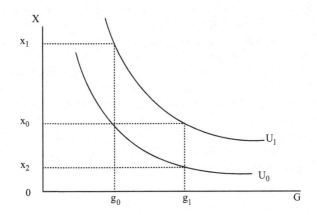

FIGURE 8.2 Convex to the origin indifference curves and WTA/WTP.

demand for the good to the Allen-Uzawa elasticity of substitution between the good and the numeraire.[2]

As such, the large WTA/WTP disparities that are observed in KKT can, in principle, be reconciled with neoclassical theory. Using Figure 8.2 and measuring WTA (WTP) for changes in G from g_1 to g_0 (g_0 to g_1), one can illustrate this result: WTA $= x_1 - x_0 > x_0 - x_2 =$ WTP. Because of income (movement to a higher indifference curve) and substitution (curvature of the indifference curves) effects, neoclassical theory predicts value divergences (recall that for price changes, the difference between the compensating and equivalent variation depends simply on the income effect).

Insights on the disparity are identical if one considers movements along different segments of the same indifference curve. One can gain this intuition by choosing any point along either convex indifference curve in Figure 8.2 and moving equidistant (in g) along the indifference curve in opposite directions. Instead of both income and substitution effects causing the divergence, in this case the divergence is caused purely by convexity of the indifference curve. Depending on the structure of the utility function, the divergence observed along different segments of the same indifference curve can be greater or smaller than differences observed when moving along different indifference curves. In practice, the substitution effect likely holds more prominence in shaping the value disparity than would the income effect. The intuition behind this thought is contained in the Engel aggregation condition, which requires that the income elasticities of demand for g and x, weighted by their respective budget shares, sum to one. While this certainly limits the size of the income effect associated with g, the substitution effect can range from zero to infinity.[3]

From a review of the literature, we can see that a majority of WTA/WTP experimental studies fall into one of these two categories, having subjects moving along either different indifference curves or different portions of the same indifference curve. This means that it is impossible to distinguish between theories in such empirical exercises.

But, what about KKT? A closer inspection of their study shows that every one of their eight experiments fall into one of these two buckets (Experiments 6 and 7 are the closest to testing the theories cleanly if you compare choosers versus sellers). This means that if one desires a strict test of neoclassical theory versus endowment theory, then the eight KKT experiments are not airtight. Does that mean the KKT paper fails to provide invaluable insights? Absolutely not! The KKT paper catalyzed an entire research agenda that shows the import of these original insights. Let's turn to that next, with a consideration of what has stood the test of time and what has not.

KKT, the catalyst for an entire research area

So if KKT does not do the trick, then how might one go about testing whether such value disparities are best described by endowment theory or neoclassical theory? The solution comes in two forms: one for individual statements of value and one for individual trading rates.

To explore statements of value, the simple intuition behind the neoclassical arguments in the "KKT experiment 1" section can be tested by appropriately compensating subjects who do not receive the good so that they state that their maximum WTP moves from g_0 to g_1 along the *same* indifference curve as the endowed group (see List, 2004a). Consider KKT's Experiments 3 and 4 and assume that Group 1 is not given a mug and asked to state their maximum WTP and that Group 2 receives a mug and is asked to state theory minimum WTA. As such, in Figure 8.2, X is money and G is mugs.

In Figure 8.2, a test of theory is achieved by endowing Group 1 subjects at point (g_0, x_1) and asking those subjects to state their maximum WTP to move from g_0 to g_1. Comparing these endowment-adjusted WTP values with

WTA statements from Group 2 yields a (relatively) clean test of whether the indifference curve is reversible, as neoclassical theory predicts. Such an exercise naturally controls for both income (different indifference curves) and substitution (curvature of the indifference curves) effects.

In this experiment, if preferences are defined over changes in consumption, then one could envision a kink for Group 1 subjects at point (g_1, x_0); this would cause the indifference curve for Group 1 subjects to pivot from U_I to U_I^E, as displayed in Figure 8.3. Under neoclassical arguments, WTA should be measured as $x_1 - x_0$, but assuming the endowment effect induces the indifference curve to pivot, WTA becomes $x_3 - x_0 > x_1 - x_0$, which illustrates the agent's aversion to sacrifice a good once it becomes part of her endowment. The WTA/WTP disparity would be exacerbated if a similar kink formed for Group 2 subjects, as it would pivot their indifference curves counterclockwise from point (g_0, x_1). This seems unlikely if X represents money; nevertheless, this is the general intuition behind the endowment effect, which implies that a good's value increases once it becomes part of an individual's endowment

If one desires, the neoclassical explanation can be pushed further by exploiting the relationship between the WTA/WTP disparity and the predicted effect of income on WTP (see Sugden, 1999; List, 2004a). One advantage of such an exercise is that it provides a further use of the observed WTA/WTP ratio and permits an examination of whether the observed ratio is consistent with economic intuition. To add structure to the argument, I continue with

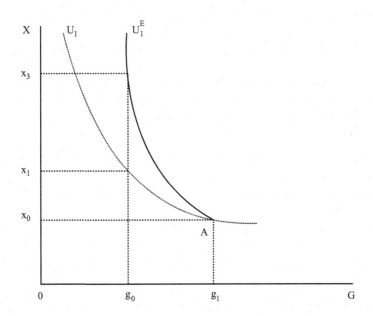

FIGURE 8.3 Endowment effects and the WTA/WTP disparity.

Figure 8.2 and assume that the initial endowment is (g_0, x_0). As previously suggested, the individual's WTP to move from g_0 to g_1 is defined as follows:

$$u(g_1, x_0 - \text{WTP}(x_0)) = u(g_0, x_0), \tag{8.1}$$

where $\text{WTP}(x_0) = x_0 - x_2$. Similarly, endowment-adjusted WTP is

$$u(g_1, x_1 - \text{WTP}(x_1)) = u(g_0, x_1), \tag{8.2}$$

where $\text{WTP}(x_1) = x_1 - x_0$. WTA is defined analogously, and thus

$$u(g_0, x_0 - \text{WTA}) = u(g_1, x_0), \tag{8.3}$$

Using the intuition that $x_1 - x_0 = \text{WTA}$, and these simple definitions of WTA and WTP, the following relationship is derived:

$$u(g_1, x_0 + \text{WTA} - \text{WTP}(x_0 + \text{WTA})) = u(g_0, x_0 + \text{WTA}) = u(g_1, x_0) \tag{8.4}$$

Equality of the first and third expressions implies $x_0 + \text{WTA} - \text{WTP}(x_0 + \text{WTA}) = x_0$, or $\text{WTP}(x_0 + \text{WTA}) = \text{WTA}$. A first-order approximation of $\text{WTP}(x_0 + \text{WTA})$ yields $\text{WTA} \approx \text{WTP} + \text{WTA} \, \partial \text{WTP} / \partial y$ (where y is income). Rewriting this leads to the basic relationship

$$\frac{\partial \text{WTP}}{\partial y} \approx 1 - \frac{\text{WTP}}{\text{WTA}}. \tag{8.5}$$

Equation 5 provides a convenient test of neoclassical theory, as $[1 - \text{WTP/WTA}]$ values can be compared to data on $\partial \text{WTP}/\partial y$, which are widely available.

A further test that makes use of individual statements of value can be explored by examining the shape and structure of Hicksian equivalent surplus and Hicksian compensating surplus measures. For example, List (2006) explores the curvature of the value function by examining individual valuation of a number of items simultaneously. This approach permits a stark test of the competing theories because in such cases the two major theories have contradictory predictions. Prospect theory predicts that Hicksian equivalent surplus will exceed Hicksian compensating surplus and that compensation demanded is *concave* in the number of relinquished goods due to "diminishing sensitivity." Neoclassical theory predicts equivalence of surplus measures and that compensation demanded is *convex* in the number of relinquished goods due to quasi-concavity of preferences.

If one would rather explore individual trading rates rather than statements of value, then the intuition is similar. Consider List (2003), who examined trading patterns of sports memorabilia on the floor of a sportscard show, and trading patterns of collector pins in a market constructed by Walt Disney World at the Epcot Center in Orlando, Florida. In one treatment a subject is endowed with good *A* and has the option to trade it for good *B*. In a second treatment, a different subject is endowed with good *B* and has the option to trade it for good *A*. Since subjects are allocated to one of the two treatments randomly, for preferences to be consistent, the proportion of subjects who choose *B* over *A* should be equal to one minus the proportion who choose *A* over *B*. Such a comparison permits a strict test of endowment theory versus neoclassical theory because it explores whether indifference curves are reversible (the interested reader should also see Knetsch, 1986, which KKT cite). I will not belabor the summary of this line of inquiry because Matthias Sutter has graciously summarized my 2003 study in his generous article (Sutter, 2021).

So, after all these years, where are we concerning KKT's two main conjectures? From this author's perspective, they were correct on one and missed on the other. They were correct on the fact that the endowment theory helps organize some of the received data – even when the experimental issues discussed in the "KKT experiment 1" section are corrected, there is a lot of evidence in favor of endowment theory, especially for inexperienced subjects. For instance, in List (2004a), I find that for inexperienced consumers the ratio of WTA/WTP ranges from 4.4 to 8, which is consistent with previous experimental studies, but is at odds with conventional economic theory. Using Equation 5, these ratios suggest that if an agent were instantly endowed with $100, he/she would spend approximately $80 on the used sports ticket stub I was valuing in the experiment. I suspect that even the most ardent of neoclassical supporters would find this figure implausibly high. Likewise, in the case of trading rates in List (2003), I find that an inefficiently low number of trades occur for naive traders, consistent with endowment theory. The literature broadly conforms to these sorts of data patterns.

Yet, where KKT seemingly over-interpreted their data was in their second conjecture: that their evidence shows the endowment effect is a fundamental characteristic of preferences that will not be eliminated by market experience. In a series of early papers (List, 2003, 2004a, b), I found that market experience mattered a lot, as people with vast market experience behaved much less in accord with endowment theory and much more in line with neoclassical theory (and, in the lab see, e.g., Shogren et al., 1994; 2001). The thrust of those early experience results have been broadly replicated in both the lab and field settings (see, e.g., Feng and Seasholes, 2005; Kermer et al., 2006; Dhar and Zhu, 2006; List, 2006; Gächter et al., 2009; Greenwood and Nagel, 2009; Engelmann and Hollard, 2010; Isoni et al., 2011; List, 2011; Seru et al., 2010; De Sousa and Munro, 2012; Ratan, 2013; Metilda, 2014; Tunçel and Hammitt, 2014; Brown and Bell, 2015; Humphrey et al., 2017; Anagol et al., 2018; Choe and Eom, 2019; Lindsay, 2019 – see also Sutter, 2021). And, there is now neurological evidence supporting the result and providing a basis for the experience insights (Tong et al., 2016 – see next section).

Epilogue

The theory of riskless choice, as pioneered by Jeremy Bentham and James Mill, characterizes utility maximization as an individual process whereby decision makers' preferences follow key tenets. Behavioral economics has provided us with a toolkit to understand when such tenets hold and when they are systematically violated. KKT provided key early evidence on what has proven to be an important consideration: the basic independence assumption.

Debating too hard whether or not certain aspects of the KKT study are right or wrong in some sense short-changes its contribution. In this spirit, KKT was an important cog in stimulating broad recognition of behavioral economics, and more parochially it represented a key catalyst that continued important work on non-standard preferences. In this manner, it played an integral role in the give-and-take between theory and empirical work that represents the crux of scientific advance.

In this sense, while we will all certainly have a different view of how this literature has matured in economics, my longitudinal view goes as follows: from the field arose data from surveys (contingent valuation) that suggested anomalous behavior existed and that individual endowments might matter, Kahneman and Tversky (1979) created a seminal theory, there was important laboratory work in the 1980s and 1990s that showed such behaviors conformed to endowment theory (KKT was a key paper in this regard), people took this to the field and found that the endowment effect is not a fundamental characteristic of preferences that is immutable by market experience (List, 2003, 2004a, b), lab and field studies replicated the experience results (see earlier citations), and a new insightful theory has been introduced (e.g., Kőszegi and Rabin, 2006).

Yet, the process did not stop there. Tong et al. (2016) have gone back to the lab and dug a bit deeper into the experience results of List (2003, 2004a, b). They conducted two functional MRI (fMRI) studies to investigate how experience changes neural correlates of the endowment effect. In Study 1, professional and inexperienced traders indicated the price that they were willing to pay to buy (WTP) and willing to accept to sell (WTA) each of several different products using a slider bar. They scanned these participants while they made decisions about buying and selling these items at different prices. In Study 2, they scanned inexperienced traders on the Study 1 paradigm before and after incentivizing the participants to sell items on eBay over a two-month period.

In both studies, they found that experience matters in a spirit similar to what List reported. But, more importantly, they report convergent evidence that the influence of trading experience on the endowment effect is mediated, in part, by lower sensitivity of the right anterior insula during selling. This result is robust across both studies despite the different populations, procedures, and incentives used, as well as corresponding differences on behavioral effect size and other whole-brain effects. The decreased insula activity suggests that trading experience causes agents to experience less loss aversion during selling. This finding is consistent with List's (2003, 2004a) observation that most inexperienced traders have substantial buying but not selling experience. Overall, these findings suggest that trading mitigates negative affective responses in the context of selling, consonant with the literature on experience effects that finds a convergence of WTA and WTP because of WTA lessening with experience (2004a).

In the end, does the conclusion that market experience attenuates the endowment effect lead one to conclude that KKT has no value outside of theory? Absolutely not. Parochially, in my own work I have taken the ideas from the literature to the field with meaningful success. In Hossain and List (2012), we collaborated with a Chinese electronics company to implement a simple framing experiment where a random subsample of workers was promised a bonus, to be paid at the end of the week if a productivity threshold was met. Others were provisionally given a salary enhancement, which was claimed back at the end of the week in the event of low productivity. We find that even such a weak framing treatment raises productivity of teams of workers relative to the economically isomorphic bonus treatment, framed in a conventional sense (see also the insightful work of Abeler et al., 2011). Fryer et al. (2012) complement this work by providing financial incentives to school teachers to increase productivity, as measured by the performance of their students. They find that leveraging loss aversion via a penalty regime is quite effective. Similar results are obtained when incentivizing students, rather than teachers (Levitt et al., 2012).[4]

Clearly the story is not complete and will continue to evolve, but what is satisfying about this literature's maturation is the give-and-take between theory and empiricism, between lab and field, between scholars and practitioners, and between scholars across quite disparate literatures. This is not synchronicity; rather, it is an amalgamation of studies over time, where, without knowing it, each serves a principle purpose of knowledge generation that the conductor, KKT, served to orchestrate.

Notes

1 Thanks to Ariel Listo, Lina Ramirez, Haruka Uchida, and Atom Vayalinkal for their incredible research support. Daniel Kahneman, Jack Knetsch, Mark Pingle, and Richard Thaler provided insightful discussions about the study.

2 The astute reader will note that the curvature of the indifference curves could be thought of as merely a reflection of convexity of the expenditure function in g. And, if one assumes utility is quasi-convex in g, then a corner solution emerges rather than an interior solution. In this case, indifference curves are concave and the substitution effect becomes positive, rather than negative.

3 Care should be taken not to dismiss income effects out of hand, however. Under certain scenarios, the spacing of the indifference curves is quite important. While in Figure 8.2 I have implicitly assumed a unitary income elasticity by making the indifference curves for U_0 and U_1 parallel displacements, if I assumed an income elasticity greater than 1, or that the marginal rate of substitution increased along any ray from the origin, the WTA/WTP disparity would

increase. The opposite would occur, of course, if G were an inferior good – the marginal rate of substitution would decrease along any ray from the origin.

4 Loss aversion does not always appear to affect behavior. Hossain and List (2012) fail to document that the claw-back regime enhances the productivity of individual (as opposed to teams of) workers, and List and Samek (2015) do not find that loss aversion helps dieticians affect children's food choices. Understanding the boundary conditions of loss aversion remains an important yet underresearched line of work. The interested reader should also see Imas et al. (2016), De Quidt (2018), and Bulte et al. (2019).

References

Abeler, J., Falk, A., Goette, L., Huffman, D., 2011. Reference points and effort provision. *American Economic Review* 101(2), 470–492.

Anagol, S., Balasubramaniam, V., Ramadorai, T., 2018. Endowment effects in the field: Evidence from India's IPO lotteries. *The Review of Economic Studies* 85(4), 1971–2004.

Bishop, R.C., Boyle, K.J., Carson, R.T., Chapman, D., Hanemann, W.M., 2017. Putting a value on injuries to natural assets: The BP oil spill. *Science* 356(6335), 253–254.

Brown, T., Bell, P.A., 2015. Exchange asymmetry in experimental settings. *Journal of Economic Behavior and Organization* 120, 104–116.

Bulte, E., John A. List, J.A., Van Soest, D., 2019. Toward an understanding of the welfare effects of nudges: Evidence from a field experiment in Uganda. NBER Working Papers 26286, National Bureau of Economic Research.

Choe, H., Eom, Y., 2019. The disposition effect and investment performance in the futures market. *Journal of Futures Markets: Futures, Options, and Other Derivative Products* 29(6), 496–522.

Ciriacy-Wantrup, S.V., 1947. Capital returns from soil-conservation practices. *Journal of Farm Economics* 29(4), 1181–1196.

Cummings, R.G., Brookshire, D.S., Schulze, W.D., 1986. *Valuing Environmental Goods: An Assessment of the Contingent Valuation Method*. Totowa, NJ: Rowman and Allanheld Publishers.

De Quidt, J., 2018. Your loss is my gain: A recruitment experiment with framed incentives. *Journal of the European Economic Association* 16(2), 522–559.

De Sousa, Y.F., Munro, A., 2012. Truck, barter and exchange versus the endowment effect: Virtual field experiments in an online game environment. *Journal of Economic Psychology* 33(3), 482–493.

Dhar, Ravi, Zhu, N., 2006. Up close and personal: Investor sophistication and the disposition effect. *Management Science* 52(5), 726–740.

Engelmann, D., Hollard, G., 2010. Reconsidering the effect of market experience on the endowment effect. *Econometrica* 78(6), 2005–2019.

Feng, L., Seasholes, M.S., 2005. Do investor sophistication and trading experience eliminate behavioral biases in financial markets? *Review of Finance* 9(3), 305–351.

Fryer, R., Levitt, S. List, J.A., Sadoff, S., 2012. Enhancing the efficacy of teacher incentives through loss aversion: A field experiment. NBER Working Paper 18237.

Gächter, S., Orzen, H., Renner, E., Starmer, C., 2009. Are experimental economists prone to framing effects? A natural field experiment. *Journal of Economic Behavior and Organization* 70(3), 443–446.

Greenwood, R., Nagel, S., 2009. Inexperienced investors and bubbles. *Journal of Financial Economics* 93(2), 239–258.

Hammack, J., Brown, G.M., 1974. *Waterfowl and Wetlands: Toward Bioeconomic Analysis*. Baltimore, MD and London: John Hopkins University Press.

Hossain, T. and J.A. List, 2012. The behaviouralist visits the factory: Increasing productivity using simple framing manipulations. *Management Science* 58(12), 2151–2167.

Humphrey, S.J., Lindsay, L., Starmer, C., 2017. Consumption experience, choice experience and the endowment effect. *Journal of the Economic Science Association* 3(2), 109–120.

Imas, A., Sadoff, S., Samek, A., 2016. Do people anticipate loss aversion? *Management Science* 63(5): 1271–1284.

Isoni, A., Loomes, G., Sugden, R., 2011. The willingness to pay—willingness to accept gap, the endowment effect, subject misconceptions, and experimental procedures for eliciting valuations: Comment. *American Economic Review* 101(2), 991–1011.

Kahneman, D., Knetsch, J.L., Thaler, R., 1986a. Fairness as a constraint on profit seeking: Entitlements in the market. *The American Economic Review* 74(4), 728–741.

Kahneman, D., Knetsch, J.L., Thaler, R., 1986b. Fairness and the assumptions of economics. *Journal of Business* 59(4), S285–S300.

Kahneman, D., Knetsch, J.L., Thaler, R., 1990. Experimental tests of the endowment effect and the Coase theorem. *Journal of Economy* 98(6), 132–1348.

Kahneman, D., Knetsch, J.L., Thaler, R., 1991. Anomalies: The endowment effect, loss aversion, and status quo bias. *Journal of Economic Perspectives* 5(1), 193–206.

Kermer, D.A., Driver-Linn, E., Wilson, T.D., Gilbert, D.T., 2006. Loss aversion is an affective forecasting error. *Psychological Science* 17(8), 649–653.

Knetsch, J.L., 1986. The endowment effect and evidence of nonreversible indifference curves. *The American Economic Review* 79(5), 1277–1284.

Knetsch, J.L., Sinden, J.A., 1984. Willingness to pay and compensation demanded: Experimental evidence of an unexpected disparity in measures of value. *The Quarterly Journal of Economics* 99(3), 507–521.

Kőszegi, B., Rabin, M., 2006. A model of reference-dependent preferences. *The Quarterly Journal of Economics* 121(4), 1133–1165.

Levitt, S., List, J.A., Neckermann, S., Sadoff, S., 2012. The behaviouralist goes to school: Leveraging behavioural economics to improve educational performance. NBER Working Paper 18165.

Lindsay, L., 2019. Adaptive loss aversion and market experience. *Journal of Economic Behavior and Organization* 168(C), 43–61.

List, J A., 2003. Does market experience eliminate market anomalies? *Quarterly Journal of Economics* 118(1), 41–71.

List, J.A., 2004a. Substitutability, experience, and the value disparity: Evidence from the marketplace. *Journal of Environmental Economics and Management* 47(3), 486–509.

List, J.A., 2004b. Neoclassical theory versus prospect theory: Evidence from the marketplace. *Econometrica* 72(2), 615–625.

List, J.A., 2006. Using Hicksian surplus measures to examine consistency of individual preferences: Evidence from a field experiment. *Scandinavian Journal of Economics* 108(1), 115–134.

List, J.A., 2011. Does market experience eliminate market anomalies? The case of exogenous market experience. *American Economic Review* 101(3), 313–317.

List, J.A., Samek, A.S., 2015. The behavioralist as nutritionist: leveraging behavioral economics to improve child food choice and consumption. *Journal of Health Economics* 39,135–146.

Metilda, J., 2014. Mutual fund investor and loss aversion: A study on the influence of gender, experience and investor type. *International Business Management* 8, 30–35.

Ratan, A., 2013. Anticipated regret or endowment effect? A reconsideration of exchange asymmetry in laboratory experiments. *The BE Journal of Economic Analysis and Policy* 14(1), 277–298.

Rowe, R.D., d'Arge, R.C., Brookshire, D.S., 1980. An experiment on the economic value of visibility. *Journal of Environmental Economics and Management* 7(1), 1–19.

Seru, A., Shumway, T., Stoffman, N., 2010. Learning by trading. *The Review of Financial Studies* 23(2), 705–739.

Shogren, J.F., Cho, S., Koo, C., List, J.A., Park, C., Polo, P., Wilhelmi, R., 2001. Auction mechanisms and the measurement of WTP and WTA. *Resource and Energy Economics* 23(2), 97–109.

Shogren, J.F., Shin, S.Y., Hayes, D.J., Kliebenstein, J.B., 1994. Resolving differences in willingness to pay and willingness to accept. *American Economic Review* 84(1), 255–270.

Sugden, R., 1999. Alternatives to the neoclassical theory of choice. *Valuing Environmental Preferences*, 152–180.

Sutter, M., 2021. Review: Does market experience eliminate market anomalies? In: Charness, G., Pingle, M. (Eds.). *The Art of Experimental Economics: Twenty Top Papers Reviewed*. New York: Routledge, 176–181.

Tong, L.C.P., Ye, K.J., Asai, K., Ertac, S., List, J.A., Nusbaum, H.C., Hortaçsu, A., 2016. Trading experience modulates anterior insula to reduce the endowment effect. Proceedings of the National Academy of the Sciences. https://doi.org/10.1073/pnas.1519853113

Tunçel, T., Hammitt, J.K., 2014. A new meta-analysis on the WTP/WTA disparity. *Journal of Environmental Economics and Management* 68(1), 175–187.

Tversky, A., Kahneman, D., 1979. Prospect theory: An analysis of decision under risk. *Econometrica* 47(2), 263–291.

9

BARGAINING AND MARKET BEHAVIOR IN JERUSALEM, LJUBLJANA, PITTSBURGH, AND TOKYO: AN EXPERIMENTAL STUDY (BY ALVIN E. ROTH, VESNA PRASNIKAR, MASAHIRO OKUNO-FUJIWARA, AND SHMUEL ZAMIR)

Armin Falk

Introduction

The paper produced by Roth, Prasnikar, Okuno-Fujiwara, and Zamir (1991), hereafter RPOZ, has been influential for two main reasons. First, it took seriously the idea that studying different subject pools – e.g., with respect to cultural background – is an important step forward in uncovering human motivation above and beyond the over-simplistic assumptions common to mainstream economics. Second, it highlighted the "puzzle" that behavior seems to be guided by fairness or reciprocity considerations in bargaining environments, yet "selfish" outcomes seem to prevail in competitive environments. This apparent contradiction has stimulated many discussions and has inspired models of fairness and reciprocity.

Experimental design

The experiment was performed in four different countries: Israel, Japan, the United States, and Yugoslavia. It comprised two distinct types of treatments: (1) a two-person bargaining game, the ultimatum game, and (2) a simple market with buyer competition. Each participant completed only one of the two types of treatments, either the ultimatum game or the market game. Within a treatment, the game was repeated ten times, with random matching, to allow for experience effects and learning, and to study potential convergence.

Ultimatum Game (Two-Person Bargaining). The two-person bargaining game is a standard ultimatum game in which the first bargainer proposes a split of the available money and the second person can either reject or

DOI: 10.4324/9781003019121-9

accept. In case of acceptance, each bargainer receives the proposed amount of money. If the proposal is rejected, both earn nothing.

Multi-person Market Environment. The market environment is a simple, one-period market with one seller and nine buyers. In this setup, the seller owns an indivisible object that is worth nothing to him, but that is worth the same amount to each buyer. First, each buyer can make an offer.

Subsequently, the seller can reject or accept the highest price offered. If the seller rejects, no player receives anything. If the seller accepts, the seller earns the highest price offered and the buyer who has made the offer receives the object's value minus the offered price, while the remaining buyers receive nothing. In case of two or more highest offers, the buyer is randomly drawn. At the end of each period, all subjects learn whether and at what price the object was sold.

Both games have a subgame perfect equilibrium in which one player receives (almost) all the money (actually, there is either one or two equilibria, depending on whether a buyer/receiver accepts an offer of zero). In the ultimatum game, the first player offers (close to) nothing while the second player accepts, which leaves the first player with (nearly) all of the money. Similarly, in the market environment, the seller earns (almost) all while all buyers receive (virtually) no money.

Cultural Differences. In addition to studying differences between bargaining and market environments, RPOZ also investigated potential cultural differences. In this respect, they do not suggest a particular hypothesis, but raise several important issues about how to control for differences other than culture that may confound a "cultural explanation." In particular, they discuss the role of using different experimenters at different locations, how to approach translation into different languages, and how to handle different country-specific currencies.

RPOZ suggested and implemented various ways in which to deal with these issues. Regarding the experimenter effect, each experimenter conducted one session in Pittsburgh before running the remaining sessions in the other countries. This way, operational procedures could be assimilated, and any pure experimenter effect should also be detectable by comparing the respective sessions in Pittsburgh. To avoid language-driven effects, the authors first wrote the English instructions together in terms that could subsequently be faithfully translated into the other languages. In addition, instructions for both environments (bargaining and markets) were phrased at the same time using the same vocabulary, thus ensuring that differences between the environments cannot be attributed to differences in the phrasing of the respective environment. With respect to currency effects, the authors adapted payments to the respective purchasing power of the country. By using the same number of tokens (1,000) for each game in each country, the authors additionally controlled for differences that may arise from specific currency scales and so-called prominent numbers, i.e., the fact that individuals tend to choose round numbers (see e.g. Albers and Albers [1983]).

Experimental implementation and results

In each of the four countries, two market and three bargaining sessions were conducted. In each session, there were (up to) 20 subjects per session. Subjects were mainly economics students, recruited from the University of Pittsburgh, the University of Ljubljana, the Hebrew University, Keio University, and the University of Tokyo.

For markets, the observed outcomes converged to the predicted equilibrium for all four country samples. Moreover, with increased experience, the inter-country differences became smaller and ultimately vanished.

However, the picture strongly differed for the bargaining environment. First, in every country, the observed behavior significantly differed from the predicted subgame perfect equilibrium. Second, RPOZ found substantial differences in behavior between countries, and the differences increased with experience.

In particular, the distributions of offers made by the proposer significantly varied across countries. In both the US and the Yugoslavian sample, the modal proposal was 500 (50% of the pie), while in Japan and Israel the modal proposal was 400.

Unsurprisingly, within a country, the probability that an offer was rejected decreased with the level of the offer. However, between countries, RPOZ found that those with lower offers did not have higher rejection rates. Instead, subjects rejected a given offer with a lower probability in countries where proposers made lower offers. This suggests that countries differ in what is considered fair and appropriate: If it is acceptable to offer less, relatively low offers will be offered and accepted.

Discussion

In my view, the two main contributions of this paper are (1) the contrasting of "fair" and "unfair" outcomes in bargaining and market environments, respectively, and (2) shifting the focus to studying experimental outcomes in different cultures. That is, the paper pushed the frontier in two domains of study: social preferences and cultural heterogeneity.

With respect to preferences, the paper presents a seemingly contradictory pattern. Behavior in markets converges well with the "selfish" subgame perfect equilibrium (irrespective of cultural background), but outcomes are much "fairer" in the ultimatum game. In the bargaining context, responders reject low offers, forcing proposers to offer relatively high and fair shares. Why is this not happening in markets? In their paper, RPOZ summarize:

> At the same time, the failure of observed behavior in the bargaining games even to approach the equilibrium prediction (and in particular the readiness of sellers in that game to earn zero by rejecting offers that would give them positive earnings) raises questions about the auxiliary assumption under which the equilibrium predictions were made,

namely, that the players are attempting to maximize their earnings. However, if players are not attempting to maximize their earnings, then why do the equilibrium predictions made under that assumption for the market games do so well?

Referring to discussions in the scientific community at that time, they continue:

> Preliminary discussions with various investigators in this area suggest at least two possible explanations. One is that the observed bargaining behavior is dominated by concerns about fairness which are context-dependent and do not arise in the market environment. Another is that whatever non-monetary concerns enter bargainers' preferences do so in both environments, but the competitive pressure toward equilibrium in the market overwhelms any such factors in players' preferences.

Research that occurred after this paper was published has led the scientific community to favor the second explanation, which does not, of course, imply that contextual effects in general are irrelevant. In fact, one of the "breakthroughs" in the study of social preferences was that this puzzling behavior could be explained using simple models of fairness, such as those provided by Fehr and Schmidt (1999), Bolton and Ockenfels (2000), and Falk and Fischbacher (2006). These models reconcile the seemingly contradictory evidence that bilateral interactions yield outcomes that are "fair," while competitive markets often produce "unfair" outcomes.

Analyzing exactly the market game with proposer competition discussed here, Falk and Fischbacher (2006) show that in their reciprocity equilibrium at least two proposers offer the maximum offer of 1,000, which the responder accepts. The striking feature of this prediction is that fair-minded or reciprocal proposers who are unwilling to accept low offers in the ultimatum game accept very unfair offers in a competitive environment.

The intuition is that in a competitive market a proposer cannot achieve a "fair" outcome. To see this more clearly, assume that a reciprocal proposer i refuses to offer more than 500 in a market game with two proposers. By infinitesimally overbidding player i's offer, proposer j can increase his material payoff by a positive amount (because he can increase the winning probability from 0.5 to 1). However, the disutility resulting from the unfair relation to the responder only changes infinitesimally, which means that player i's refusal to propose more than 500 is not an effective tool for achieving a "fair" outcome. Consequently, he tries to outbid the other proposer to obtain at least a minimal share of the pie. This mutual "overbidding" inevitably leads to the "selfish" equilibrium prediction. It is important to note that welfare is "low" for reciprocal or fair-minded proposers in this equilibrium, because they care for fair outcomes. However, they cannot prevent its emergence in the competitive environment.

A very differently formulated (but not entirely unrelated) explanation of these results comes from models of learning in games. Roth and Erev (1995) considered how reinforcement learning would change players' behavior as they gained experience in these games. They found that, in ultimatum games, proposers learned not to make small offers faster than responders learned not to reject them (because the stakes involved in rejecting small offers are small, so learning not to reject small offers is slow). Over time, what participants learned as they gained experience was influenced by the initial distributions of offers and rejections in the country in which they were participating. But in market games, demanding a low price is not reinforced whenever that price is not the winning bid in the auction. So what players learn from experience is that high bids are necessary, regardless of the initial distribution of bids in the country where they were participating.

The second important contribution of the paper is that it demonstrates the usefulness of using experimental economics to examine cultural effects. Given today's methodological standards, one would probably be cautious when basing statements about culture on (very) small numbers of observations and college student samples. This is particularly true here, given that the composition of the samples was slightly peculiar, as acknowledged RPOZ. The recognition of these limitations in this paper motivated researchers to go beyond convenience samples, which is one of the most important developments in experimental economics. Recognizing heterogeneity as a fundamental source of different outcomes (i.e., age, gender, specific socioeconomic factors, etc., along with culture) has enormously increased our understanding of the motives guiding human behavior.

By recognizing the key role heterogeneity can play, behavioral economics has freed itself from the "socio-psychological imperative" of explaining variation only in terms of treatments or contexts, a characteristic of first-generation behavioral economics. Instead, it has started to integrate a "personality-psychology" perspective, relying on individual differences as a major source of variation in outcomes. In response, many studies now use representative samples, exploiting the wealth of variation in social background, age, or education, which is impossible using convenient college samples. An example in the realm of fairness and reciprocity (as in the present paper) is Dohmen et al. (2009), which measures reciprocal inclinations in a large, representative survey and relates these measures to real-world labor market behavior and life outcomes.

Researchers have also taken up the idea of running experimental and survey studies in different countries and cultures. In their paper on "Antisocial Punishment Across Societies," Herrmann, Thöni, and Gächter (2008), for example, collected data on public goods experiments that they conducted in 16 comparable participant pools around the world. They document a considerable cross-societal variation in antisocial punishment and relate it to norms of civic cooperation and the weakness of the rule of law in a country. Another more recent example following the role model discussed here is Falk et al. (2018), which provides the first global account on economic preferences, based on a sample of 76 representative country samples.

In sum, this is an important and beautiful paper, full of ideas and innovations. Congrats!

References

Albers, W., Albers, G., 1983. On the prominence structure of the decimal system. *Advances in Psychology* 16, 271–287.

Bolton, G. E., Ockenfels, A., 2000. ERC: A theory of equity, reciprocity, and competition. *American Economic Review* 90(1), 166–193.

Dohmen, T., Falk, A., Huffman, D., Sunde, U., 2009. Homo reciprocans: Survey evidence on behavioural outcomes. *The Economic Journal* 119(536), 592–612.

Falk, A., Becker, A., Dohmen, T., Enke, B., Huffman, D., Sunde, U., 2018. Global evidence on economic preferences. *The Quarterly Journal of Economics* 133(4), 1645–1692.

Falk, A., Fischbacher, U., 2006. A theory of reciprocity. *Games and Economic Behavior* 54, 293–315.

Fehr, E., Schmidt, K. M., 1999. A theory of fairness, competition, and cooperation. *The Quarterly Journal of Economics* 114(3), 817–868.

Herrmann, B., Thöni, C., Gächter, S., 2008. Antisocial punishment across societies. *Science* 319(5868), 1362–1367.

Roth, A.E., Erev, I., 1995. Learning in extensive-form games: Experimental data and simple dynamic models in the intermediate term. *Games and Economic Behavior* 8, Special Issue: Nobel Symposium, 164–212.

Roth, A.E., Prasnikar, V., Masahiro Okuno-Fujiwara, M., Zamir, S., 1991. Bargaining and market mehavior in Jerusalem, Ljubljana, Pittsburgh, and Tokyo: An experimental study. *American Economic Review* 81(5), 1068–1095.

10

UNRAVELING IN GUESSING GAMES: AN EXPERIMENTAL STUDY (BY ROSEMARIE NAGEL)

John H. Kagel and Antonio Penta

Introduction

The inclusion of Nagel's "Guessing Game" experiment in this volume is well deserved. The paper is heavily cited (over 1,800 Google Scholar citations, and counting), and helped kick off theorists' and experimenters' interest in models of level-k reasoning, of which there are an enormous number of interesting and insightful papers (see Crawford, Costa-Gomes, and Iriberri, 2013 for a survey of the literature). The paper is a staple of reading lists in experimental economics classes, and has been widely applied to a number of different subject populations, as well as serving as a handy illustration of limited deductive reasoning on the part of real people, as opposed to the ideal economic man.

Nagel (1995) was the first paper to experimentally investigate the *Beauty Contest*, or p-guessing game. In its baseline version, subjects simultaneously announce a number between 0 and 100. The subject whose number is closest to a fraction p of the average report wins a monetary prize.[1] First note that, unless $p = 1$, this game is dominance solvable: if $p < 1$, the only rationalizable profile (and, hence, the only Nash equilibrium) is for everybody to report 0; if $p > 1$, the only rationalizable profile is for everybody to report 100, but 0 is also an equilibrium. In Nagel's (1995) experiment p values were $p = 1/2$, $p = 2/3$, and $p = 4/3$. The same game is repeated four times, with the same parameter and the same subjects, given full information about all choices, winning numbers, and targets of the previous period.

The first period behavior is separately analyzed from the remaining periods as subjects do not have information, unlike when they repeat the same game. The same level-k model (explained below) is used for the initial behavior and behavior over time, with the main difference being that level 0 is differently measured, precisely due to the different information structure.

DOI: 10.4324/9781003019121-10

The directional learning model (Selten and Stoeker, 1986) is adapted for the analysis of behavior over time.

However, it is worth stressing that the literature has focused almost entirely on *initial responses* to the game.[2] That is subjects' behavior when they have no previous experience with the game, with no feedback about others' choices. This eliminates learning about others' choices, relying strictly on introspective reasoning. Figure 10.1 shows Nagel's results.

A few things are immediately apparent from the figure. First, very few agents play the unique rationalizable action. (In fact, given the actual distribution of play, the Nash equilibrium action 0 would *not* be a "winning" choice.) Second, these spikes vary systematically with p. In particular when $p = \frac{1}{2}$ there are spikes at 25 and 12.5, corresponding to $p \cdot 50$ and $p^2 \cdot 50$, and with $p = 2/3$ at 33.3 and 22.2, corresponding to $p \cdot 50$ and $p^2 \cdot 50$. The striking regularities of these patterns have been confirmed in a number of other studies, showing that the deviations from Nash equilibrium are systematic, indicating that individuals follow distinct reasoning procedures, of which they typically perform only a few steps.[3]

To account for these regularities, Nagel (1995) introduced a model of *level-k reasoning*. In the baseline version of the model, each individual is described by an exogenous type k, which corresponds to the number of rounds of iterated reasoning performed. *Level-0* individuals represent nonstrategic types (which perhaps only exist in other players' minds), which follow some exogenously specified, typically random, behavior; *level-1* individuals best respond to *level-0*, *level-2* individuals to *level-1*, and so on. Taking the *level-0* action as equal to the uniform distribution (which plays the role of a *Laplacian conjecture* from the viewpoint of *level-1* players), this very parsimonious model makes sense of the spikes observed in her experiment. Following systematic variation with the p-parameter, each *level-k* in the p-guessing game plays action $p^k \cdot 50$, with the Nash equilibrium action corresponding to *level-∞*. Since Nagel's (1995) seminal work, level-k models have proven remarkably successful in explaining behavior in a number of variations in the baseline guessing game, and for a variety of subject populations. However, beyond replicability and extensive validation, the real sign of the significance of the paper is that the model has helped spawn a number of interesting papers. We focus on a few such papers, the choice of which is idiosyncratic to our own research interests.

At the top of this list is "One, Two, (Three), Infinity, …: Newspaper and Lab Beauty-Contest Experiments" (Bosch-Domènech, García-Montalvo, Nagel, and Satorra, 2002). This paper reports the results of the beauty-contest game in three newspapers. It stands out on two dimensions: (1) its application outside the lab with different populations, and (2) the analysis of the comments submitted by the different participants. Examples of different types of reasoning are reported in the Appendix accompanying the paper. The newspaper experiments immediately address two of the standard objections to lab experiments: What can we learn from college sophomores?

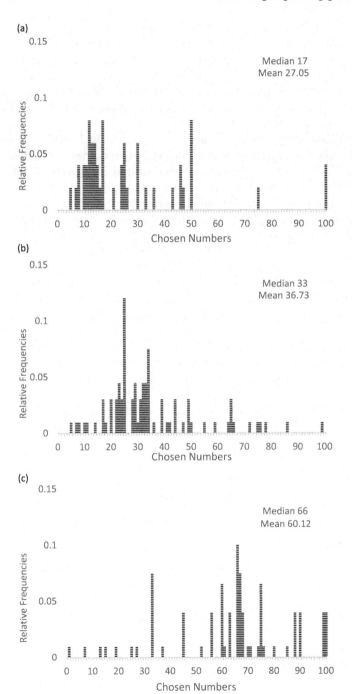

FIGURE 10.1 Choices in first round of Nagel (1995) experiment: Panel A p = 1/2; Panel B p = 2/3; Panel C p = 4/3.

What would happen with increased incentives, as the lab payoffs are not substantial enough? With respect to the latter, incentives ranged from two Club Class tickets from England to New York or Chicago by British Airways, valued at $800 and $600, to the winners in the Spanish and German contests. In addition, they asked contestants to provide written explanations of their choices to get at their underlying thought processes, the results of which are quite interesting.

The newspaper contests used $p = 2/3$. Figure 10.2 shows the distribution of choices averaged over the three newspaper contests. There are spikes around 33, equal to 2/3 of 50 and a spike around 22, equal to 2/3 of 33, just as in the original experiment. A detailed classification of comments showed that a majority (64%) of responders used what Nagel characterized as an IBRd argument; a model of iterated best response to the belief that others are one level less sophisticated, with level *1* players assuming a uniform prior over the interval [0, 100]. To quote a level-*1* player: "If all the numbers had the same probability of being chosen, the mean would be 50, and the choice would be 2/3 50 = 33.33. However, I have estimated a percentage of deviation around 33.33 of 10% and, therefore, I chose the number 30." Some contestants recognized that iterated reasoning to the end point of level-*k* yields the conclusion that "at the end you get 0! However, I chose, despite that logic, 2.32323." Perhaps most interesting of all is that a number of contestants ran their own experiments before submitting their answer, with the result that, on average, their choices came closest to the winning answer.

Another interesting experiment based on Nagel's paper is one in which 6,000 chess players took part in an online experiment announced in "ChessBase newspages" using the p = 2/3 version of the game, with numbers over

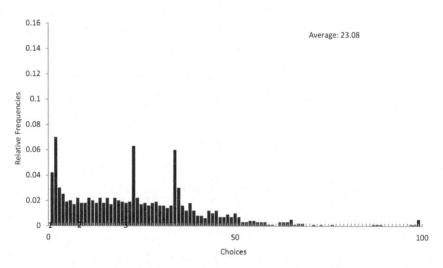

FIGURE 10.2 Choice frequencies from three newspaper experiments.

the interval [0, 100] (Bühren and Frank, 2012). The winning guess in this case was 21.5, close to the spike in the newspaper experiments. Chess players are often thought to employ greater depths of reasoning than the average person. However, regardless of whether you conclude that the correct answer should be 0, chess players, like everyone else, have the problem of guessing the average of what everyone else will choose as part of their deductive reasoning process.

Based on the limited deductive reasoning demonstrated in the original Nagel paper and the newspaper contests, a number of theorists have employed level-k models to characterize outcomes in a number of different environments. One notable example is Crawford and Iriberri's (2007) use of level-k reasoning to explain outcomes in both independent private value and common value auctions, without invoking the joy of winning, risk aversion, or cognitive biases. They investigate behavior in both first- and second-price auction experiments, as well as a number of other private value and common value auction experiments, focusing on inexperienced bidders in early auction rounds. They econometrically compare predictions from equilibrium bidding, Eyster and Rabin's (2005) cursed equilibrium, and results from mixture models with level-k bidders distributed over types L0, L1 and L2. Random L0 bidders bid randomly, and truthful L0 bidders bid based on their induced valuations. The results are mixed, as might well be expected. With independent private values, level-k coincides with equilibrium bidding in second-price auctions and in first-price auctions when bidders' induced valuations are i.i.d. over a uniform distribution, neither of which matches the data. Level-k models do a much better job in common value auctions. For first-price auctions, random L1 types constitute the highest percentage of bidders (59%), with the second highest being truthful L1 types (18%). For these auctions, the level-k model performs better than the equilibrium bidding model, but slightly worse than Eyster and Rabin's cursed equilibrium. In second-price common value auctions data, the distribution of types is quite different than in the first-price auctions, with the estimated frequency for random L1 types at 21%. Crawford and Iriberri (2007) go on to offer a plausible explanation for the difference between first and second-price common value auctions. While it is clear that level-k models do not uniformly outperform equilibrium bidding, the fact that they can organize behavior in first- and second-price auctions with three bidder types (L0, L1, and L2) is novel and interesting.

Aside from its ability to account for patterns of behavior that depart from classical solution concepts, the level-k literature has been especially important for uncovering some of the main features of reasoning processes when agents face novel strategic situations. Initial responses are important to shed light on behavior in the many situations where agents have no previous experience, or knowledge, about other players' behavior (e.g., when an individual purchases a house, or when investors face a stock's Initial Public Offering, or in the early phases of a financial bubble or crisis, etc.). In these settings, decisions are often based on introspective reasoning, which can be very different from equilibrium logic. It is well known that, in the absence of learning or other kinds of adaptive dynamics, the possibility of players achieving equilibrium coordination is problematic, even from a purely theoretical viewpoint (see, e.g., Bernheim, 1984 and Pearce, 1984). In addition, when multiple equilibria exist, the eventual outcome is often dependent on agents' initial actions (see, for example, Brandts and Holt, 1993 and Fudenberg and Vespa, 2019).

Nagel's levels of reasoning model has provided an important unifying framework to organize initial responses. The cleverness of the beauty-contest game, and particularly the structure of the best responses it induces, has shown how standard experimental methods based on choice data can uncover features of individuals' reasoning processes. The paper has played a central role in fostering a rich and increasingly active area of research, which aims to go beyond the mere ex-post organization of behavior in a game, focusing directly on deliberation processes, with the objective of developing structural models of reasoning capable of generating reliable predictions across games. This recent area, which often combines techniques and methodologies from economics, psychology, and cognitive sciences, has helped us better understand important points of level-k reasoning, which were not fully resolved by first-generation models.

Standard level-k models are agnostic about whether level-k behavior is driven by an individual's inability to conceive of more steps of reasoning, or merely by her beliefs about the anticipated level of reasoning that others employ. A recent exception is the Endogenous Depth of Reasoning (EDR) model of Alaoui and Penta (2016), in which a subject's understanding of a game (*cognitive level*, or *capacity*) is distinct from her *behavioral level*.[4] In their model, holding constant an individual's cognitive level, choices will vary depending on beliefs about their opponents' depth of reasoning.[5] Higher-order belief effects are also possible. That is, a player's beliefs about her opponent's behavioral level may depend on her beliefs about the opponent's beliefs about *her* own cognitive level.

Alaoui and Penta (2016) test the predictions of the EDR model with a series of experiments on initial responses in the *acyclical 11–20 game*. In this game, subjects are matched in pairs and are asked to simultaneously call out an integer between 11 and 20. Each agent obtains a number of tokens equal to his own announcement, plus an extra 20 tokens if it is *exactly one less* than his opponent's, or an extra 10 tokens if the two announcements are the same. Note that 19 is the best-response (the L1 action) for several specifications of L0, including 20 (the action that maximizes payoffs ignoring strategic considerations), or the mixing uniformly over the possible reports. Given this, L2 plays 18, L3 plays 17, and so on, until the action for all levels higher than 9 is playing 11.[6] This means that each number from 12 to 20 is associated with a unique level-k action in this game, which will change depending on one's beliefs about the opponent's level of strategic reasoning.

To investigate the EDR model, Alaoui and Penta (2016) divide their subject pool into two groups, according to two classification criteria. In half of the pool, subjects are labeled based on their area of study, into "humanities" and "math and sciences." In the other half, subjects are labeled as "high" or "low" types based on a test taken at the beginning of the experiment (the test is designed to be indicative of their cognitive ability). Subjects know their own label, with labels used to induce variation in their beliefs about their opponents' likely levels of reasoning. In the *homogeneous treatment [Hom]*, two subjects with the same label play against each other (e.g., math vs. math, or high score vs. high score). In the *heterogeneous treatment [Het]*, subjects with different labels were matched against each other. In the *higher-order beliefs treatment [HOB]*, subjects classified under a label play against the action that subjects from the other label used in the homogeneous treatment.

The experimental results show clear belief effects: The distribution of choices made by math and sciences subjects, for instance, shifts upwards going from the [Hom] to the [Het] treatment, and then further from the [Het] to the [HOB] treatment. This indicates that math and science majors expect that humanities majors will choose higher numbers (i.e., play according to lower levels) than their fellow math and sciences majors, and that they expect humanities majors to choose lower numbers (i.e., play according higher levels) when they face a math and science major, than when they play among themselves. The patterns are reversed for humanities subjects: The distribution of actions shifts downwards (i.e., toward higher levels) when they move from the [Hom] to the [Het] treatment, but, as predicted by the EDR model, no further shift is observed in this case going from the [Het] to the [HOB] treatment. [7]

The EDR model also predicts that a player's *cognitive level* will vary with the stakes of the game, which they confirm as well.[8] These results show that implied levels of reasoning change systematically as incentives and beliefs are varied, requiring caution in interpreting levels of play as revealing cognitive abilities alone. That is, there is an endogeneity problem in identifying players' level of reasoning. Once taken into account, however, this endogeneity may enable level-k models to make predictions across games, including ones not normally associated with level-k reasoning.[9]

In the EDR model, cognitive levels are determined endogenously by players trading off their costs of reasoning (a function of their cognitive ability) and the incentives to reason provided by the payoffs of the game. Alaoui and Penta (2018) provide an axiomatic foundation to a cost-benefit approach to reasoning and extend the EDR model to account for *response time data*. Recent papers have shown that the extension of level-k models to include response time data can be particularly fruitful.[10]

Alós-Ferrer and Buckenmeier (2019) investigate the relation between deliberation time, a well-known correlate of cognitive effort, and level-k reasoning, adding the assumption that the per-step deliberation time decreases as the benefits of that step increase. This assumption is based on a well-known phenomenon in neuroeconomics and psychometrics, according to which deliberation times are longer for alternatives that are more similar to each other. The model delivers the following predictions: 1. As incentives increase, the depth of reasoning (weakly) increases. 2. For fixed incentives, deliberation time increases with depth of reasoning. 3. Holding the depth of reasoning constant, larger incentives induce (weakly) shorter deliberation times. As a result, when incentives are increased, the impact on deliberation time is indeterminate, as it increases the total number of steps taken, but it decreases the time associated with each of them.

Applying this logic to a version of Nagel's (1995) beauty contest, as well as several variations of the 11–20 game based on Alaoui and Penta (2016) and Goeree et al. (2018), they report several main findings. First, both response time and the observed behavioral levels increase with incentives. Second, in games for which level-k seems an obvious way of reasoning (e.g., the Beauty Contest), there is clear evidence of a direct connection between response time and depth of reasoning. However, in some variations of Goeree et al.'s (2016) 11–20 game, this connection is loose or non-existent, suggesting that in some games the deliberation process departs from that posited by standard level-k reasoning.

Applications of level-k reasoning to neuroeconomic studies show promising avenues for connecting level-k to more explicit, mechanistic models of individuals' reasoning processes. Coricelli and Nagel (2009) used functional-MRI to measure subjects' brain activity in the beauty-contest game. They implement treatments in which subjects play against a computer programmed to play randomly or against other humans. They find that higher levels of reasoning (level-2 or higher), and a measure of strategic IQ (related to winning the game), correlate with neural activity in the medial prefrontal cortex (mPFC), an area of the brain commonly associated with thinking about other people's thinking. This shows a clear neural basis for levels of play related to thinking about other players' level of strategic reasoning. These results, as well as those discussed earlier, show that Nagel's (1995) simple level-k model is much more than just a parsimonious way of characterizing initial choices. Rather, it provides insight into reasoning processes that individuals apply in strategic situations.

Notes

1 The prize was split between winners in case of ties.
2 There are some experimental papers which also model learning over time using level-k. See Stahl (1996) for the guessing game, Georganas and Nagel (2011) in toehold auctions. Behavioral macroeconomics, especially the seminal paper by Garcia-Schmidt and Woodford (2019), has used level-k to explain inertia over time in their discussion on forward guidance puzzles. For a review of this recently emerging literature, see Mauersberger and Nagel (2018) and Mauersberger, Nagel, and Bühren (2020). There is also a new emerging literature on level-k in repeated games, see Garcia-Pola, and Iriberri (2019).
3 See for example Ho, Camerer, and Weigelt (1998), Nagel (1998), Camerer, Ho, and Chong (2004), and Kovalchick, Camerer, Grether, Plott, and Allman (2005). Camerer (2003, p. 217) shows similar patterns across a variety of subject populations including CEOs, portfolio managers, high school students, and economics students.
4 See also Strzalecki (2014) and Georganas, Healy, and Weber (2015).
5 Recall the comments of some of the players in the newspaper context.

6 This game is a modified version of Arad and Rubinstein's (2012) original 11–20 game, the only difference being the addition of the reward in case of tie, which ensures that all choices other than 11 correspond to a unique level-k.

7 See Agranov, Potamites, Schotter, and Tergiman (2012) for related results in the beauty contest game.

8 Other predictions of the EDR model are investigated in Alaoui, Janezic, and Penta (2020), who develop methods to determine whether subjects account for others' incentives, as well as disentangling whether a subject's choice is due to his cognitive bound or his beliefs about others' beliefs (see also Friedenberg, Kets, and Kneeland, 2018).

9 Alaoui and Penta (2016) illustrate this point using Goeree and Holt's (2001) "little treasures" experiments. They show that a specification of the EDR model with a single free parameter, calibrated to match the data in one of Goeree and Holt's games, generates predictions that are consistent with Goeree and Holt's findings from the other games.

10 Alaoui and Penta (2018) apply their model of endogenous response time to explain Avoyan and Schotter's (2019) experiment on attention allocation.

References

Agranov, M., Potamites, E., Schotter, A., Tergiman, C., 2012. Beliefs and endogenous cognitive levels: An experimental study. *Games and Economic Behavior* 75(2), 449–463.

Alaoui, L., Janezic, K.A., Penta, A., 2020. Reasoning about others' reasoning. Forthcoming *Journal of Economic Theory* 186(C), doi: 10.1016/j.jet.2020.105091.

Alaoui, L., Penta, A., 2016. Endogenous depth of reasoning. *Review of Economic Studies* 83(4), 1297–1333.

Alaoui, L., Penta, A., 2018. Cost-benefit analysis in reasoning. *mimeo.*

Alós-Ferrer, C., Buckenmaier, J., 2019. Cognitive sophistication and deliberation times. University of Zurich, Department of Economics, Working Paper No. 292.

Arad, A., Rubinstein, A., 2012. The 11–20 money request game: A level-*k* reasoning study. *American Economic Review* 102(7), 3561–3573.

Avoyan, A., Schotter, A., 2019. Attention in games: An experimental study. *mimeo.*

Bernheim, B.D., 1984. Rationalizable strategic behavior. *Econometrica* 52(4), 1007–1028.

Bosch-Domènech, A., García-Montalvo, J., Nagel, N., Satorra, A., 2002. One, two, (three), infinity…: Newspaper and lab beauty-contest experiments. *American Economic Review* 92(5), 687–1701.

Brandts, J., Holt, C.A., 1993. Adjustment patterns and equilibrium selection in experimental signaling games. *International Journal of Game Theory* 22(3), 279–302.

Bühren, C., Frank, B., 2012. Chess players' performance beyond 64 squares: A case study on the limitations of cognitive abilities transfer. *Talent Development and Excellence* 4(2), 157–169.

Camerer, C.F., 2003. *Behavioral Game Theory: Experiments in Strategic Interaction.* New York, NY: Russell Sage.

Camerer, C.F., Ho, T.K., Chong, J.K., 2004. A cognitive hierarchy model of games. *Quarterly Journal of Economics* 119(3), 861–898.

Coricelli, G., Rosemarie Nagel, R., 2009. Neural correlates of depth of strategic reasoning in medial prefrontal cortex. *PNAS* 106(23), 9163–9168.

Crawford, V.P., Costa-Gomes, M.A., and Iriberri, N., 2013. Structural models of nonequilibrium strategic thinking: Theory, evidence, and applications. *Journal of Economic Literature* 51(1), 5–62.

Crawford, V.P., Iriberri, N., 2007. Level-*k* auctions: Can a nonequilibrium model of strategic thinking explain the winner's curse and overbidding in private-value auctions? *Econometrica* 75(6), 1721–1770.

Eyster, E., Rabin, M., 2005. Cursed equilibrium. *Econometrica* 73(5), 1623–1672.

Friedenberg, A., Kets, W., Kneeland, T., 2018. Is Bounded rationality driven by limited ability? *mimeo.*

Fudenberg, D., Vespa, E., 2019. Learning and heterogeneous play in a signaling-game experiment. *AEJ: Microeconomics* 11(4), 186–215.

Garcia-Pola, B., Iriberri, N., 2019. Naivete and sophistication in initial and repeated play in games. CEPR Discussion Paper No. DP14088, SSRN: https://ssrn.com/abstract=3486237.

Garcia-Schmidt, M., Woodford, M., 2019. Are low interest rates deflationary? A paradox of perfect-foresight analysis. *American Economic Review* 109(1), 86–120.

Georganas, S., Healy, P.J., Weber, R.A., 2015. On the persistence of strategic sophistication. *Journal of Economic Theory* 159(a), 369–400.

Georganas, S., Nagel, R., 2011. Auctions with toeholds: An experimental study of company takeovers. *International Journal of Industrial Organization* 29(1), 34–45.

Goeree, J.K., Holt, C.A., 2001. Ten little treasures of game theory and ten intuitive contradictions. *American Economic Review* 91(5), 1402–1422.

Goeree, J.K., Louis, P., Zhang, J., 2018. Noisy introspection in the 11–20 game. *Economic Journal* 128(611), 1509–1530.

Ho, T.H., Camerer, C.F., Weigelt, K., 1998. Iterated dominance and iterated best-response in p-beauty contests. *American Economic Review* 88(4), 947–969.

Kovalchick, S., Camerer, C.F., Grether, D.M., Plott, C.R., Allman, J.M., 2005. Aging and decision making: A broad comparative study of decision behavior in neurologically healthy elderly and young individuals. *Journal of Economic Behavior and Organization* 58(1), 79–94.

Mauersberger, F., Nagel, R., 2018. Levels of reasoning in Keynesian beauty contests: A generative framework. In Hommes, C., LeBaron, B. (Eds.). *Handbook of Computational Economics, Volume 4, Heterogeneous Agents.* Amsterdam: North-Holland, 541–634.

Mauersberger, F., Nagel, R., Bühren, C., 2020. Bounded rationality in Keynesian beauty contests: A lesson for central bankers? *Economics - The Open-Access, Kiel Institute for the World Economy (IfW)* 14, 1–38.

Nagel, R., 1995. Unraveling in guessing games: An experimental study. *American Economic Review* 85(5), 1313–1326.

Nagel, R., 1998. A survey on experimental "beauty-contest games": Bounded rationality and learning. In: Budescu, D., Erev, I., Zwick, R. (Eds.). *Games and Human Behavior: Essays in Honor of Amnon Rapoport.* New York, NY: Taylor & Francis Group, 105–142.

Pearce, D.G., 1984. Rationalizable strategic behavior and the problem of perfection. *Econometrica* 52(4), 1029–1050.

Selten, R., Stoecker, R., 1986. End behavior in sequences of finite prisoner's dilemma supergames: A learning theory approach. *Journal of Economic Behavior and Organization* 7(1), 47–70.

Stahl, D.O., 1996. Boundedly rational rule learning in a guessing game. *Games and Economic Behavior* 6(2), 303–330.

Strzalecki, T., 2014. Depth of reasoning and higher-order beliefs. *Journal of Economic Behavior and Organization* 108, 108–122.

11

TRUST, RECIPROCITY, AND SOCIAL HISTORY (BY JOYCE BERG, JOHN DICKHAUT, AND KEVIN MCCABE)

Vernon L. Smith[1]

Introduction

In 1995, Joyce Berg, John Dickhaut, and Kevin McCabe (hereafter BDM) inaugurated entirely new directions of experimental investigation, business research, and human sociability in their study of trust and trustworthiness (BDM called it trust and reciprocity). Building on research results from the study of ultimatum and dictator games, BDM ignited widespread research interest – Google Scholar indicates 5,242 citations through September 2019. Johnson and Mislin (2011) offer a meta-analysis of BDM, using data from 162 replications across 35 countries and 23,000 subjects, but replications and extensions have continued unabated since these data were assembled. Few experiments have approached the status of BDM in launching such extensive further investigation.

What accounts for the incredible scholarly popularity of the BDM protocol and its many derivative studies?

Subjects in the BDM protocol chose unexpectedly high levels of cooperative other-regarding action, under conditions of strict privacy and anonymity that invited self-interested action under a heavy cloak of secrecy. Their findings seem at odds with dictator games in which similar conditions of anonymity and secrecy had greatly reduced dictator game "generosity." After all, BDM was "merely" a two-stage dictator game. The observations also appeared to be at complete odds with the own-regarding actions that had dominated market experiments beginning a half century earlier (Chamberlin, 1948; Smith, 1962; see Holt, 2019, pp 1–35 for a historical summary).[2] The BDM investment game challenged the beliefs underlying economic modelling, altered research directions, and ignited a search for understanding – for reconciling disparate bodies of data, each highly replicable and coming from people in the same sampling populations. Can these

DOI: 10.4324/9781003019121-11

distinct and contradictory patterns be reconciled in one underlying theory, or are we stuck with a two-regime theoretical justification?

This evaluation begins with the BDM protocol – itself a methodological contribution – and the experimental findings. The question of the replicability and robustness of these unexpected results is addressed next in a summary of two subsequent experimental papers. We follow with a discussion of two attempts to explain qua understand the BDM findings; both, however, have methodological deficiencies – Reciprocity and Social Preference explanations. Finally, we offer a brief on Adam Smith's (1759, 1853; hereafter in the text *Sentiments*) model of human sociability, based on strictly self-interested actors, that culminates in propositions that (1) account for trust game choices and (2) predict action in new variations on trust game designs that, in the absence of Smith's model, would be neither natural nor well-motivated.

The BDM protocol: first results and "social history" replication

Across three sessions, BDM recruited 32 pairs of subjects. In each session half the individuals were recruited for Room A and half for Room B.[3] Each received ten $1 bills as an upfront payment for showing up on time – an intentional form of earned compensation that belongs to the individual. Each person in Room A is free to select from their money payment any number, from zero to ten $1 bills to be sent to their anonymous and randomly paired counterpart in Room B. En route, the sum is tripled before delivery to the person's counterpart in Room B. BDM implemented a double-anonymity protocol wherein each pair is anonymous with respect to each other and to any and all third parties, including the experimenters. No one can know who sent whom how much money.

This procedure was a departure from commonly practiced protocols and generated some entirely appropriate controversy that we will discuss as part of our reexamination and review.[4] Methodological challenges – what does it mean to test a theory? – are part of daily life in any and all experimental sciences. That meaning emerges out of the personal experiences and conversation of experimentalists whose "knowledge in science is not made but discovered, and as such it claims to establish contact with reality beyond the clues on which it relies [...]. For we live in it as in the garment of our own skin" (Polanyi, 1962 p 64; also see Mayo, 1996 on the role of experimental methodology in reducing belief error).

The dictator game as a precursor to the investment trust game

The dictator game (DG) evolved from the study of the ultimatum game (UG) as part of explorations designed to better understand the unexpected findings by Guth, Schmittberger, and Schwarze (1982) who originated the UG. In this game, the Proposer offers to split M $1 bills with the Responder, yielding (Proposer payoff, Responder payoff) = (M—X, X). M is commonly $10 or $20. Play then passes to the Responder who either accepts the offer, in which case the imputation is (M—X, X), or rejects the offer, in which case the outcome is (0, 0). If the players are each strictly self-interested and always choose dominant own payoff outcomes, the predicted equilibrium offer is (M—1, 1), since $1 clearly dominates 0, and the Responder is predicted to accept. On average, Proposers offer about 0.45M, and Responders accept almost all offers. Responders routinely tend to reject infrequent offers of $1 or $2 and even of $3.

The predominance of offers of $4 and $5 led to the *ex post hoc* explanation that people have a strong preference for "fairness" or an equal-outcome division of M. This interpretation was challenged by Forsythe et al. (1994). They argued that if the results were driven by a strong preference for equal split "fairness" then the results would not be effected by eliminating the Responder's right to veto the Proposer's offer. Hence, they compare UG treatments with and without the Responder being allowed to veto the offer, and report mean offers of 0.47M when Responder can veto, and (the significantly lower) 0.24M when Responder cannot veto (see Camerer, 2003, Tables 2.2 and 2.3, pp 50–55; and 2.4, pp 57–58; he conveniently reports data from all the early studies). The no-veto treatment quickly became known as the DG and took on an experimental life of its own.

Next – in this scenario from UG to DG to BDM – enters Hoffman et al. (1994; hereafter HMSS) who report many treatment variations on the UG and the DG.[5] In particular, although DG offers are significantly lower than UG offers reported in Forsythe et al. (1994), HMSS were intrigued and impressed by the fact that dictators were nevertheless giving away 24% of their endowments. To stress the boundary of these unexpected but persistent DG results, they introduce a "double-blind" procedure to see if DG generosity is materially reduced, or stubbornly resistant, to this treatment protocol.[6]

Legitimacy of the double-blind treatment component

The double-blind treatment procedures used by HMSS and by BDM has been criticized as representing an illegitimate experimenter-demand effect "by too clearly indicating the goals of the experimenter" (Kagel and Roth, 1995, p 303). This constitutes a misunderstanding of the purpose and objectives behind this protocol. BDM and HMSS, in controlling for reputation and other social effects, intentionally sought to invite and encourage strictly self-serving action by making it surveillance-safe and transparent – the idea that it is okay not to send money, and okay to keep any money received. (Smith, 1982, refers to such explorations as "boundary experiments.") HMSS found that the procedure substantially (as well as significantly) lowered dictator giving (on average from 0.24 to 0.10M, with the percent giving nothing rising from 20 to 60%). Similarly, in BDM, which is merely a two-stage DG, we have a doubling of the opportunity to secretly give nothing. If cooperation fails, we have evidence of the power of self-interested motivation – Max-U(own) – to be expressed under the cloak of secrecy as a control for social value and influence. If cooperation persists, we meaningfully expand the range of conditions where the standard "strangers" model fails. In exploring the boundaries of that persistence, the BDM experiment either expands the range of self-interested action, or launches us into explorations of why robust cooperation trumps the temptation to serve private advantage.

We were not to be disappointed in this polarizing stress test, for BDM find that the dramatic effect found by HMSS in reduced DG giving does not carry over to the trust game. Moreover, far from reducing cooperation, it is substantially increased. Hence, the interpretation that people in the BDM trust game see it in a completely different way than they see the DG. The trust game is indeed very different from a sequential DG – the tripling of any amount sent implies gains from trust/trustee interaction, a synergy that is absent in DG, and it is this leveraging of the reward stakes that seems to invite a much different experiential response, such as BDM's emphasis on "reciprocity."

The important learning from these experiments is that other-regarding actions trump and robustly survive instructional treatments designed strongly to encourage self-interested actions. This powerful finding demonstrates the strength of human sociability, and robustly falsifies the traditional economic and game-theoretic modeling based on self-interested action. Methodologies that preclude such boundary experiments because of unexamined hypothetical experimenter-demand effects fail to afford opportunities for identifying the edges of validity of new and unexpected findings – or establish that there are no edges.

Beyond the moral imperative that subjects be treated with respect, dignity, payment for their earnest service, and strict adherence to the principle that the experimenter shalt not bear false witness (don't lie to the subjects or anyone else), experimental methods must be free and open to new means of learning.[7]

For a non-cooperative equilibrium of the game, sufficient conditions are that (1) all are strictly self-interested, (2) this is common knowledge, and (3) each chooses to maximize their own utilitarian outcome. It follows that individuals in Room A are predicted to send nothing; those in Room B return nothing if any money is sent. This prediction does badly even under the supposed favorable condition where no one, not even the experimenter, knows the identity of any individual actor. The primary implication was that it was a good idea for researchers to seek better ways of thinking about two-person connectedness. Any massive prediction failure ought to motivate re-evaluation and new learning on a similar scale. As we aim to show here, that failure was not newsworthy within the framework of *Sentiments*, published over 250 years before BDM's paper. Moreover, this classical contribution to social psychology expands the range of new experimental designs and prediction. Our only excuse was that we were either ignorant of *Sentiments* or did not understand its message for embracing BDM and their aftermath.

BDM results

On average, individuals in Room A sent $5.16, but the average amount returned was $4.66; two subjects sent zero and five sent $10; 28 of 32 people in Room A sent more than $1. Since sending money yielded an overall loss, senders' beliefs in the game appeared mistaken. Hence, BDM followed with their "social history" treatment in which new subjects, informed by a summary of the first experiment's results, could adapt and correct their beliefs. The social history summary treatment reported the number of subjects sending each amount from $1.00 to $10.00, the average amount returned and average profit of the sender; the only net profitable amounts sent were $5 and $10.

However, BDM's conjecture that subjects would correct their belief error was not supported: Now, the average amount sent increases slightly to $5.36, but the average returned increases to $6.46. The baseline norm, "be generous in sending" does not unravel in the social history treatment, while the trustworthy norm, "be generous in rewarding trust" is enhanced; 3 of 28 sent nothing, half (14) of those in Room A sent $5 or $10, with only one recipient in Room B keeping all that was sent.

Skeptics challenge the BDM results, find only confirming evidence, and significantly extend the domain of BDM applicability

In the large subsequent literature, two studies, both by scholars skeptical of the robustness of these remarkable findings, continued to observe results inconsistent with Max-U (own payoff) rationality in experiments motivated by BDM's findings. In the first, Andreas Ortmann, John Fitzgerald, and Carl Boeing (2000; hereafter OFB) comprehensively replicated and reexamined the BDM experiments, adding new treatments that they hypothesized would change the findings.

They study five treatments:

First, a baseline "No History" treatment, which replicated the original BDM experiments.

Second, a replication of the BDM "Social History" treatment by presenting the results from the first baseline treatment, precisely as did BDM, by simply presenting the values of previous investments and returns in a table.[8]

Third, a "Social History" treatment framing the previous experimental results in terms of the portion that Room B participants returned to A, clearly showing Room A participants that the returns were not equitable.

Fourth, a second "baseline No History treatment" characterized, however, by several key modifications.

Specifically, OFB included a questionnaire for the Room A participants, which they were to complete prior to their decision. Specifically, this questionnaire had two purposes. First, it was to ensure that Room A subjects understood the design and considered their decisions carefully before making them. Second, it was to help subjects determine how much to invest by encouraging them to think carefully (prompting strategic reasoning)[9] about the consequences of their decisions before they made them. The subjects were asked the following four questions:

1. How much money do you think you will send?
2. How much money will your Room B counterpart receive if you send this much?
3. How much money do you think will be returned to you?
4. How much money would you return if you were in Room B?

The authors hypothesized that changing the presentation format in Treatment 3 and prompting strategic reasoning in Treatment 4 would cause significant drops in both the amounts sent to Room B from A, and consequently the amounts returned to Room A from B. As we shall see, however, these modifications had no effect.

Fifth, Treatment 5 and 5R each applied the combined modifications of Treatments 3 and 4, with 5R a replication of Treatment 5 designed to further test the statistical significance finding in Treatment 5. "When Berg et al. used their social history treatment, contributions did not change much. The median remained at $5 and only 3 out of 28 subjects sent zero [...] none of our treatments led to significantly different results. This means that neither the way information is presented (BDM presentation, OFB presentation) nor strategic reasoning prompts (the questionnaire) matter statistically to our subject pool. In fact, as the results for treatment Five and its replication show, nor do these two modifications to the original design matter jointly if we pool the data" (Ortmann, et al., 2000, pp 85–86). In their abstract, OFB express the unexpectedness of their findings: "To our surprise, none of our various treatments led to a reduction in the amount invested."

A second skeptical examination of BDM substantially alters the BDM framework, while polarizing the potential outcome depending upon how the subjects' respond (McCabe and Smith, 2000; hereafter MS). Senders in the BDM game can choose any one of 11 amounts from 0 to $10 to send to their counterpart; if $X are sent ($0 \leq X \leq 10$), receivers can return any amounts from zero up to and including $3X.

MS dichotomize the choices for each of the players so that each can choose only two starkly contrasting actions. The MS payoffs are motivated by BDM, but the BDM context – two people matched in a sending, tripling, and returning money relationship – is stripped out of the MS narrative. One of only two actions by each of the players provides the largest self-interested outcome, the other a "fair" equal split of the joint gains. Thus, Player 1 can choose to send nothing – the self-interested "best" outcome, yielding the payoff: (Player 1= $10; Player 2 = $10). Or, alternatively, Player 1 chooses to send the entire $10, which is tripled to $30. Player 2 can only respond with either of two actions: split the $30 equally with Player 1, yielding the payoff (Player 1 = $15; Player 2 = $25 = $10 + $15), or take all the money resulting in the payoff (Player 1= $0; Player 2 = $40 =$10 + $ 30). In the first option, Player 1 receives a 50% larger amount than if nothing is sent. However, Player 2 receives an increase that is 150% larger than if Player 1 sent nothing. Clearly, Player 2 is made strictly and asymmetrically better off. In the second option, however, Player 1 can end with nothing.

By removing all context and starkly focusing on the hazards to any Player 1 who passes to Player 2, MS intentionally probe the boundary of validity of the BDM's original results, hypothesizing that this would discourage cooperative play.

Remarkably and surprisingly, the frequencies with which subjects offered and accepted the cooperative chose actions that were trusting and trustworthy were high enough that, on average, the earnings of both players increased relative to the self-interested equilibrium payoffs. Of 24 undergraduates, 12 Player 1s (50%) passed play to their counterpart Player 2 and 9 of those 12 responded cooperatively (75%), with only 3 taking all the money (25%).

MS also report data for 28 graduate PhD students who played the same game twice, knowing that they will retain the same pairing.

> First Play: Twenty-one (75%) pass to their counterpart Player 2, of which 16 (76%) choose to cooperate, and only five (24%) take all the money. Second Play: Fourteen (50%) of Player 1s pass to their Player 2s of which nine (64%) cooperate, and only five (36%) defect.

Far from failing this simplified, alleged self-interest promoting test, the MS subjects were even more other-regarding in rejecting non-cooperative action and tended to earn more money than in the BDM game. Thus, MS introduced a simplified design that enabled subjects to better coordinate actions designed to achieve their cooperative intentions.

How are we to explain these findings, so bizarre by traditional economic standards?

Reciprocity and social preference explanations

As indicated in their title, reciprocity as an explanation of trusting and trustworthy behavior was very much part of how BDM thought about their discovery. Their title was not "Trust, Trustworthiness, and Social History"; trustworthiness was identified with reciprocity in a non-market exchange.

By sending money, the first mover in the BDM game is offering to cooperate; by returning money, the second mover is accepting the offer in an exchange – "reciprocity" is simply a word for describing those two actions.[10] How can a description of what transpires be an explanation of why we observe the behavior? The argument is circular (Smith and Wilson, 2019).[11]

Social Preference Theory had its origins in the proposition that other-regarding action is a direct consequence of other-regarding preference or utility functions (Fehr and Fischbacher, 2002). What seemed to fail in BDM was the neoclassical assumption that people cared only about their own payoff. Thus – for generations of economists brought up on utility as the cause of all action – it was natural to explain the new findings with a utility of the form U(own payoff, other payoff) in which actions reflected the actors' concern about other as well as own payoff in the trust game. But if social preference is to be the predictor of action, we need to know the form of the Utility function in advance. For example, suppose Player 1 has social preferences such that they want to transfer money to Player 2. Suppose Player 1 passes to Player 2, and Player 2 defects; that may be a better outcome than if Player 2 chooses the cooperative outcome. Social Preference Theory cannot assume that defection hurts Player 1. If Player 1 is given the opportunity to punish defection by Player 2, some do, but most do not. The methodology is that of retrofitting utility to actions discovered empirically, then looking for "epi-cycle" parameters that accommodate the observation.[12]

Attempts to solve the puzzle – how do we explain and reconcile other-regarding action in BDM and its extensions with the self-interested acts of the same individuals in markets and other contexts – led to decades of experimental explorations. The puzzle also contributed to the discovery that *Sentiments* provided an independent means of interpreting and modelling action, wherein all individuals are strictly self-interested in preference, but follow rules that are other-regarding. That development and its history in recounted in (Smith and Wilson, 2019, pp. xiii–xx).

Humanomics of trust and trustworthiness: why strictly self-interested actors can make good neighbors

The subtitle of *Sentiments* states succinctly its message – "An Essay towards an Analysis of the Principles by which Men Naturally Judge the Conduct and Character, First of their neighbors and then of themselves" (Smith, 1759, 1853, title page).

In *Sentiments*, we learn an alternative to reciprocity and social preference explanations of cooperation in our lives and in our experimental trust game data. Cooperation stems from human sociability and is governed by our rule-following conduct; the very word "conduct" suggests a pattern of proper manners emanating from our judgement of each other. Our actions are other-regarding as well as own-regarding. Moreover, these actions are not direct consequences of our preferences, which are strictly self-interested, and are not in any way conflictual with our actions either in markets or in our social world. To understand *Sentiments,* as economists who study behavior, we must distinguish between our self-interested preferences and our actions, which need not take the form of acting in accordance with this principle; that is, action *need not have the form*: Action if and only if Max-U(own).

> Though it may be true, therefore, that every individual, in his own breast, naturally prefers himself to all mankind, yet he dares not look mankind in the face, and avow that he acts according to this principle. He feels that in this preference they can never go along with him, and that how natural soever it may be to him, it must always appear excessive and extravagant to them. When be views himself in the light in which he is conscious that others will view him he sees that to them be is but one of the multitude, in no respect better than any other in it. If he would act so as that the impartial spectator[13] may enter into the principles of his conduct, which is what of all things he has the greatest desire to do, he must upon this, as upon all other occasions, humble the arrogance of his self-love, and bring it down to something which other men can go along with.
>
> *(Smith, 1759, 1853, p 120)*

In fact, common knowledge that we are all self-interested is a necessary part of how we automatically know that a context-specific action is beneficial or hurtful to another and are, thus, able to implement the rules we follow in interacting with our neighbors (Smith, 1759, 1853, p 112).

What are the circumstances of life that determine this rule-following means of disciplining our actions?

Smith observes that about the time we start to school and "mix with equals" we find that our play-fellows do not show the "indulgent partiality" of our parents in tolerating our expressions of anger; they use punishment to express their displeasure with our hurtful actions towards them, and find ways to reward our beneficent actions toward them. Thus, we enter "the great school of self-command" in "which the practice of the longest life is very seldom sufficient to bring to complete perfection" (Smith, 1759, 1853, pp 204, 206).[14]

The first proposition implied by the analysis in *Sentiments* – and which drives the experimental observations in BDM, OFB, and MS – is the following: "Actions of a beneficent tendency, which proceed from proper motives, seem alone to require a reward; because such alone are the approved objects of gratitude, or excite the sympathetic gratitude of the spectator" (Smith, 1759, 1853, p 112).

By proper motives, Smith is referring to intentionality: I do something good for you because I wanted to do something good for you. And he is here asserting the strong directive that such action alone induces in us a compulsion to reward the action, and this is because of the spontaneous fellow-feeling of gratitude that we experience. Furthermore, this is not just what the individual who is the target of the action experiences and responds to, but it also commands the agreement of every indifferent spectator. That is, every third-party observer easily agrees, or fellow-feels, with the target of the action.[15] In modern language we would call it a "social norm," and here Smith is articulating a theory with specific a priori predictions of its action consequences.

Regrettably, our abysmal ignorance of *Sentiments* prevented us, in the 1990s, from hypothesizing the implied behavior before we observed it.[16]

Later, Smith uses this proposition to derive "reciprocity" (logically, as an implication) although he does not use that word in that context. Rather, he asks who above all we should be kind to. Those who have been kind to us. Thus, "[k]indness is the parent of kindness" (Smith, 1759, 1853, p 331). This is called the Principle of Beneficent Reciprocity by Smith and Wilson (2014, p 16). Hence, *Sentiments* provides the underlying explanation for reciprocity, and is not circular as in the original trust game literature.

Let us now think through the application of Smith's first beneficence proposition to BDM (OFB) and MS. The first mover is clearly under no obligation to send any money, nor the recipient to return money if any is sent. Moreover, the first mover is clearly at risk of getting nothing back. Knowing this, the recipient of any money sent can only infer that money was sent intentionally – an action that obviously and unambiguously benefits the recipient. Smith's proposition predicts that the recipient feels gratitude and is motivated to reward the action by returning some money. How much? Well, more in positive relation to the benefit and gratitude felt – "the greater exertions of that virtue appear to deserve the highest reward. By being productive of the greatest good, they are the natural and approved objects of the liveliest gratitude" (Smith, 1759, 1853, p 117). Smith's theory, culminating in this proposition, predicts the tendency expressed in the data of BDM and OFB, and is found more prominently in MS.

Over and over, *Sentiments* stresses the importance of context, and across the BDM, OFC, and MS treatments, context is varied (also see Hoffman, McCabe, and Smith, 2000). The data show clearly that context matters; the three studies all confirm the findings in *Sentiments* relative to utilitarian action in the self-interest, but actions in the MS game are most strongly consistent with Smith's first proposition on beneficence. In MS, Player 1 sends a strong and unambiguous signal of benefit, or none, and this dichotomy, we can conjecture, accounts for the proposition's greater consistency with MS.

It should be noticed how natural it is to think about how *Sentiments* applies to the actions of the subjects. If the model fails, we know where to look for the cause. Gratitude may not be felt, as with sociopathic tendencies. Or, gratitude might be felt, but may be insufficient to overcome the temptation to defect, suggesting further experiments that vary payoffs. In contrast, if the traditional dominant-strategy, self-interested choice model fails, it says nothing about what to do next. We are left with no guidelines as to the next scientific step.

I will close by quoting a second proposition in *Sentiments* on beneficence and applying it to a new trust game in the MS framework:

> Beneficence is always free, it cannot be extorted by force, the mere want of it exposes to no punishment; because the mere want of benef- icence tends to do no real positive evil. It may disappoint of the good which might reasonably have been expected, and upon that account it may justly excite dislike and disapprobation: it cannot, however, pro- voke any resentment which mankind will go along with.
>
> *(Smith, 1759, 1853, p 112)*

Two recent experimental studies are directly motivated by this important proposition in which the benefit-reward calculus governed by the first prop- osition is said to be voided if there is any threat of coercion, thus predictively bounding the domain of conditions over which the first applies.

The first study observes that the literature on the UG is replete with evi- dence that Responders feel and express much anger which in turn explains the pattern of rejections across UG treatments. Since UG participation is always involuntarily assigned by the experimenter, this suggests a treat- ment effect emanating from the influence of coercion—the implicit threat of veto by the Responder. In new UG experiments, the Responders move first, choosing to either exit the game along with their paired Proposer, each receiving $1, or voluntarily entering the UG stage by passing to the Pro- poser who choose between an equal split of $24, or the equilibrium outcome (Player 1 = $2. Player 2 = $22). Ninety-four percent of Responders signal willingness-to-play by passing play to the Proposer. Remarkably, forty per- cent of the proposers offer the equilibrium option, and sixty-one percent accept—the highest known rate of equilibrium play, and of acceptance re- corded in the extensive UG literature (Smith and Wilson, 2019, pp 135–141).[17]

The second study directly tests Adam Smith's second beneficent proposi- tion in a new trust game, with the same extensive form structure as in MS, but [with] different payoffs. Player 1's have two options: (1) pass to Player 2, who chooses the equilibrium ($12, $12), or ($10, $10); (2) pass to Player 2, who chooses either (Payoff 1, Payoff 2) = ($18, $30), or ($6, $42). If Player 1 de- cides to not cooperate and choose[s] the equilibrium option (1), and if Player 2 wishes to punish Player I at a cost, we have the outcome ($10, $10). No Player 2 so chooses: Of thirty-eight pairs in this game, twenty-three Player 1's select option (1), but none choose to punish the action (Smith and Wilson, 2019, pp 135–141).[18]

Conclusions

That "Trust, Reciprocity and Social History" was a landmark paper in the history of experimental economics is indicated by several measures of academic impact: Citations, of course, but more precisely the results were unexpected, surprising, and continue to inspire new trust game experiments; the results were replicable and robust; and they defined, along with the ultimatum game, the canonical structure and protocol for using trust games to examine human sociality.

However, with the discovery that the results are consistent with key propositions in *Sentiments* – the lesser-known first book written by the founder of economics, Adam Smith – I believe the paper became an important part of demonstrating the relevance of that monumental work for contemporary economics and the moral foundations of the human career.

Notes

1 I am grateful to Andreas Ortmann for his careful reading of two earlier drafts of this paper and providing extensive comments, while not absolving myself from responsibility for any errors that remain. Author Website: www.chapman. edu/research/institutes-and-centers/economic-science-institute/about-us/vernon-smith-personal/index.aspx

2 As we shall see below, these appearances were not correct; both own-regarding and other-regarding human actions are consistent with strictly self-interested preferences in Smith (1759, 1853). The path-breaking work of BDM has helped immeasurably in enabling the rehabilitation of Smith's classical work.

3 When the subjects were recruited, they were told to come to either Room A or B, making it credible that there really were two rooms (no deception); a monitor was chosen in each room to carry envelops to the other room, further making it evident that real people were paired with real people and no deception was possible. Also, by not meeting in one room first, there was additional social control in support of the concept of paired "strangers."

4 Every experimental science depends on an immense body of "experimental knowledge," a specialized form of human capital based on practice and the on-going evaluation, and re-evaluation, of the state of that knowledge; this is the life-blood of any experimental science. (Mayo, 1996; Smith, 2008, Chapter 13)

5 The reader should note that the four papers in this scenario were all published in 1994–1995 as the various authors were all in contact with each other and working from pre-publication drafts of their respective papers.

6 The term "double-blind" is used here in the sense that subject identity is protected (1) between and among the subjects participating in a ("single-blind") experiment, but is also protected (2) between the subject, the experimenter, and any other potential observer.

7 Psychological research traditions are not self-bound by any such moral imperative although the latter is rooted in the experimental research of the psychologist, Sydney Siegel, one of the early founders of experimental economics (Smith, 2017).

8 Experimental economists often encounter editorial resistance from journals to publishing "mere replications," especially in the leading ones that seek to pioneer new and innovative work, while personally placing high priority on the scientific importance of replications. The solution to this challenge for many has taken the form of combining replication with new treatment variations on the original motivating study (Smith, 1994, p 128).

9 Hoffman, McCabe, and Smith (2000) used instructions to "prompt" subjects to think about what their paired counterpart would do in the UG, but it simply focused them on the prospect that Responder might veto the proposal (not on the strategic idea that $1 was better than nothing, which ought to be acceptable), and their offers became more generous.

10 Many of us fell into that pattern. Smith (1998) elevates reciprocity to the key to an understanding of the connection between Adam Smith's (1759, 1776) two books. This is neither wrong, nor very profound, as an explanation of the results in BDM and the large subsequent literature demonstrating the robustness of their results.

11 The same circular reasoning has been accepted to explain the strong tendency toward equal-split outcomes in the UG. The preference for "fair" outcomes is said to be the explanation and the cause. However, equal-split "fair" outcomes also constitute what is observed, which itself cannot serve as an explanation and a cause. It is correct to state that "[t]he (UG) data falsify the assumption that players maximize their own payoffs as clearly as experimental data can" which recognizes the contradiction between prediction and observation. But it is leading and questionable to add: "Since the equilibria are so simple to compute, [...] the ultimatum game is a crisp way to measure social preferences rather than a deep test of strategic thinking" (Camerer, 2003, p 43). This inference follows only if all action is a direct consequence of preference, but it takes only one non-preference-based model of action to negate it. *Sentiments* performs that function.

12 Added to this procedure is the fact that "there is a professional tendency to view utility explanations as final—once a result is deemed due to utility the conversation stops, implying that there is nothing left to explain or test" Hoffman, McCabe, and Smith (2008, p 415).

13 The "impartial spectator" in *Sentiments* is a metaphor for the means by which we learn to judge our own actions in the light of their impact on others – based on our sympathetic fellow-feeling toward others – and to choose in a manner that is properly other-regarding, and not only self-regarding.

> We endeavour to examine our own conduct as we imagine any other fair and impartial spectator would examine it. If, upon placing ourselves in his situation, we thoroughly enter into all the passions and motives which influenced it, we approve of it, by sympathy with the approbation of this supposed equitable judge. If otherwise, we enter into his disapprobation, and condemn it.
>
> *(Smith, 1759, 1853, p 162)*

14 For Adam Smith self-command (or self-government) is the omnipresent gatekeeper of virtue and many situations may allow the "voice of human weakness" to undermine this self-command (Smith, 1759, 1853, p 29). Consequently, higher stakes may tempt a decrease in trust/trustworthiness. But meta-analysis finds this not to be the case; generally the results documented by BDM and OFB were further validated, indicating bedrock support for trust and trustworthiness as expressions of human beneficence even under conditions of anonymity (Johnson and Mislin, 2011, p 874).

15 Note the critical role for human fellow-feeling in *Sentiments* and the following corroborating results of trust game meta-analysis showing that it is important for senders to know that the receiver is a real person:

> We also find that playing with a real person is associated with significantly more sent. While researchers sometimes employ simulated confederates to play the role of the receiver in the trust game, these studies rarely use a manipulation check to confirm that the experimenter's attempts to deceive the participants have been successful. Our findings suggest that participants in such trust game experiments may in fact not all believe, as the experimenters wish them to, that they are playing with real counterparts. This could be due to flaws in the experimental procedures employed or even early participants informing later participants of the deception.
>
> *(Johnson and Mislin, 2011, p 875)*

Recall that the BDM protocol made it credible that real people were matched with each other across two rooms.

16 Harking back to those exciting discovery years, I should note that, even if we were given then our current understanding of *Sentiments*, there was reason aplenty for being skeptical that the proposition would be predictive – it might easily fail because of the deep cloak of secrecy implemented by BDM and OFB (but not MS). Hence, the BDM launch would have been no less path-breaking, by virtue of extending *Sentiments* significantly beyond its original presumed domain.

17 Of course the Proposer may or may not also feel anger; allowing the Proposer to voluntarily choose whether or not to enter the game may further impact their joint outcome.

18 Yet in sharp contrast, Justice Propositions in *Sentiments* predict that if Player 1 offers cooperation, and Player 2 defects, then – given a costly option to punish the defection – Player 1s will so choose, which indeed they do (Smith and Wilson, 2019, pp 152–153). Hence, Adam Smith states general conditions that predict when people will use punishment strategies, and when they will not.

References

Berg, J., Dickhaut, J., McCabe, K.A., 1995. Trust, reciprocity, and social history. *Games and Economic Behavior* 10, 122–142.

Camerer, C., 2003. *Behavioral Game Theory*. Princeton, NJ: Princeton University Press.

Chamberlin, E., 1948. An experimental imperfect market. *Journal of Political Economy* 56(2), 95–108.

Fehr, E., Fischbacher, U., 2002. Why social preferences matter: The impact of non-selfish motives on competition, cooperation and incentives. *Economic Journal* 112, C1–C33.

Forsythe, R., Horowitz, J.E., Savin, N.E., Sefton, M., 1994. Fairness in simple bargaining experiments. *Games and Economic Behavior* 6(3), 347–369.

Guth, W., Schmittberger, R., Schwarze, B., 1982. An experimental analysis of ultimatum bargaining. *Journal of Economic Behavior and Organization* 3(4), 367–388.

Hoffman, E., McCabe, K.A., Smith, V.L., 1994. Preferences, property rights and anonymity in bargaining games. *Games and Economic Behavior* 7(3), 346–380.

Hoffman, E., McCabe, K.A., Smith, V.L., 2000. The impact of exchange context on the activation of equity in ultimatum fames. *Experimental Economics* 3(1), 5–9.

Hoffman, E., McCabe, K.A., Smith, V.L., 2008. Reciprocity in ultimatum and dictator games: An introduction. In: Plott, C., Smith, V.L. (Eds.). *Handbook of Experimental Economics Results*. Amsterdam: North Holland, 411–416.

Holt, C.A., 2019. *Markets, Games, and Strategic Behavior: An Introduction to Experimental Economics*. Princeton, NJ: Princeton University Press.

Johnson, N.D., Mislin, A.A., 2011. Trust games: A meta-analysis. *Journal of Economic Psychology* 32, 865–889.

Kagel, J.H., Roth, A.E., 1995. *Handbook of Experimental Economics*. Princeton, NJ: Princeton University Press.

Mayo, D., 1996. *Error and the Growth of Experimental Knowledge*. Chicago, IL: University of Chicago Press.

McCabe, K.A., Smith, V.L., 2000. A comparison of naïve and sophisticated subject behavior with game theoretic predictions. *Proceedings of the National Academy of Sciences* 97(7), 3777–3781.

Ortmann, A., Fitzgerald, J., Boeing, C., 2000. Trust, reciprocity, and social History: A re-examination. *Experimental Economics* 3(1), 81–100.

Polanyi, M., 1962. *Personal Knowledge*. Chicago, IL: University of Chicago Press.

Smith, A. (1759, 1853) *The Theory of Moral Sentiments; or, An Essay Towards an Analysis of the Principles by which Men Naturally Judge the Conduct and Character, First of their neighbors and then of Themselves*. With a Biographical Critical Memoir of the Author, by Dugald Stewart, Second Edition. London: Henry G. Bohm.

Smith, V.L., 1962. An experimental study of competitive market behavior. *Journal of Political Economy* 70(2), 111–137.

Smith, V.L., 1982. Microeconomic systems as an experiential science. *The American Economic Review* 72(5), 923–955.

Smith, V.L., 1994. Economics in the laboratory. *Journal of Economic Perspectives* 8(1), 113–131.

Smith, V.L., 1998. The two faces of Adam Smith: Southern economic association distinguished guest lecture. *Southern Economic Journal* 65 (1), 1–19.

Smith, V.L., 2008. *Rationality in Economics Constructionist and Ecological Forms*. Cambridge: Cambridge University Press.

Smith, V.L., 2017. Tribute to Sidney Siegel (1916–1961): A founder of experimental economics. *Southern Economic Journal* 83(3), 664–667.

Smith, V.L., Wilson, B.J., 2014. Fair and impartial spectators in experimental economic behavior. *Review of Behavioral Economics* 1(1–2), 1–26.

Smith, V.L., Wilson, B.J., 2018. Equilibrium play in voluntary ultimatum games: Beneficence cannot be extorted. *Games and Economic Behavior* 109(C), 452–464.

Smith, V.L., Wilson, B.J., 2019. *HUMANOMICS Moral Sentiments and the Wealth of Nations for the Twenty-First Century*. Cambridge: Cambridge University Press.

12

COOPERATION AND PUNISHMENT IN PUBLIC GOODS EXPERIMENTS (BY ERNST FEHR AND SIMON GÄCHTER)

Yan Chen[1]

Introduction

The inclusion of "Cooperation and Punishment in Public Goods Experiments" in this volume of foundationally important papers is a testament to its influence on different fields of research across the social sciences. The paper has inspired a significant body of research, garnering 4,808 Google Scholar citations.[2] I am honored to have the opportunity to review this important work and its role within the social preference space in behavioral and experimental economics research. This work provides a striking puzzle that cannot be explained by classic game theoretic solutions with players who care only about their own payoffs. In addition, from a design perspective, this work provides a simple and intuitive behavioral mechanism that alleviates the free-rider problem in public goods provision and differs from both Nash-efficient public goods mechanisms (Groves and Ledyard, 1977, 1987) and their extensive-form counterparts (Varian, 1994).

Summary of the paper

The 2000 paper by Ernst Fehr and Simon Ga¨chter uses a laboratory experiment to show that, in a linear public goods game with voluntary contribution mechanisms and peer punishment opportunities, cooperators are willing to punish free-riders, even when the punishment is costly to the punisher and entails no future benefits. Consequently, punishment by the cooperators cannot be explained by the self-interest motive, and there is much less free-riding in the presence punishment.

DOI: 10.4324/9781003019121-12

Motivation for their experimental design

When I first read Fehr and Gächter's (FG) work, I was intrigued by their experimental design, given my own background in mechanism design. In considering their design, I looked at two possible inspirations for their design choice.

My first conjecture was that they had been culturally influenced by their experience with the strong norm enforcement culture present in Switzerland, where they resided during the time they conducted their study. Having lived in Germany and having visited Switzerland frequently over the years, I have noted a distinctive willingness to abide by rules and enforce norms in German-speaking countries. For instance, it is common to see pedestrians wait for a crosswalk indication before crossing the street, even when no cars are around. Interestingly, while the possibility that design reflected observed cultural behavior patterns did not turn out to be a direct motivation for their study, though the notion was not completely off base either. Indeed, Orley Ashenfelter, the editor of the *AER* handling the paper at the time, suggested the paper be subtitled, "Evidence from Germany," when he meant "Evidence from Switzerland," perhaps reflecting a similar conjecture that their observed behavior reflected cultural norms.

My second thought was that their design was motivated by the existing literature at the time. Indeed, the authors mention that Ostrom et al. (1992) report costly punishment in a repeated common pool resource game. However, since Ostrom et al. (1992) observe the *same* group of subjects interacting for an *ex-ante* unknown number of periods, they are unable to establish the effect of costly punishments, as their subjects could develop individual reputations. Fehr and Gächter eliminated both features in their experiment design to rule out any possibility that selfish motives could drive punishment. Therefore, if systematic punishment occurs, it must be attributed to some sort of social preference. However, a conversation with Simon Gächter revealed that FG were not aware of Ostrom et al.'s work when they first developed their design. As Gächter remarked, "To read political science journals, we had to go to another building."[3]

Interviews with both authors reveal that the idea for their paper actually came from a deep dive into their own research. In a summer workshop in Linz in 1994, they conducted a gift-exchange experiment among soldiers. The control condition was a market without gift exchange, with an excess supply of labor. In the experiment, when the gift exchange was shut down, wages continued to decline. Between Periods 5 and 6 of the game, one subject (worker) shouted, "Let's have a union!" and for the next two periods, no one accepted a single offer. Essentially workers were on strike, albeit temporarily. At the end of the session, the subjects filled out a questionnaire. When asked if they were angry at the employers, they answered, "Yes, we are angry at the employers." However, when asked if they were angry at their

co-workers, they answered, "Yes, we are very, very angry at our co-workers."
In this context, the higher wage is a public good, whereas accepting a lower
wage is equivalent to free-riding. In another public goods experiment with
communication, Gächter and Fehr (1999) placed subjects into groups of
four and allowed them to communicate with each other before and after the
experiment. In one of the post-experiment discussions, one subject admitted
that he was a free-rider. A young woman said, "Because of people like you,
the world goes to the dogs." Observing the subjects' emotional responses to
the act of free-riding inspired FG to design an experiment to explore the extent to which subjects would go in order to punish and potentially alleviate
free-riding.

Experiment design

To address this issue, FG designed an experiment with a 2×2 factorial design, with the first factor being partners versus strangers (between subjects),
and the second factor being with and without peer punishment opportunities (within subjects, counterbalanced order). This design, thus, yields
four experimental conditions: strangers with and without punishment, and
partners with and without punishment. In the partner treatments, the same
group of four subjects play a finitely repeated public goods game for ten
periods. By contrast, in the stranger treatments, 24 subjects are randomly
grouped into $n = 4$ for each of the ten periods.

FG conduct four experimental sessions with 24 subjects in each session
and one session with 16 subjects, allowing the subjects to interact with each
other anonymously through computers in a laboratory. Sessions 1–3 are
stranger treatments (18 groups of size $n = 4$). In sessions 1 and 2, subjects
play ten periods of the punishment condition, followed by ten periods without punishment. In Session 3, the order is reversed. In comparison, Sessions
4 and 5 are partner treatments (10 groups of size $n = 4$), with session 4 starting with ten periods of the punishment condition followed by ten periods
without, and Session 5 in the reverse order.

To facilitate comparisons with findings in linear public good experiments, FG use standard parameters in their voluntary contribution stage,
with the payoff function for each subject i in each period without punishment represented by

$$\pi_i^1 = y - g_i + a \sum_{j=1}^{n} g_j,$$

where $y = 20$ is the initial endowment, g_i is i's contribution to the public
good, $a = 0.4$ is the marginal per capita return from a contribution to the
public good, and $n = 4$ is the group size. With this parameter combination,
full free-riding ($g_i = 0$) is a dominant strategy, the sum of group payoff is
maximized if each group member fully cooperates ($g_i = y$, for all i).

In treatments with punishment opportunities, after the voluntary contribution stage in each period, subjects are first informed of other group members' individual contributions and then given the opportunity to simultaneously punish each other via a system of punishment points. That is, group member j can punish group member i by assigning punishment points p_i^j to i. For each punishment point received, i's first-stage payoff, π_i^1, is reduced by 10%. Therefore, the pecuniary payoff of subject p_i^j at the end of the punishment stage is given by:

$$\pi_1 = \pi_i^1\left[1 - P^i / n\right] - \sum_{i \neq j} c\left(p_i^j\right),$$

where $P^i = min\left\{\sum_{i \neq j} p_i^j, 10\right\}$ is the total number of payoff effective punishment points subject I receives, and $\sum_{i \neq j} c\left(p_i^j\right)$ is the total number of punishment points subject I sends out to others.

The key innovation in FG's experiment design is their inclusion of a peer punishment stage. Their experiment is not the first to incorporate a punishment stage (see Ostrom et al., 1992). However, their design is the first to isolate non-selfish motivational sources and to examine the effects of punishment choices. Ostrom et al. (1992) use the *same* group of subjects interacting for an *ex-ante* unknown number of periods, it is possible that their subjects could develop individual and collective reputations that may lead to selfish motivations in punishment decisions. FG eliminate both features in their experiment design. Therefore, it is a much-improved design.

Results

In 1997, I participated in the Bounded Rationality Workshop in Bonn, a watershed event in the history of experimental economics. The dominant themes that emerged from that workshop – social preferences, learning in games, and neuroeconomics – were harbingers of the direction experimental economics would take in the new millennium. During the Q&A session, after the cluster of papers on learning had been presented, I recall Ernst Fehr walking up to the overhead projector, putting up a transparency showing Figure 1 in FG, and challenging those working on learning to explain the discontinuity between Periods 10 and 11. At the time, Fang-Fang Tang and I were working on a paper examining learning and incentive compatible mechanisms for public goods provision (Chen and Tang, 1998). At the conference, I carefully studied the figure that Ernst showed us and concluded that none of the learning models we had discussed could have predicted the dramatic discontinuity observed between Periods 10 and 11.

This discontinuity, summarized in Result 1, shows that the existence of punishment opportunities causes a large rise in the average contribution level in the stranger-treatment. On average, FG find that contribution rates amount to 58% of the endowment.[4]

FG further find that, in the stranger treatments, subjects contribute between two and four times more than in the no-punishment condition. Over time, these contributions do not decrease and indeed may even increase. Lastly, they find that while the punishment condition yields no stable contribution level, the no-punishment condition contribution becomes stable at 0 (free-riding).

By contrast, FG find that punishment creates a steep increase in the average contribution level in the partner treatment. Further, in the no-punishment condition, average contributions decrease over time, converging to 0 (full free-riding), while in the punishment condition, contributions converge toward full cooperation. Five out of ten groups in their punishment condition actually reach full cooperation.

FG also find that, in both the stranger and partner treatments, subjects with contributions well below the average receive a greater punishment, to the point where subjects might receive a payoff loss. However, the relative payoff gain remains positive in the punishment condition, with about a 20% gain in the partner treatment and a 10% gain in the stranger treatment, relative to the respective no-punishment treatments.

In what follows, I organize my discussion of their main results around a series of questions these results evoke that, in turn, have set the stage for research in the field.

What explains their observed increase in contributions when subjects are given the opportunity to punish?

In a conversation between myself and Simon Gächter, he indicated that they saw punishment as "an emotional thing." These emotional motivations are synthesized as envy and guilt in Fehr and Schmidt (1999), who use an inequality aversion model to reconcile theory with the FG finding. Specifically, Proposition 5 in Fehr and Schmidt (1999) predicts that full cooperation can be sustained as an equilibrium outcome if there is a group of "conditionally cooperative enforcers." In fact, one such enforcer may be enough if that individual is sufficiently concerned about inequality leading to her disadvantage.

What explains the jump in contribution levels between the treatments in Figure 1?

This jump is one of the more striking findings and indicates that subject belief is an important component in modeling behavior in public goods games.[5] In their context, it is plausible that subjects form beliefs about the new institution they will experience and best respond given these beliefs. In a subsequent experiment that measures both beliefs and preferences in linear public goods games, Fischbacher and Gächter (2010) find that belief is significant, in that there is conditional cooperation on top of contribution preferences in one of their treatment conditions.

Which subjects choose to punish?

A robust result that came out of the linear public goods literature is the heterogeneity of individual strategies and behaviors. Starting with Fischbacher et al. (2001), researchers have subsequently used a simplified strategy method in a one-shot linear public goods game to type subjects into behavior categories such as free-riders and conditional cooperators. In repeated interactions, this exercise is identical to modeling repeated game strategies using finite automata (Rubinstein, 1986; Abreu and Rubinstein, 1988).

One subsequent study of note is that of Weber et al. (2018). Using the strategy method pioneered by Fischbacher et al. (2001), Weber et al. (2018) first classify participants into either dispositional free-riders or conditional cooperators. The subjects then participate in a real time one-shot linear public goods game either with or without punishment. Weber et al. (2018) discover that dispositional free-riders and conditional cooperators are similar in their punishment levels, frequencies, and motives. Therefore, in their subject pool, the "burden of cooperation" is carried by a larger set of individuals than previously assumed.

What is the welfare effect of peer punishment in the short and long run?

Finally, FG's study has motivated researchers to examine the welfare effect of punishment. In the subgame perfect implementation literature, since punishment is intended to deter off-the-equilibrium-path behavior, there should be no punishment present in equilibrium. This is seen in the classic tale of Solomon, who proposed the solution of dividing a baby in two when presented with two women claiming the same child. The woman who begged him to give the baby to the other rather than cut him in two was deemed the true mother. In experiments, off-the-equilibrium-path strategies are often observed, especially in the initial rounds of an experiment. In this context, if punishment is used to increase cooperation, a reasonable question is whether the cost of punishment is worth the gain from the increased cooperation or not.

In a typical FG experiment, which lasts for ten rounds, the option of costly punishment increases the amount of cooperation but not the average payoff of the group, when compared to the control condition with no such option (Dreber et al., 2008). By contrast, Gächter et al. (2008) find that average net earnings are significantly higher in a long-run (50 periods) setting, but not in a short-run (10 periods) setting, compared to the corresponding control conditions with no peer punishment.

Robustness, generalizability, and future directions

In addition to the research their study has inspired, the FG paper has stood the test of time. The public goods game with peer punishment introduced by FG has been played in experimental settings around the globe. While studies consistently find the presence of punishment, the nature of this punishment has been found to vary with subjects' cultural experiences. In a sequence of experiments conducted in 16 comparable participant pools around the world, Herrmann et al. (2008) find that pro-social punishment, directed towards low contributors, is observed in countries where the rule of law is strong. By contrast, they find that anti-social punishment, directed towards both low and high contributors, is more likely to occur in countries with weak norms of civic cooperation and weak rule of law. Taken together, their findings suggest that punishment opportunities are socially beneficial only if they are complemented by strong social norms of cooperation. Further grouping these 16 subject pools into six different world cultures, Gächter et al. (2010) find that culture has a substantial influence on the extent of cooperation, beyond the effect of individual heterogeneity and group-level differences.

Extensions of FG include allowing subjects to choose institutions in public goods environments, as well as enabling peer rewards. When subjects are given the opportunity to choose institutions, despite the high initial cost caused by peer punishment, Gürerk et al. (2006) find that subjects prefer environments with a peer punishment and reward opportunity over one without. To separate the effects of peer punishment from those due to peer reward, Gürerk et al. (2014) implement a treatment where subjects choose between a standard VCM and an institution with costly peer punishment, as well as another treatment where subjects choose between a standard VCM and an institution with costly peer reward. They find that a community that allows peer punishment is the most successful with regard to public goods provision and that (additional) reward opportunities do not improve on this.

The findings in FG also suggest avenues for future research examining the mechanism driving their effects. While social preference theory generates predictions consistent with the effects observed in their experiment, it is also plausible that the driving force for human cooperation in environments with public goods and externalities is an underlying social norm (Fehr and Schurtenberger, 2018). One open question is whether we can endogenize social norms through social preferences in a broad class of games. On the theoretical front, Chen and Chen (2011) derive descriptive norms from group-contingent social preferences in the context of coordination games. Future research could examine additional contexts. Another open question is whether we can empirically distinguish between social preferences and social norms. On the empirical front, future research might use structural estimation in combination with established protocols for norm elicitation (Krupka and Weber, 2009).

Another fruitful area of further research applies the insights gained from FG to the real world to help us better understand why certain communities succeed in providing public goods while others fail. In one study, Kosfeld and Rustagi (2015) conduct a lab-in-the-field experiment among leaders of forest user groups in a large forest commons management program in Ethiopia. They use a one-shot, third-party punishment game to identify the types of leaders associated with group success and find that leaders who emphasize equality and efficiency see positive forest outcomes, whereas antisocial leaders who punish indiscriminately see relatively negative forest outcomes.

Another future area of research extends FG's insights to help us design new institutions that align human social preferences with market designers' goals. In one study, Bolton et al. (2013) draw on the tendency toward altruistic punishment and reciprocity to suggest designs for online reputation systems. Online marketplaces, such as eBay and Amazon, rely on participants' feedback about their transaction partners to facilitate trading among strangers. In these settings, feedback information is largely a public good since it helps traders manage the risks involved in trusting an unknown transaction partner. Traders who do not follow the social norm may receive a negative rating, which punishes the trader while providing useful information to others. However, punishments can often be counter-punished, which is known to reduce the effectiveness of punishment as a means of promoting cooperation. Therefore, designing reputation systems that elicit truthful feedback while reducing retaliation is an ongoing design challenge for economists and computer scientists alike (Chen et al., forthcoming).

The important work of FG in the field of public goods provision has prompted a large number of studies examining the role of punishment and reward as a means of encouraging cooperation. Human cooperation in providing public goods has always been and will continue to be an important area of research, as we encounter the commons problem in villages (Ostrom, 1990), team production issues in organizations (Groves and Ledyard, 1977), and global challenges, such as climate change and the COVID-19 pandemic. Discovering that people are willing to enforce a norm of contribution at a cost to themselves has important policy implications in many real-world domains.

Notes

1 I thank Ernst Fehr and Simon Gächter for conversations that helped me understand the process through which this influential paper emerged, and for their insightful comments on the first draft of this review.
2 Google Scholar: retrieved on July 6, 2020.
3 As context, prior to the advent of the internet, universities had access to only hard copy versions of academic journals, which were housed in respective

discipline libraries. The highly decentralized setting of Swiss universities meant that the authors had to travel across Zürich to obtain the article in question.
4 The partner treatment amplifies this effect but there are confounds in the partner treatment, such as reputation concerns.
5 To fully explain the jump, it would be desirable to decompose the total effect attributed to punishment opportunities as well as restart.

References

Abreu, D., Rubinstein, A., 1988. The structure of Nash equilibrium in repeated games with finite automata. *Econometrica* 56(6), 1259–1281.

Bolton, G., Greiner, B., Ockenfels, A., 2013. Engineering trust: Reciprocity in the production of reputation information. *Management Science* 59(2), 265–285.

Chen, R., Chen, Y., 2011. The potential of social identity for equilibrium selection. *American Economic Review* 101(6), 2562–2589.

Chen, Y., Cramton, P., List, J.A., Ockenfels, A., 2020. Market design, human behavior and management. *Management Science*, Published Online: 9 Sep 2020, https://doi-org.proxy.library.ucsb.edu:9443/10.1287/mnsc.2020.3659

Chen, Y., Tang, F.F., 1998. Learning and incentive compatible mechanisms for public goods provision: An experimental study. *Journal of Political Economy* 106(3), 633–662.

Dreber, A., Rand, D.G., Fudenberg, D., Nowak, M.A., 2008. Winners don't punish. *Nature* 452(7185), 348–351.

Fehr, E., Gächter, S., 2000. Cooperation and punishment in public goods experiment. *American Economic Review* 90(4), 980–994.

Fehr, E., Schmidt, K.M., 1999. The theory of fairness, competition, and cooperation. *Quarterly Journal of Economics* 114(3), 817–868.

Fehr, E., Schurtenberger, I., 2018. Normative foundations of human cooperation. *Nature Human Behaviour* 2(7), 458–468.

Fischbacher, U., Gächter, S., 2010. Social preferences, beliefs, and the dynamics of free riding in public goods experiments. *American Economic Review* 100(1), 541–556.

Fischbacher, U., Gächter, S., Fehr, E., 2001. Are people conditionally cooperative? Evidence from a public goods experiment. *Economics Letters* 71(3), 397–404.

Gächter, S. Fehr, E., 1999. Collective action as a social exchange. *Journal of Economic Behavior and Organization* 39(4), 341–369.

Gächter, S., Herrmann, B., Tho"ni, C., 2010. Culture and cooperation. *Philosophical Transactions of the Royal Society B: Biological Sciences* 365(1553), 2651–2661.

Gächter, S., Renner, E., Sefton, M., 2008. The long-run benefits of punishment, *Science* 322(5907), 1510–1510.

Groves, T., Ledyard, J.O., 1977. Optimal allocation of public goods: A solution to the "free rider" problem. *Econometrica* 45(4), 783–809.

Groves, T., Ledyard, J.O., 1987. Incentive compatibility since 1972. In: Groves, T. Radner, R., Reiter, S. (Eds.). *Information, Incentives and Economic Mechanisms: Essays in Honor of Leonid Hurwicz.* Minneapolis: University of Minnesota Press, 48–111.

Gü rerk, O., Irlenbusch, B., Rockenbach, B., 2006. The competitive advantage of sanctioning institutions. *Science* 312(5770), 108–111.

Gü rerk, O., Irlenbusch, B., Rockenbach, B., 2014. On cooperation in open communities. *Journal of Public Economics* 120, 220–230.

Herrmann, B., Tho¨ni, C., Gächter, S., 2008. Antisocial punishment across societies. *Science* 319(5868), 1362–1367.

Kosfeld, Michael and Devesh Rustagi, 2015. Leader punishment and cooperation in groups: Experimental field evidence from commons management in Ethiopia. *American Economic Review* 105(2), 747–783.

Krupka, E., Weber, R.A., 2009. The focusing and informational effects of norms on pro-social behavior. *Journal of Economic Psychology* 30(3), 307–320.

Ostrom, E., 1990. *Governing the Commons: The Evolution of Institutions for Collective Action (Canto Classics)*. Cambridge: Cambridge University Press.

Ostrom, E., Walker, J., Gardner, R., 1992. Covenants with and without a Sword: Self-Governance Is Possible. *American Political Science Review* 86(2), 404–417.

Rubinstein, A., 1986. Finite automata play the repeated prisoner's dilemma. *Journal of Economic Theory* 39(1), 83–96.

Varian, H., 1994. A solution to the problems of externalities when agents are well-informed. *American Economic Review* 84(5), 1278–1293.

Weber, T.O., Weisel, O., Gächter, S., 2018. Dispositional free riders do not free ride on punishment. *Nature Communications* 9(1). doi: 10.1038/s41467-018-04775-8.

13

A FINE IS A PRICE (BY URI GNEEZY AND ALDO RUSTICHINI)

Alex Imas

Introduction

In October of 2015, the American Medical Association – the largest organization of physicians and medical students in the US – held a meeting of experts. The topic: how to incentivize physicians so that quality of care would be high while also ensuring that the costs would not overwhelm the medical system. As healthcare progressively became more and more expensive, both policy makers and advocacy groups began focusing on how physicians are paid. Some have argued that the pay-for-service system – where doctors are compensated based on the number of procedures performed – exacerbates medical costs by encouraging unnecessary procedures; the proposed alternative is to instead pay for performance, i.e., incentivize the healthcare outcomes themselves. While some experts invited by the AMA held medical degrees, the majority were social scientists. They were here because the association was worried that introducing extrinsic incentives for performance would actually lead to worse outcomes – that paying doctors based on performance may *crowd out* their intrinsic motivation to help their patients.

The idea that financially incentivizing performance can degrade performance is more than just counterintuitive – it goes against one of the most central tenets of economic analysis. Effort is costly, so increasing the benefits of exerting it through monetary incentives should only make people work harder. Two seminal papers by Uri Gneezy and Aldo Rustichini, both published in the same year, challenge this very basic prediction. In "A Fine is a Price" (Gneezy & Rustichini, 2000a), which is the focus of this chapter, the authors partnered with day-care centers who sought to decrease the incidence of parents showing up late to pick up their kids. Half the day cares introduced a fine for late pick-ups, while the others did not. Standard models would naturally predict that increasing the cost of an action should

DOI: 10.4324/9781003019121-13

discourage people from doing it. This is not what the authors found: More parents showed up late at the day cares that introduced the fine; some weeks, the number of late arrivals was double that of the no-fine control group. Importantly, removing the fine did not help, as parents who had faced a fine continued to come in late at higher rates than those who never did. In the related "Pay Enough or Don't Pay at All" (Gneezy & Rustichini, 2000b), the authors showed that the introduction of small incentives for activities such as solving intelligence puzzles or collecting money for charity decreased performance. While output did increase when incentives were raised further, paying people nothing resulted in significantly better performance than offering small (but positive) payments. In both papers, the authors argue that the introduction of monetary incentives (or disincentives, in the case of fines) may backfire if they crowd out people's intrinsic desire to perform a task or activity.

Every year when teaching behavioral economics, I end the first class by highlighting pieces of research that I believe best exemplify the field. Both these papers by Gneezy and Rustichini lead the discussion. Why is this the case? First, like all the best work in behavioral economics, it demonstrates how taking psychology seriously is important for thinking about the most basic economic principles. Incentive design is a hallmark of economic analysis. In turn, gaining a better understanding of how people actually react to different incentive schemes is of broad interest to economists – especially if the results completely reverse a key prediction of standard theory. Cognitive psychologists such as Deci (1971) have shown that the introduction of tangible rewards lower children's motivation for engaging in a variety of activities.[1] Gneezy and Rustichini (2000a, b) brought these insights into economics by demonstrating the potentially detrimental effects of monetary compensation in settings that are of clear interest to the field. As discussed later in the "Contribution" section, this led to the launch of an entire literature of both theoretical (Bénabou & Tirole, 2003) and empirical (Ariely, Brach, & Meier, 2009) work that explores the factors that affect the crowding out of intrinsic motivation. Second, the papers were unique in their methodology in that both featured a field experiment. While field experiments are common today, in 2000 it was rare to see one published in an economics journal, especially in the field of behavioral economics (Card, DellaVigna, & Malmendier, 2011). The conceptual innovation of the Gneezy and Rustichini papers – as well as the impact they quickly had on the literature – likely motivated many researchers to run field experiments of their own. Lastly, as exemplified by the opening paragraph, this work had a significant impact on the way that researchers and policy makers think about incentives more broadly.

The rest of the chapter proceeds as follows. The "Paper summary" section provides a more in-depth summary of the papers. The "Contribution" section discusses the influence on theory, methodology, and impact on the broader literature. The "Conclusion" section discusses policy implications and concludes.

Paper summary

In "A Fine is a Price" and the closely related "Pay Enough or Don't Pay at All," Gneezy and Rustichini demonstrate that the introduction of monetary incentives or fines can potentially backfire.

The central component of "A Fine is a Price" is a field experiment looking at the effect of fines on the frequency of parents' late arrival to collect their children from day-care centers. The authors partnered with ten day-care centers in the city of Haifa and ran the study over a period of 20 weeks. Four day-care centers served as the control group and never implemented a penalty for late arrival, and six served as the test group, introducing a late-arrival fine in the fourth week. The fine was a flat fee of 10 NIS (New Israeli Shekel) for a delay of 10 minutes or more.

In the initial four weeks, there was no significant difference in the behavior of the test and the control group, and no significant trend was observed in the test group. This validates the critical assumption that the control and test groups saw similar levels of late arrivals. In the seventh week, the fine was removed for the test group. In contrast to standard theory – which predicts that a monetary penalty would discourage the targeted behavior – the introduction of the fine led to an *increase* in late arrivals amongst parents in the test group. Importantly, even after the fine was removed, the higher level of late arrivals persisted until the end of the study. This result is consistent with idea of the fine crowding out parents' intrinsic motivation for picking up their kids on time; once this motivation is gone, it is hard to restore even when the monetary penalty is removed. The authors also discuss an alternative explanation, where parents are uncertain about the penalty of arriving late. The fine clarifies the exact monetary cost. For some parents – particularly those who are risk averse or who may have thought the cost was higher than the fine – spending more time at work or doing errands around the house may be worth paying the price.

"Pay Enough or Don't Pay at All" pairs a laboratory experiment with a field experiment to demonstrate the deleterious effects of introducing low monetary incentives on performance. The laboratory experiment was conducted at the University of Haifa in Israel. In the experiment, a group of 160 undergraduate students was evenly assigned to four different treatment groups, and each student was asked to answer a set of 50 IQ test questions. These questions were chosen so that the probability of a correct answer depended on participants' effort, involving reasoning and computation rather than general knowledge. All four groups received a fixed amount of 60 NIS for participating in the study. The first group was simply asked to answer as many questions as possible. The second group would receive an additional 10 cents of a NIS per correct answer. The third group would receive 1 NIS per correct answer, and the fourth group would receive 3 NIS for each of the questions answered correctly. The authors observed that the average number of questions answered correctly was significantly lower for the second group (23.1 questions) than the first group (28.4 questions). The third and fourth groups had significantly higher averages than the first two groups with 34.7 and 34.1 questions, respectively.

The second study was run in the field, using a sample of high school students doing volunteer work. Annually, high school students in Israel go from house to house and collect monetary donations for charities. In the experiment, 180 students were divided into three groups: the first was the control group and did not receive any monetary compensation; the second received 1% of the total amount collected; the third group received 10% of the total amount collected. All students were told in advance that the payment for the reward was financed by the researchers, separate from the donations collected. The authors found that the amount collected was the largest in the first group, which did not receive any payment (238.6 NIS), followed by the third group with the 10% compensation rate (219.3 NIS). Notably, the second group, which received a higher monetary payment than the first, collected the least amount for charity (153.6 NIS).

While "A Fine is a Price" demonstrated that the introduction of fines can *increase* behavior that the penalties are meant to deter, "Pay Enough or Don't Pay at All" showed that adding positive monetary incentives can have an analogous effect in *decreasing* behavior that the compensation is meant to encourage. In both sets of studies, the authors argue that monetary incentives – whether in the form of prices or payments for effort – can backfire by crowding out intrinsic motivation.

Contribution

Together, these two papers have had a substantial impact on how academics, practitioners, and policy makers think about incentives. The study of incentives is a cornerstone of economic analysis, with whole subfields – both empirical (e.g., labor economics) and theoretical (e.g., contract theory, mechanism design) – devoted to studying them. In the simple settings examined by Gneezy and Rustichini, the standard framework makes a clear prediction on how the introduction of incentives should affect behavior: Agents attempt to maximize income while minimizing the costs of effort and any potential risk involved. Since the tasks are held constant, increasing the outcome-contingent compensation (or price) will increase (or decrease) the targeted behavior. The authors showed that the introduction of incentives may lead to behavior that actually goes in the opposite of the hypothesized direction. This dramatic violation of the most basic of predictions launched a body of literature that sought to take the psychology of incentives more seriously.

Bénabou and Tirole (2003) were one of the first to formally model the crowding out of intrinsic motivation as part of a principal-agent framework. They extend the standard model by allowing incentives to convey information to the agent about the rewards from a task or her own ability to perform it. To see the intuition, suppose that an agent is offered a task (e.g., solving word problems) by a principal. The agent may not know how rewarding these word problems are to herself – they may be intellectually enriching – and she may be uncertain about her ability to solve them. Without incentives, she may infer that solving these problems are rewarding in their own right – they may be enriching or fun to work on. Moreover, she would not expect them to be that difficult where these intrinsic rewards are out of reach. However, if the principal offers a monetary incentive, this conveys information that this task cannot be *that* fun to work on – otherwise payment would not be necessary. If the compensation is fairly low, this extrinsic reward may not be enough to counteract the change in the agent's beliefs about the task's intrinsic reward; in turn, the agent will work less hard than in the case without incentives. In this framework, incentives "crowd out" intrinsic motivation by shifting the agent's perception of the task. Importantly, when incentives are removed, their initial introduction yields a strictly negative outcome for the principal: beliefs about the intrinsic value of the task do not change, but the extrinsic incentive is no longer there to even weakly motivate the agent. In this way, extrinsic incentives are weak reinforcers of behavior in the short run and negative reinforcers in the long run. Besides rationalizing the behavioral patterns in the Gneezy and Rustichini papers – particularly the long-run consequences of fines in the day-care setting – the framework of Bénabou and Tirole (2003) makes a number of other predictions about the role of incentives in principal-agent relationships, such as when crowding out can be reversed or not.

Bénabou and Tirole (2006, 2011) demonstrate how extrinsic incentives can backfire when intrinsic motivation is linked to one's social- or self-image. They note that people may engage in an activity such as recycling in order to signal to others or themselves that they are a good person. This signaling mechanism is driven by the assumption that people do not have perfect insight about an individual's "type" – whether they are prosocial or not. Because moral and charitable types are more likely to engage in a prosocial activity in equilibrium, the individual will perform this activity at least in part for its signaling value. In the case of social signaling (Bénabou & Tirole, 2006), individuals act prosocially in order to signal their type to others; in the case of self-signaling (Bénabou & Tirole, 2011), prosocial choices act as signals to the self. The introduction of extrinsic incentives decreases the informativeness of the signal because it is no longer clear, for example, whether a person recycles because she would like to help the environment or to earn the monetary reward. Here, monetary rewards crowd out intrinsic motivation by lowering an activity's signaling value; extrinsic incentives backfire when the monetary reward is not large enough to compensate for this decrease in signaling value.

These papers constitute just a handful of the theoretical advances inspired by the work of Gneezy and Rustichini (see also, e.g., Sliwka, 2007). The theoretical literature has been accompanied by a similar stream of empirical investigations. Ariely, Bracha, and Meier (2009) show that introducing monetary incentives for prosocial tasks indeed decreases effort, but only when incentives are publicly revealed. Heyman and Ariely (2004) distinguish between monetary and social markets. The authors argue and provide evidence that crowding out will only be observed for monetary incentives – in-kind or social incentives do not lead to decreased effort. Falk and Kosfeld (2006) demonstrate that incentives which decrease an agent's sense of control by, for example, setting a minimum performance benchmark are more likely to backfire than less restrictive alternatives. Fehr and List (2004) show that the insights from Gneezy and Rustichini extend to sophisticated decision-makers such as company CEOs. There, they show that just like students, CEOs respond to the prospect of punitive incentives by being less trustworthy.

Gneezy and Rustichini's work also had a lasting impact on management literature, inspiring papers on the relationship between pay, intrinsic and extrinsic motivations, and performance. Ederer and Manso (2013) find that the standard pay-for-performance incentive schemes are less effective in motivating innovation than an incentive scheme that tolerates early failure and rewards long-term success. Lin (2007) examines the role of both extrinsic and intrinsic motivators in employees' knowledge-sharing attitudes and shows that these attitudes are strongly associated with intrinsic motivation for sharing knowledge. On the other hand, extrinsic incentives in the form of expected organizational rewards have no significant influence on employees' attitudes. Hossain and Li (2014) designed a field experiment in which they frame a task in two different ways: a natural *work* frame and a prosocial *social* frame. They find that small monetary rewards reduce labor participation under the social frame but not under the work frame, demonstrating that the crowding-out effect relies on the framing of the work environment. Frey and Osterloh (2005) argue that linking managers' and directors' compensation to firm performance crowds out intrinsic motivation and reinforces selfish behavior, which can increase the incidence of corporate scandals.

Conclusion

Besides academic research in economics and management (see Kamenica, 2012 for review), the insights from Gneezy and Rustichini have also contributed to popular discourse on motivation more broadly. The studies are prominently featured in best-selling books such as *Drive: The Surprising Truth About What Motivates Us* by Daniel Pink (2011), *Happiness: Lessons from a New Science* by Richard Layard (2011), and *Predictably Irrational* by Dan Ariely (2008). Management texts for practitioners commonly discuss the potential pitfalls of using extrinsic rewards and methods that harness rather than crowd out intrinsic motivation.

Gneezy and Rustichini's work is especially critical for policy makers who intend to utilize incentives to influence people's behavior. Without a careful design that takes crowding-out and other psychological factors into account, reforms may be ineffective – or worse, may bring about the opposite effect. For example, the Civil Service Reform Act in 1978 established a pay-for-performance plan for mid-level managers and supervisors in order to improve performance. However, it was soon discontinued as many studies found that the new pay system did not improve performance or employee satisfaction (Kellough & Lu 1993; Rainey & Kellough 2000). School districts also frequently adopt different reforms to increase student achievement and reduce differences between racial groups. Providing schools and teachers with monetary incentives positively affected student performance (Lavy, 2002), whereas providing financial incentives to students improved performance only when the incentives were tied to input but not output (Fryer Jr, 2011). Pecuniary incentives are also widely used to change individuals' health-related behaviors, such as weight loss, smoking cessation, regular health checkups, and blood donation. No significant differences in weight loss were observed between the incentivized and control groups in a weight-loss program (Paul-Ebhohimhen & Avenell, 2008). When a monetary reward for blood donation was introduced, the supply of donors decreased by almost half, with a significant crowding-out effect in women (Mellström & Johannesson, 2008). This small sample of findings serves to highlight the need for further study of the psychological factors affecting motivation and performance under various incentive schemes.

The influence of Gneezy and Rustichini's research across both academic and practical applications highlights its importance in behavioral and experimental economics. I believe this influence will only grow as follow up work continues to expand on the research – both in highlighting its boundary conditions and finding new applications for it. Moreover, the seamless blend between deep psychological insights and important economic principles is sure to keep these papers on class syllabi for decades to come.

Note

1 While the idea that extrinsic incentives could potentially backfire was first introduced by Richard Titmuss (1970), he argued that proving rewards for activities such as donating blood may weaken a person's sense of civic duty but did not provide evidence for this claim.

References

Ariely, D., 2008. *Predictably Irrational*. New York, NY: Harper Audio.

Ariely, D., Bracha, A., Meier, S., 2009. Doing good or doing well? Image motivation and monetary incentives in behaving prosocially. *American Economic Review* 99(1), 544–555.

Bénabou, R., Tirole, J., 2003. Intrinsic and extrinsic motivation. *The Review of Economic Studies* 70(3), 489–520.

Bénabou, R., Tirole, J., 2006. Incentives and prosocial behavior. *American Economic Review* 96(5), 1652–1678.

Bénabou, R., Tirole, J., 2011. Identity, morals, and taboos: Beliefs as assets. *The Quarterly Journal of Economics* 126(2), 805–855.

Card, D., DellaVigna, S., Malmendier, U., 2011. The role of theory in field experiments. *Journal of Economic Perspectives* 25(3), 39–62.

Deci, E.L., 1971. Effects of externally mediated rewards on intrinsic motivation. *Journal of Personality and Social Psychology* 18(1), 105–115.

Ederer, F., Manso, G., 2013. Is pay for performance detrimental to innovation? *Management Science* 59(7), 1496–1513.

Falk, A., Kosfeld, M., 2006. The hidden costs of control. *American Economic Review* 96(5), 1611–1630.

Fehr, E., List, J.A. (2004). The hidden costs and returns of incentives—trust and trustworthiness among CEOs. *Journal of the European Economic Association* 2(5), 743–771.

Frey, B.S., Osterloh, M. (2005). Yes, managers should be paid like bureaucrats. *Journal of Management Inquiry* 14(1), 96–111.

Fryer Jr, R.G. (2011). Financial incentives and student achievement: Evidence from randomized trials. *The Quarterly Journal of Economics* 126(4), 1755–1798.

Gneezy, U., Rustichini, A., 2000a. A fine is a price. The Journal of Legal Studies 29(1), 1–17.

Gneezy, U., Rustichini, A., 2000b. Pay enough or don't pay at all. *The Quarterly Journal of Economics* 115(3), 791–810.

Heyman, J., Ariely, D., 2004. Effort for payment: A tale of two markets. *Psychological Science* 15(11), 787–793.

Hossain, T., Li, K.K., 2014. Crowding out in the labor market: A prosocial setting is necessary. *Management Science* 60(5), 1148–1160.

Kamenica, E., 2012. Behavioral economics and psychology of incentives. *Annual Review of Economics* 4(1), 427–452.

Kellough, J.E., Lu, H., 1993. The paradox of merit pay in the public sector: Persistence of a problematic procedure. *Review of Public Personnel Administration* 13(2), 45–64.

Layard, R., 2011. *Happiness: Lessons from a New Science.* London, UK: Penguin Books.

Lavy, V., 2002. Evaluating the effect of teachers' group performance incentives on pupil achievement. *Journal of Political Economy* 110(6), 1286–1317.

Lin, H.F., 2007. Effects of extrinsic and intrinsic motivation on employee knowledge sharing intentions. *Journal of Information Science* 33(2), 135–149.

Mellström, C., Johannesson, M., 2008. Crowding out in blood donation: Was Titmuss right? *Journal of the European Economic Association* 6(4), 845–863.

Paul-Ebhohimhen, V., Avenell, A., 2008. Systematic review of the use of financial incentives in treatments for obesity and overweight. *Obesity Reviews* 9(4), 355–367.

Pink, D.H., 2011. *Drive: The Surprising Truth about What Motivates Us.* London: Penguin Books.

Rainey, H.G., Kellough, J.E., 2000. Civil service reform and incentives in the public service. In: Pfiffner, J.P., Brook, D.A., (Eds.). *The Future of Merit: Twenty Years after the Civil Service Reform Act.* Baltimore, MD: John Hopkins University Press, 127–145.

Sliwka, D., 2007. Trust as a signal of a social norm and the hidden costs of incentive schemes. *American Economic Review* 97(3), 999–1012.

Titmuss, R.M., 1970. *The Gift Relationship.* London: Allen and Unwin.

14

GIVING ACCORDING TO GARP: AN EXPERIMENTAL TEST OF THE CONSISTENCY OF PREFERENCES FOR ALTRUISM (BY JAMES ANDREONI AND JOHN MILLER)

Catherine Eckel

Research question and experimental design

Since Forsythe et al. (1994) first proposed and tested the behavior of subjects in the dictator game, economists have been aware that many individuals will give away money in the lab, voluntarily sharing resources with their fellow subjects. Andreoni and Miller (2002) were the first to ask whether donations to other individuals behave in much the same way as purchases one might make, responding to price and income in predictable, systematic ways. If subjects' donations are like other expenditures, then utility functions and indifference maps for such transfers should behave as they would for purchase of goods. Their paper introduces a setting where this idea can be explored. Andreoni and Miller design a laboratory experiment to test the responsiveness of donations to standard elements of budget constraints – prices and income – thereby eliciting subject's utility function for altruistic giving. Their study tests whether donations obey the axioms of revealed preference, which impose consistency on choices that subjects make.

Subjects make a series of modified dictator-game allocation decisions between themselves and another person; these decisions vary the dictator's endowment and the relative price of transferring money to another individual. The subject chooses how much to keep and how much to pass under each of these budget constraints. The authors then test whether the observed behavior conforms to the requirements of the General Axiom of Revealed Preference (GARP).[1]

Analysis and findings

Andreoni and Miller find that the majority of their subjects exhibit behavior that is consistent with maximizing a quasi-concave utility function. Behavior

DOI: 10.4324/9781003019121-14

in the standard game, with a 1/1 price of giving, are quite similar to earlier studies using a fixed endowment and a single decision, with subjects giving away 23% of their endowment on average. This indicates that embedding the standard game in the modified design has not distorted behavior overall.

Of the 176 subjects in the study, 18 violated GARP at least once. Andreoni and Miller use Afriat's (1972) Critical Cost Efficiency Index (CCEI) to measure the severity of violations. The CCEI is the largest value by which the endowments must multiplied to transform violations into rational decisions. The closer the value of the index to 1, the smaller the change necessary to avoid violations. They found that three subjects' violations fell below their chosen threshold of 0.95. This is quite a high level of rationality, and indicates that subjects' decisions about how much to give to another person behave very much like decisions over any other good.

The authors then go on to determine the form of subjects' utility functions. First they classify subjects into types. The most common type had selfish preferences: 22.7% behaved perfectly selfishly, keeping all tokens in all decisions; hence, their utility functions put no weight on the payoffs of other subjects. Twenty-five subjects (14.2%) always divided payoffs equally, showing Leontief preferences with a kink at equality. Eleven subjects (6.2%) maximized efficiency by giving all of the endowment to the person who had the highest value (lowest price) for tokens. These subjects treated payoffs as perfect substitutes. The remaining subjects were classified by estimating the distance between their choices and each of these types of preferences and allocating them to the closest type, leading to a distribution of "weak" types with 43% weak Selfish, 28.5% weak Leontief, and 28.5% weak Perfect Substitutes.

The authors estimate three utility functions, one with each of the defined subsets of the weak-type subjects. The functional form they select is CES (Constant Elasticity of Substitution), chosen because it fit the data well. (For the pure types, the parameters can just be calculated.) The estimation focuses on two parameters, one measuring the weight on one's own payoff, i.e., the degree of selfishness, and the other the convexity of preferences, i.e., the tradeoff between one's own and the other's payoff. The estimated parameters show clear differences across types, consistent with expectations. Using the estimated utility functions, the authors then "predict" behavior in dictator, public goods games, and prisoner's dilemma games, and compare their estimates with data from other studies. The fit, you might say, is pretty darn good.

A second part of the paper, largely forgotten in the literature, tests whether subjects are motivated by envy. Here Andreoni and Miller design decisions to test for jealous preferences – the willingness of a subject to sacrifice their own earnings in order to reduce another person's earnings. Subjects face five upward-sloping budget constraints with different slopes. The steepest slope, where inequality is advantageous to the decision maker, gives 13 tokens to self for every 1 token to the other person, and the flattest slope, where inequality is disadvantageous, is the opposite, with 1/1 in the middle. Most subjects choose the endpoint of the budget constraints, earning for themselves (and the other person) as much as possible. But for the two decisions with high disadvantageous inequality, about 20% of subjects hedged a little, choosing an interior allocation point. Subjects clearly don't mind inequality if it is advantageous, but do, to some extent, when it is disadvantageous.

Contribution

The most important contribution of this paper is to show that giving to others obeys the laws of rationality. Giving behavior is not random noise or a manifestation of experimenter demand, but instead exhibits systematic responses to changes in prices and endowment. Perhaps equally important is the demonstration that there are different types of individuals in the population, ranging from the own-payoff maximizers found in economist's models to equal-splitters. Very few pure altruists – those who give away everything in the dictator game – turn up in the lab. While a substantial number of participants are selfish, most give something away, at least some of the time, and give more when the cost of doing so is low. Andreoni and Miller left it to later studies to tease out the implications of this for public policy, particularly redistributive policy, and fundraising. Many later studies were inspired by this work, as discussed below.

Methodological choices

In any experiment, a researcher has dozens of design decisions to make, some of which may seem minor, but at the same time could be consequential for the results. The impact of these design choices are often revealed over time, as other researchers explore alternative design choices. Of all the games that experimentalists have explored, the dictator game is the most sensitive to context, so design changes are likely to matter for the results. This could be problematic for the use of dictator games as individual-level measures of altruism, and at the very least mean that the researcher should take particular care with the details, where the devil surely resides.

Subject pool. First, the subject population may affect the outcome. The authors' choice was to recruit student subjects from intermediate and upper-level economics courses. The use of econ students might be questioned by current reviewers as potentially biasing the results in the direction of more selfish decisions, as compared with students from other majors. The superior selfishness of economists was first asserted by Marwell and Ames (1981) and, at this point, everyone knows econ students are more selfish, though, to be fair, the result has been both supported and refuted by many studies since.[2] On the other hand, folks outside the world of experimental research often criticize the use of student subjects to conclude anything about how people behave in general. They assume that students in a lab will be overly generous with one another. But dictator games conducted with people who are not students tend to show much higher levels of giving, and more equal division (see the meta-analysis by Engel 2011). As far as we know, the consequences of using economics majors or student subjects has not been explored in an experiment with multiple budget constraints such as this one. The use of these particular subjects is unlikely to have affected the rationality result, but it might have affected the estimate of the proportions of each type.

Context. The setting may also impact results. The study was run by hand in a classroom. This setting might make the subjects feel more "observed" than in more anonymous, computer-mediated decisions, whether in a lab or online. This might in turn lead to more generous decisions. Subjects are less generous in settings where their anonymity is assured (Hoffman et al. 1994), and merely adding eyes to a computer screen seems to enhance the feeling of being observed enough to increase giving (Haley and Fessler 2005). As many clever experimentalists have shown, it is possible to design games or discover contexts where subjects behave more like the income-maximizing agents that populate our models. Experiments conducted at a sports-card convention show much more limited generosity (see Levitt and List 2007 for a summary), and a field experiment at a bus stop in Las Vegas (where subjects didn't know they were in an experiment) showed none at all (Winking and Mizer 2013).[3] As with the subject population, these different contexts are unlikely to have affected the degree of rationality in the decisions, but clearly would have affected the estimates of the proportions of different types.

Payment and incentives. A more subtle effect may have arisen from the payment procedure. Here, subjects were paid for two randomly selected decisions, each with a different pairing: every subject was paid for one decision as dictator, and also for being a recipient for someone else's dictator decision. This is clear when reading the instructions, so the subjects likely understood it, but is not clear from the text. Why would a researcher do this? This procedure is a way of getting dictator decisions from all subjects in a study, thereby not wasting money on mere recipients, while making the dictator game decision salient for everyone (since all subjects get paid for one of their decisions as dictator). On the other hand, someone has to be a recipient for all those decisions, and the simplest thing is just to use the subjects on hand. Seems innocent. But this "playing both roles" procedure has been shown to lead to different outcomes than if the decision maker is paid only once, for one of his own decisions. If you think about it, this could go either way. If the subject is more sympathetic to the recipient by virtue of knowing he'll be one, then he might give more. On the other hand, if he knows he is going to get paid as a recipient, he might expect others to mirror his own decisions, and therefore keep everything for himself, expecting his paired recipient to do the same. Either way, this procedure could substantially affect the estimation of the proportions of subjects who fall into each of the categories above.

Two studies have attempted to figure this out. Grech and Nax (2020) develop a theoretical model to predict how a subject with various elements of social preferences might behave under two procedures, amounting to playing one role (either dictator or recipient) or playing both roles (being paid, as in Andreoni and Miller). As in any standard model, egoists (selfish people) always keep everything, and altruists (those who care only about others' payoffs) will give away everything. An efficiency maximizer will give everything to the lowest-cost recipient (whether himself or the other person). But if the decision maker cares about the payoffs of both players, then the playing-both-roles payment procedure turns the dictator game into a real strategic game: this is the important insight of the paper. A subject's decision then depends on what he believes his counterpart will do. The authors then characterize the set of equilibria, which depend on beliefs about the types in the population. Their experiments replicate the design of Andreoni and Miller, varying only whether the subject is paid in one role or two. They find a small but significantly higher level of transfers at every price level, and a substantially lower proportion of zero donors, in the paying-both-roles protocol.[4] Transfers are also more responsive to price in the both-role protocol.

Zhan et al. (2020) also replicate the Andreoni and Miller design, varying whether a subject is paid for one role (as dictator or recipient) or two (with one decision paid for each role). Their instructions and procedure swerve closer to the original study, and the results for the both-role protocol are, on the money, the same as the original study. In contrast to Grech and Nax, their subjects give less in the both-role treatment except at the very lowest price of giving (.25). However, they also find that giving is more responsive to price in the both-roles setting. Categorizing subjects, the single-role treatment produces significantly fewer purely selfish subjects, and more equality focused subjects. Thus, the implications of this study, that paying for both roles reduces generosity, are the opposite of that from Grech and Nax. This study also extends previous work by testing whether the expectation of payment from another source accounts for the difference in behavior, and find a small effect that does not fully offset the difference in the two payment schemes.[5]

Replications and extensions

Many researchers have built on the work of Andreoni and Miller. These include gender differences, charitable giving, and political support for redistribution. Each of these is discussed briefly.

Gender differences. Andreoni and Vesterlund (2001) replicated the procedure in Andreoni and Miller, focusing on gender differences.[6] Their protocol did not call attention to gender, they merely collected information on the gender of their subjects.[7] We had published a standard dictator game study showing that women were more generous than men (Eckel and Grossman

1998), and this study expanded our work to a larger set of prices and endowments. Andreoni and Vesterlund found that women and men both almost always comply with GARP, but that they differ in the distribution of preference types. Including both strong and weak type classifications, women in their study were twice as likely to be have Leontief (equal division) preferences (54% of women as compared to 25% of men), while men were three times as likely to have efficiency preferences (9% compared to 27%) and somewhat more likely to be selfish (37% compared to 47%). In aggregate, this study found that women are not always more generous. Their study is frequently billed as showing mixed evidence of women's generosity, but the evidence not very mixed. Women in their study are only less generous when the price of giving is very low (.5 or below), at which point men tend to favor efficiency by giving away everything, while women try to achieve an equal division of the available resources, given the exchange rates. Men are more generous only when efficiency dictates it.[8]

Charitable giving. One of the criticisms of the dictator game is that subjects have little reason to give. After all, the other subject is a student, too, and unlikely to be particularly needy or deserving of support. In Eckel and Grossman (1996), we pointed this out using a "real donation" game – a dictator game with a charity recipient. Subjects gave a lot more to a charity than an anonymous subjects down the hall, an indication that the "benefit" of giving affects allocations. We subsequently used a modified version with varying prices and endowments, to look at the effect of price subsidies (matching and rebates) on charitable giving (Eckel and Grossman 2003). Although this paper focused on a comparison of two types of subsidies, it clearly was influenced by Andreoni and Miller and cites the working paper version of it. We found that subjects were responsive to the price of giving, but the form of the subsidy mattered, with a matching subsidy more effective than a rebate subsidy. Many subsequent studies used variations on the real donation game, but to my knowledge no one has fully replicated the Andreoni Miller protocol with a charitable recipient.[9]

One important result arising from the real donation literature is that, apart from price or endowment, subjects discriminate in their donations, varying what they give in response to the characteristics of the recipient. Subjects are willing to transfer larger amounts to deserving recipients or causes, an indication that the quality of the donation – the value to the recipients – plays an important role, similar to the role quality would play in any economic transaction. Examples of studies that explore heterogeneity in giving with respect to the deservingness of the recipient include (among many others): Fong (2007), Fong and Luttmer (2009), Eckel et al. (2018), and Candelo et al. (2019).

Extension and relation to political preferences. A significant modification of the Andreoni/Miller approach appeared in Fisman et al. (2007). The authors developed a new graphic interface, using budget constraints with slider bars, that was designed to make it easier for subjects to understand the allocations and faster for them to make decisions. They also include two other types of decisions in their study, one with three-person dictator games, where one person determines payoffs to two others at varying prices, and one with step-shaped budget constraints. Subjects complete 50 decisions in a computer interface. The results for the two-person dictator games confirm the findings of Andreoni and Miller, in that subjects' decisions conform to GARP for the most part, and there is a great deal of heterogeneity in giving behavior with types corresponding to those identified in the original study. Their main contribution is to explore the relationship between preferences for giving, and what they term "social preferences," in their case meaning the preferences that someone has about the distribution of income among others (hence the use of the three-person games).

Fisman et al. (2015) returns to this question, and further explores the relationship between giving and distributional preferences using their 50-question protocol. The authors compare the giving behavior of a sample of "elite" subjects – students at Yale Law School – with a sample of adults from the American Life Panel, and compare them on two dimensions: self-ish vs. fair-minded (egalitarian) and efficiency or equality focused, roughly corresponding to the two parameters of the CEI utility function. The elite sample is more selfish and more efficiency focused as compared with the sample of adults. Unfortunately, the procedures used in these experiments were different. The YLS students were paid for two decisions, as in the original study, but the ALS subjects were paid only once as dictators, with recipients chosen from non-participants in the study. As noted by Grech and Nax and by Zhan et al., the variation in procedures is likely to have affected the results, calling into question the validity of the comparison.

In Fisman et al. (2017), the protocol is repeated for a sample of adult Americans in order to examine the heterogeneity in preferences across demographic groups, and relationship between these preferences and voting behavior. This study also uses the ALF panel with subjects being paid for one decision. The authors find substantial heterogeneity. Using the same two-dimensional categorization as in the previous study, they find that more educated, higher-income subjects are more selfish (less egalitarian), and that younger, lower-income subjects and African Americans show a greater efficiency focus while women show a greater equality focus.

Relationship to other fairness studies

Andreoni and Miller first circulated their paper in 1996, which means that it substantially predated the dominant theories of fairness preferences that were published around the same time or soon after (Fehr and Schmidt 1999; Bolton and Ockenfels 2000; Charness and Rabin 2002). Fehr and Schmidt cite the 1996 working paper; Bolton and Ockenfels the 1998 working paper; and Charness and Rabin the 2002 published version, meaning that all of them were aware of the work. Andreoni and Miller differs from these subsequent studies of social preferences in that it does not propose a theory of motives for giving. However, it did provide grist for their mills, and likely helped shape those theories. For example, the preference for efficiency, which is neglected in the first two theories, plays an important role in the third. It is clearly present in Andreoni and Miller's data, for a subset of subjects. Andreoni and Miller is frequently cited in studies that test one or more of the fairness theories.

Conclusion

Andreoni and Miller broke new ground with their 2002 paper, showing for the first time that the somewhat surprising levels of generosity seen by subjects in the lab obey the laws of rationality. Using careful experimental design and sophisticated statistical methods, Andreoni and Miller established that, whatever their motive, subjects' transfers to others respond to price and endowment in much the same way that consumers respond when purchasing goods. The notable heterogeneity across subjects established for the first time that people differ markedly in their preferences for giving. The paper has been highly influential in that both its methodology and its subject matter have been the subject of much subsequent investigation.

Notes

1 If a consumer chooses a bundle of goods A over B, and then chooses B over A, that would violate the Weak Axiom of Revealed Preference (WARP). If A is chosen over B and B over C, then choosing C over A would violate the Strong Axiom of Revealed Preference (SARP). The General Axiom of Revealed Preference (GARP) extends these intuitive axioms to cases of indifference between budgets, and is necessary and sufficient for the existence of well-behaved preferences, given linear budget constraints. This is why GARP is useful for the current study. See p. 739 for more detail.
2 And they are still at it. See Girardi et al. (2020) for a current example.
3 Levitt and List argue that little can be learned about the preferences of individuals from their behavior in the lab. For an eloquent response to this assertion, see Camerer (2015) who also summarizes some of the main studies that find a positive relation between lab and field behavior.
4 The Grech and Nax protocol has some other differences from the original Andreoni Miller. It may be important that the allocation decisions are presented in random order, instead of all on one page, as in the original. The experiment was conducted online, which shouldn't have affected comparative statics, but who knows. The instructions make the payment structure really explicit. To me, the most puzzling aspect of their study is the difference in giving at a price of 1, with the dual-role subjects giving about 10% more. Unless I missed it, they do not explicitly conduct a comparison of their results with Andreoni and Miller. Recall that Andreoni and Miller find the same level of giving for a price of one as in other studies that have only a single decision. Zhan et al. replicate this finding as well.
5 In their second experiment, Zhan et al. create a lottery payment that mimics the distribution of payoffs in the first experiment. Subjects draw a card to determine their lottery payment. This extra payment does increase giving slightly

compared with the standard single-role game, but does not account for the difference between the single- and dual-role treatments. The proportions of purely selfish, equality-focused (Leontief) and efficiency-focused subjects is not affected by this treatment, and remains the same as the single-role protocol.

6 Though it was published first, Andreoni and Vesterlund clearly draws upon the protocols developed in Andreoni and Miller, which first circulated as a working paper in 1996.

7 For some reason, experimental economists were long reluctant even to collect information on the individual characteristics of their subjects, perhaps because the agents in most formal models were anonymous and identical. Much of the data we can recover from early experimental studies does not contain any information about gender. Only when the study was explicitly about gender was this information gathered. Sadly, this makes it impossible to go back and re-analyze old data for individual differences. I expect Andreoni and Miller did not record the gender of their participants, so new data had to be collected to test for gender differences. Most labs now routinely collect basic demographic information.

8 This study has been cited over 1,500 times on Google Scholar, so I expect it has been replicated. But I did not find a replication.

9 A number of studies have look at individual differences in the real donation game. I'll just mention a couple of results. In our rebate-match paper, we found that women gave more than men on average, but we did not test for gender differences by price. A recent meta-analysis finds that women are more generous than men in dictator games, especially when the recipient is a charitable organization (Bilén et al. 2020). Carpenter et al. (2008) report results of a representative real donation game, and find that students are less generous than older community members, consistent with the results above on the standard dictator game with students and non-students.

References

Andreoni, J., Miller, J.H., 1996. Giving according to GARP: An experimental study of rationality and altruism. Working paper, Wisconsin Madison-Social Systems.

Andreoni, J., Miller, J., 2002. Giving according to GARP: An experimental test of the consistency of preferences for altruism. *Econometrica* 70(2), 737–753.

Andreoni, J., Vesterlund, L., 2001. Which is the fair sex? Gender differences in altruism. *The Quarterly Journal of Economics* 116(1), 293–312.

Bilén, D., Dreber, A., Johanneson, M., 2020. Are women more generous than men? A meta-analysis. Available at SSRN: https://ssrn.com/abstract=3578038 or http://dx.doi.org/10.2139/ssrn.3578038

Bolton, G.E., Ockenfels, A., 2000. ERC: A theory of equity, reciprocity, and competition. *American Economic Review* 90(1), 166–193.

Camerer, Colin F., 2015. The promise and success of lab-field generalizability in experimental economics: A critical reply to Levitt and List. In Fréchette, G.R. and Schotter, A. (Eds.). *Handbook of Experimental Economic Methodology*. Oxford: Oxford University Press, 249–295.

Candelo, N., de Oliveira, A.C., Eckel, C., 2019. Worthiness versus self-interest in charitable giving: Evidence from a low-income, minority neighborhood. *Southern Economic Journal* 85(4), 1196–1216.

Carpenter, J., Connolly, C., Myers, C.K., 2008. Altruistic behavior in a representative dictator experiment. *Experimental Economics* 11(3), 282–298.

Charness, G., Rabin, M., 2002. Understanding social preferences with simple tests. *The Quarterly Journal of Economics* 117(3), 817–869.

Eckel, C.C., Grossman, P.J., 1996. Altruism in anonymous dictator games. *Games and Economic Behavior* 16(2), 181–191.

Eckel, C.C., Grossman, P.J., 1998. Are women less selfish than men?: Evidence from dictator experiments. *The Economic Journal* 108(448), 726–735.

Eckel, C.C., Grossman, P.J., 2003. Rebate versus matching: does how we subsidize charitable contributions matter? *Journal of Public Economics* 87(3–4), 681–701.

Eckel, C.C., Priday, B.A. and Wilson, R.K., 2018. Charity begins at home: A lab-in-the-field experiment on charitable giving. *Games* 9(4), 95, https://doi.org/10.3390/g9040095.

Engel, C., 2011. Dictator games: A meta study. *Experimental Economics* 14(4), 583–610.

Fehr, E., Schmidt, K.M., 1999. A theory of fairness, competition, and cooperation. *The Quarterly Journal of Economics* 114(3), 817–868.

Fisman, R., Jakiela, P., Kariv, S., 2017. Distributional preferences and political behavior. *Journal of Public Economics* 155, 1–10.

Fisman, R., Jakiela, P., Kariv, S., Markovits, D., 2015. The distributional preferences of an elite. *Science* 349(6254), https://doi:10.1126/science.aab0096.

Fisman, R., Kariv, S. Markovits, D., 2007. Individual preferences for giving. *American Economic Review* 97(5), 1858–1876.

Fong, C.M., 2007. Evidence from an experiment on charity to welfare recipients: Reciprocity, altruism and the empathic responsiveness hypothesis. *The Economic Journal* 117(522), pp.1008–1024.

Fong, C.M., Luttmer, E.F., 2009. What determines giving to Hurricane Katrina victims? Experimental evidence on racial group loyalty. *American Economic Journal: Applied Economics* 1(2), 64–87.

Forsythe, R., Horowitz, J.L., Savin, N.E., Sefton, M., 1994. Fairness in simple bargaining experiments. *Games and Economic Behavior* 6(3), 347–369.

Girardi, D., Mamunuru, S.M., Halliday, S.D., Bowles, S., 2020. Does economics make you selfish? Working paper.

Grech, P.D., Nax, H.H., 2020, Rational altruism? On preference estimation and dictator game experiments. *Games and Economic Behavior* 119, 309–338.

Haley, K.J., Fessler, D.M., 2005. Nobody's watching? Subtle cues affect generosity in an anonymous economic game. *Evolution and Human Behavior* 26(3), 245–256.

Hoffman, E., McCabe, K., Shachat, K., Smith, V., 1994. Preferences, property rights, and anonymity in bargaining games. *Games and Economic Behavior* 7(3), 346–380.

Levitt, S.D., List, J.A., 2007. What do laboratory experiments measuring social preferences reveal about the real world? *Journal of Economic Perspectives* 21(2), 153–174.

Marwell, G., Ames, R.E., 1981. Economists free ride, does anyone else? *Journal of Public Economics* 15(3), 295–310.

Winking, J., Mizer, N., 2013. Natural-field dictator game shows no altruistic giving. *Evolution and Human Behavior* 34(4), 288–293.

Zhan, W., Eckel, C., Grossman, P., 2020, *Does How We Measure Altruism Matter? Playing Both Roles in Dictator Games*. Melbourne: Monash University. Pre-print, ISSN: 114-5429. Discussion number 05/20. Available at: www.monash.edu/__data/assets/pdf_file/0008/2228732/Does-how-we-measure-altruism-matter-Playing-both-roles-in-dictator-games.pdf.

15

RISK AVERSION AND INCENTIVE EFFECTS (BY CHARLES HOLT AND SUSAN LAURY)

Kevin McCabe

Introduction

The primary goal of economics is to understand how institutions, operating in different economic environments, incentivize peoples' actions, thus producing societal outcomes.

The microeconomic systems approach from Hurwicz (1973) provides a framework for achieving this goal. A microeconomic system defines an environment representing the system's state and an institution that accepts messages and causes state transitions. While Hurwicz and many others were mainly interested in the design of institutions whereby theoretical agents would produce desired societal outcomes, Smith (1982) adapted this framework as a method to study human behavior in controlled experiments.

In both theory and experiment, the ability to characterize preferences separately from cognition is critical to crafting informed microeconomic policy. Preferences in a microeconomic system, together with ownership rights, knowledge, and natural events, make up the economic environment.

Institutions consist of a set of rules governing the messages decision-makers can send and, based on the messages, a set of rules that produce salient outcomes. In an experiment, the decision-makers are human subjects who use cognitive strategies to decide on their messages. As subjects send messages, the microeconomic system's state moves from an initial state set by the experimenter to a final state determined by the subjects. One of the main results of the experimental economics literature is that the messages subjects send depend on the rules of the institution and what subjects learn during state transitions. As a computational exercise, the decision-maker can be replaced by a theoretical agent and be used to simulate the microeconomic system by modeling the agent's strategy, defined as state-contingent messages to the institution.

DOI: 10.4324/9781003019121-15

Most microeconomic systems introduce some form of risk for decision-makers. The presence of risk makes it essential to know the risk preferences that are used to construct a decision-maker's strategy. In running experiments, economists can control for subjects' risk preferences or infer subjects' risk preferences from choices. Each approach has its own advantages and disadvantages. Controlling for preferences allows us to specify the risk coefficients subjects will use in making their choices, but what remains unknown is the cognitive process for translating induced valuations into internalized values. Inferring risk preferences lets us estimate the subjects' risk-preference coefficients if one is willing to make strong assumptions about the functional form of subjects' preferences. Alternatively, the approach can be used to make general qualitative, non-parametric inferences about factors that tend to increase risk aversion or preference. In practice, it has been challenging to control for risk preferences, leading experimental economists to choose inference over control (see, for example, Selten, Sadrieh, and Abbink, 1999).

In the literature on inferring risk preferences, some authors following the psychology tradition refer to the different procedures used to measure risk preferences as instruments. In this article, I prefer the term "mechanism" to better link these procedures to the microeconomic systems approach. When the experimenter chooses a risk-inference mechanism, they are choosing both an environment and an institution that may, or may not, incentivize subjects to reveal aspects of their risk preferences, given their message sending strategy. Also, the use of a particular mechanism may make the observed choices more or less noisy. Only with replication will we be able to better understand the behavioral properties of the different mechanisms.

The Holt-Laury Mechanism

Kogan and Wallach (1964) review a structured table of binary lottery choices used in psychology to infer a subject's risk preferences from their choices. Murnighan, Roth, and Schoumaker (1988) modify the structured table of binary lotteries by using monetary payoffs to better incentivize choices. In this new table, one option was a certain monetary payoff and the other was a lottery with monetary payoffs. The Holt-Laury Mechanism (HLM) avoids a possible certainty bias and eliminates the guaranteed option in favor of choosing between lotteries with low and high variances.

We can map the HLM into the microeconomic system's framework as follows. The environment consists of a set of lottery choices, a decision-maker with Constant Relative Risk Averse (CRRA) utility over money, and a procedure for playing lotteries to produce a monetary outcome. The institution orders the lottery choices and presents them in sequence to the decision-maker. The institution then chooses one of the decision-maker's chosen lotteries at random and uses the environment procedure to produce a monetary outcome.

The HLM environment

In the HLM, lotteries are of the form $L = (m_H, m_L, p_H)$, where $m_H > m_L > 0$ and $0 \leq p_H \leq 1$ is the probability that m_H occurs. For example, in their low-payoff sessions, Holt and Laury used the lottery templates $A = (\$2.00, \$1.60, p_H)$ and $B = (\$3.85, \$0.10, p_H)$. We can think of a pair of lotteries $[L_A(p_H), L_B(p_H)]$ as a choice between two projects. Once chosen, a project randomly returns one of two monetary outcomes according to the probability p_H.

Holt and Laury used a theory agent with preferences $U(m)$ characterized by the class of CRRA functions:

$$U(m) = m^{1-r} / (1-r), \text{ for } r \neq 1,$$
$$= \ln(m), \text{ for } r = 1,$$

where m is the monetary payoff. The coefficient, r, determines if the decision-maker is risk-neutral, $r = 0$; risk-averse, $r < 0$; or risk-loving, $r > 0$. Holt and Laury further assumed that the agent chooses between lotteries to maximize the agent's expected utility given by $EU(L) = p_H U(m_H) + p_L U(m_L)$. This results in the following decision rule, $D_r(L_A, L_B)$:

$$D_r(L_A, L_B) = L_A, \quad \text{if } EU(L_A) > EU(L_B),$$
$$= L_B, \quad \text{if } EU(L_B) > EU(L_A),$$
$$= \text{either } L_A \text{ or } L_B, \quad \text{if } EU(L_B) = EU(L_A)$$

The HLM institution

The institution constructs a lottery table where each row, denoted by $n = 1$ to 10, displays a choice between a Type A and a Type B lottery with $p_H = 0.1n$. The agent must choose a lottery $L_A(p_H)$ or $L_B(p_H)$ from each row of the lottery table. After an agent makes the choice, the institution picks a row at random, and the lottery the agent has chosen in that row is played.

Table 15.1 shows a replica of the lottery table used by Holt and Laury. (See their Figure 1, p. 1645.) As we look down the row, we see that the probability of getting the high payoff (\$2.00 for option A and \$3.85 for option B) increases while the probability of getting the low payoff (\$1.60 for option A and \$0.10 for option B) decreases.

A decision-maker chooses between Option A or Option B for each of the ten decision rows. For example, a list of lottery choices might look like [A, A, A, A, A, A, B, B, B, B], which shows the choice of Option A for the first six decision rows, and the choice of Option B for the last four decision rows.

The column labeled ΔEV in Table 15.1 shows the change in expected value. We note the difference in expected payoff, rounded to two significant digits, between Option A and Option B is $\Delta EV = (p_H 2.0 + p_L 1.6) - (p_H 3.85 + p_L 0.10)$.

When the risk coefficient r equals 0, the theoretical decision-maker is risk-neutral and will produce the choice data [A, A, A, A, B, B, B, B, B, B].

TABLE 15.1 Holt-Laury price list for low payoff

Row	Option A		Option B		ΔEV	$r = 0$ Choice	$r = 0.5$ Choice	$r = -0.8$ Choice
	$2.00	$1.60	$3.85	$0.10				
1	1/10	9/10	1/10	9/10	1.17	A	A	A
2	2/10	8/10	2/10	8/10	0.83	A	A	A
3	3/10	7/10	3/10	7/10	0.50	A	A	B
4	4/10	6/10	4/10	6/10	0.16	A	A	B
5	5/10	5/10	5/10	5/10	−0.18	B	A	B
6	6/10	4/10	6/10	4/10	−0.51	B	A	B
7	7/10	3/10	7/10	3/10	−0.85	B	B	B
8	8/10	2/10	8/10	2/10	−1.18	B	B	B
9	9/10	1/10	9/10	1/10	−1.52	B	B	B
10	10/10	0/10	10/10	0/10	−1.85	B	B	B

Since the theory agent only switches once from A to B we can characterize the theory agent's decision rule as $D_r{}^*(LT) = s$, where s is the last row of the lottery table (LT), before the agent switches from Option A to Option B. For example, $D_0{}^*(LT) = 4$. Because LT has only ten rows, there will be a range of risk coefficients that result in the same switching point. We can compute the switching point for every r, resulting in the following table that defines $Dr^*(LT)$ for the lottery table shown in Table 15.1.

$$Dr^*(LT) = \{0,1\} \text{ for } r < -0.95$$
$$= 2 \text{ for r in } (-0.95, -0.49)$$
$$= 3 \text{ for r in } (-0.49, -0.15)$$
$$= 4 \text{ for r in } (-0.15, 0.15)$$
$$= 5 \text{ for r in } (0.15, 0.41)$$
$$= 6 \text{ for r in } (0.41, 0.68)$$
$$= 7 \text{ for r in } (0.68, 0.97)$$
$$= 8 \text{ for r in } (0.97, 1.37)$$
$$= \{9,10\} \text{ for } r > 1.37$$

By examining the decision rule used by a subject and assuming that the differences are due to the CRRA risk coefficient, $D^*(r)$ allows us to infer the subject's range of risk coefficients. For r < 0, the subject is risk-averse, and for r > 0, the decision rule is risk-loving.

Procedure for running the HLM as an experiment

The procedure for running the HLM has three steps:

Step 1: Subjects are shown the lottery table and asked to make choices between Option A or Option B for each row. For example, row four is expressed as in Figure 15.1 in the subject's decision sheet.

Step 2: Holt and Laury used a ten-sided die to pick a row, n, from the lottery table.

	Option A	Option B	Your Choice A or B
Decision 4	$2.00 if the throw of die is 1-4 $1.60 if the throw of die is 5-10	$3.85 if the throw of die is 1-4 $0.10 if the throw of die is 5-10	_____

FIGURE 15.1 Example of subject decision sheet.

Step 3: The option the subject chose for row n is played as follows:

1. The ten-sided die is rolled again, and the outcome, d, is recorded;
2. If, $d \leq n$, the high payoff is awarded;
3. If $d > n$, the low payoff is awarded.

Data transformations

While the $D^*(r)$ rule above predicts that choices will only switch once, human subjects may switch more than once. Holt and Laury approached this problem by measuring a subject's total number of safe A choices as a proxy for $D^*(r)$, which we will refer to as d*. If we let num(A) be the number of A choices on a subject's decision sheet, then $d^*(r) = num(A)$.

A summary statistic can be built from this measure as follows. First, we will denote, o(j, t), as the list of ten decisions reported by subject j in treatment condition t. Note, we will denote the row k choice by subject j as $o_k(j, t)$ in {A, B}, where A denotes the choice of Option A and B denotes the choice of Option B. Furthermore, we will denote $O_t = (o(1, t), ..., o(j, t), ..., o(M, t))$ as the complete list of subjects' decisions in treatment condition t, where M is the total number of subjects in t. Then we can compute the summary statistic, $g(O_t)$, for t as

$$g(O_t) = \lfloor g_1(O_t), ..., g_k(O_t), ..., g_{10}(O_t) \rfloor \quad \text{where}$$

$$g_k(O_t) = \sum_{j=1}^{M} o_k(j, t), \text{ for } k = 1 \text{ to } 10.$$

Note, this measure has the added benefit of providing a descriptive sample statistic that can be readily displayed graphically across experiments (see, Holt and Laury, 2002, Figure 1, p. 1648).

Estimation procedure

Holt and Laury (2002) built a maximum likelihood model of subjects where the probability of choosing the lower variance option A, is defined by

$$\text{Prob.}(\text{choose } L_A) = \frac{EU_A^{1/\mu}}{EU_A^{1/\mu} + EU_B^{1/u}},$$

where μ is a noise parameter. Recognizing that the utility function must capture increasing risk aversion at higher stakes, Holt and Laury used a hybrid Expo-Power Utility Function, introduced by Saha (1993) to allow for constant relative risk aversion and constant absolute risk aversion. This function is defined by

$$U(x) = \frac{1 - \exp\left(-\alpha x^{1-r}\right)}{\alpha}.$$

The Expo-Power Utility Function approaches a CRRA utility function as α approaches 0 and a CARA utility function as r approaches 0. Holt and Laury used the proportion of safe choices, Option A, for each subject in the four real-payoff treatments to calculate maximum likelihood estimates of the expected utility parameters, μ = 0.134, r = 0.269, α = 0.029. When Holt and Laury compared the predicted proportion of safe choices to the actual proportions of safe choices (see Figure 6 in Holt and Laury, 2002), they found a high degree of correspondence.

The Holt-Laury experiment

Holt and Laury (2002) used the HLM to study inferred risk preferences when the scale of lottery payoffs is changed and depending on whether the payoffs were hypothetical (subjects were not paid the lottery payoff), or real (subjects were paid). Their first treatment variable, λ ∈ {1, 20, 50, 90}, varied the scale of payoffs in the lottery table. For example, $L(\lambda) = (\lambda m_H, \lambda m_L, p_H)$, with λ = 1 resulting in Table 15.1. Their second treatment variable, h in {hypothetical, real}, indicated whether the payoffs were hypothetical (h = hypothetical) or real (h = real). Different treatment pairs (λ, h) were then used in their experimental design as follows:

Session 1: [(1, real), (20, hypothetical), (1, real)], n = 25
Session 2: [(1, real), (20, real), (1, real)], n = 57
Session 3: [(1, real), (20, hypothetical), (20, real), (1, real)], n = 93

Holt and Laury then ran two follow up sessions as follows:

Session 4: [(1, real), (50, hypothetical), (50, real), (1, real)], n = 19
Session 5: [(1, real), (90, hypothetical), (90, real), (1, real)], n = 18

Note, running the baseline (1, real) twice in every session allowed a test for learning effects resulting from a subject's repeated exposure to the procedure. Also, to eliminate the possibility of added wealth effects between the first (1, real) task and the second (λ, real) task, where λ ∈ {20, 50, 90}, subjects were required to forfeit their earnings from the first task in order to play the second task.

Holt and Laury conclude that the low-payoff treatment (1, real), with all payoffs below $4.00, results in a positive inferred risk-aversion coefficient for roughly two-thirds of their subjects. Moreover, as the scale of payoffs is increased from 1x to 20x, 50x, and 90x, inferred risk aversion also increased significantly. However, when hypothetical payoffs were used, inferred risk parameters did not change as the scale parameter is changed from 1x to 20x, 50x, or 90x.

Order effects in the original Holt-Laury experiment

Harrison, Johnson, McInnes, and Rutstrom (2005) found that the order effect created by starting with the low-payoff scale (1, real) and moving to the high payoff scale (20, real) increases the inferred measure of risk aversion. Holt and Laury (2005) responded to this critique by running between-subjects design (one treatment per subject). They used a payoff scale of $\lambda = 1$ or 20, h = hypothetical or real, in the following sessions:

Session 6: [(1, real), (20, real)], n = 48
Session 7: [(1, real)], n = 48
Session 8: [(20, real)], n = 48
Session 9: [(1, hypothetical)], n = 36
Session 10: [(20, hypothetical)], n = 36

The second experiment confirmed the order effect produced by the estimates from Harrison et al. as well as the original Holt and Laury (2002) findings. They conclude:

> Both our new data, and Harrison et al., confirm that scaling up real payments results in a significant increase in risk aversion. Our new data further demonstrate that scaling up hypothetical payments by the same amount does not cause a significant difference in risk aversion when possible order effects are eliminated.
>
> *(Holt and Laury, 2005, p. 904)*

Replicating the Holt-Laury experiment using induced preferences

Dickhaut, Houser, Aimone, Tila, and Johnson (2013) asked the following question: Can an experimenter induce risk preferences that replicate the Holt-Laury choice data for a much smaller maximum salient payment of $2.50? To do this, they use the risk-inducing procedure used by Berg, Daley, Dickhaut, and O'Brien (1986) to induce a risk-averse CRRA utility function for each of the different λ treatments in Holt and Laury (2002). This procedure involved paying subjects in probability units (lottery tickets) using a nonlinear transformation determined by the CRRA function.

The inducing procedure pays subjects in points – see Table 3 in Dickhaut, Houser, Aimone, Tila, and Johnson (2013). The points are then used in a final lottery to earn \$2.50 or \$0.00. The probability of winning the \$2.50 equals the points earned divided by 100. A hundred-sided die is used to determine the final payment. All ten lottery choices were also played in their design, resulting in a maximum total payout of \$25. They found that subjects made the same qualitative decisions using the inducing procedure as subjects using their natural preferences for the $\lambda = 1, 20, 50, 90$ treatments. This suggests that it should be possible to run policy-oriented laboratory experiments at a reasonable cost before moving to much more costly field experiments by inducing inferred preferences.

Modifying the Holt-Laury Mechanism

The HLM environment has lottery pairs in equal probability steps of winning the high payout. When the institution orders these lotteries, it produces a potential framing effect that could bias subjects to switch in the lottery table's middle rows, the so-called "compromise effect." One way to reduce the compromise effect, suggested by Andersen, Harrison, Lau, and Rutstrom (2006) is to use a table of lotteries with unequal step size in probabilities. For example, in their skewLO treatment, the probabilities of winning the high payout in each row of the Table 15.1 are 0.1, 0.2, 0.3, 0.5, 0.7, and 1, resulting in a table with only six rows. Using this approach, Beauchamp, Benjamin, Laibson, and Chabris (2019) estimate both a compromise effect parameter and risk coefficient. They find that the compromise effect is significant and can bias the estimates of risk coefficients.

Other modifications to the HLM change how the institution elicits choices over the lotteries in the lottery table (see Harrison, Lau, Rutstrom, and Sullivan, 2005). The first modification to HLM deals with the problem that subjects may switch back and forth in making their choices. Charness, Gneezy, and Imas (2013) report several studies where subjects switch back and forth over 50% of the time. To mitigate the switching problem, Harrison, Lau, Rutstrom, and Sullivan had their subjects make one choice, i.e., the row the subject wanted to switch from Option A to Option B. While this procedure increases the consistency of choices, it may simply hide the decision problem's complexity and lead to larger behavioral errors.

A second modification to the HLM attempts to improve precision of the estimated risk coefficients. Harrison, Lau, and Rutstrom introduce an institution that recursively refines the lottery table. In this institution, a subject is asked to choose a switching point from A to B, in the original Holt-Laury Table. The switching point then determines a range of possible risk coefficients. The institution then recursively defines a new lottery table over the discovered range and again asks the subject for a switching point in the new lottery. Note that recursion can continue to get as precise a range as desired, but at some point, the payoffs used in the recursive lottery tables may become meaningless to subjects.

Modifications to the estimation procedure

Wilcox (2008) examined five stochastic models that make different identifying restrictions on the estimation of risk-preference coefficients. Three of these models, Random Preferences, Strict Utility, and Contextual Utility, are CRRA-neutral regarding scale multiples of payoffs. Wilcox shows the original Holt-Laury estimation procedure using the strict utility model imposes identifying restrictions on the econometric model that imply any increase in Lottery A's safer choice must be due to increasing relative risk aversion.

Harrison and Rutstrom (2008) added a linear function of subjects' observable characteristics to the Expo Power Utility Function by letting $r = r_0 + \beta X$ where β is a vector of linear coefficients and X is a vector of observable characteristics of the individual or task. They also look at the Holt-Laury data with alternative stochastic models. By comparing log-likelihoods, they conclude that the Holt-Laury conclusion of increasing relative risk aversion is most likely correct. In Appendix F of their paper, Harrison and Rutstrom provide the Stata scripts necessary to do their Maximum Likelihood estimations.

Building combinatoric hybrids

A reasonable assumption from the measurement of risk coefficients is that subjects are heterogeneous with respect to risk attitudes. Heterogeneity may also extend to the algorithms subjects use to evaluate lotteries. Expected Utility Theory (EUT) is one such algorithm, but an alternative one, called Prospect Theory (PT), is proposed by Kahneman and Tversky (2012). PT includes a reference point for gains and losses in outcomes and a nonlinear weighting of probabilities. Harrison and Rutstrom (2008) defined a mixture-model with a likelihood function that allows the experimenter to estimate the probability that a decision-maker uses either EUT or PT. Harrison and Rutstrom conclude that each theory explains about half of the subjects.

Drichoutis and Lusk (2016) ran experiments using both the Holt-Laury 1x table, together with a varying-payoff table. Their varying-payoff table elicits the same partition of risk coefficients as a CRRA expected utility maximizer. They hypothesized that the HLM is better suited to estimating the probability weights assumed by PT and their payoff-varying table is better suited to estimating risk coefficients. Drichoutis and Lusk then ran an experiment to parameterize a composite model based on their hypotheses and show that their composite model makes better out-of-sample predictions. Although, note that the probability-weighting aspects of PT cannot explain the strong payoff scale effects reported by Holt and Laury, who held probabilities constant across different scales.

Alternative risk elicitation mechanisms

The HLM can be used to compare alternative methods for eliciting risk preferences. Harrison and Rutstrom (2008) review many other risk elicitation methods, including the investment task first used by Gneezy and Potters (1997) and modified by Eckel and Grossman (2002). An experiment by Chetan, Eckel, Johnson, and Rojas (2010) hypothesized that mathematics skills, i.e., numeracy, may affect subjects' choices in the HLM. They then compare the HLM to the "mathematically less difficult" Investment Task Mechanism (ITM) described in Eckel and Grossman (2002). They conclude that the ITM performs better than the HLM in terms of an estimated noise parameter, μ, for low numeracy subjects. However, note that Holt and Laury used "odd" and non-integer payoffs with changing probabilities in order to hide salient risk-neutral choices, which are obvious in the Gneezy-Potters investment task and which can be determined by just adding the two payoffs for each equally likely option in the Eckel and Grossman mechanism. Testing for mathematical numeracy may help experimenters decide when to use the HLM, but comes at the cost of revealing salient risk-neutral choices.

Another task that may link a subject's affective response to their risk preferences is the Balloon Analogue Risk Task (BART), used by Lejuez et al. (2002). BART has a subject watch the simulated filling of a balloon. Each air pump adds a fixed increment of money, M, to the subject's earnings and increases the probability that the balloon will pop. Before each pump, the subject can choose to stop and take the accumulated earnings. The subject loses the accumulated earnings if the balloon pops. The resulting decision to make the nth pump is a lottery that earns $(n - 1)M$ if the balloon doesn't pop and 0 if the balloon pops. This approach has the advantage of providing "hot" emotional context, but the measurement of risk preference is truncated if the balloon pops.

An alternative to the BART mechanism is the Bomb Elicitation Risk Task (BERT) introduced by Crosetto and Filippin (2013). In the BERT mechanism, a subject is shown 100 boxes and told that there is a bomb inside one of them. In the static decision procedure, subjects pick a number k to indicate how many boxes from 1 to k to open. The choice $k = 0$ is allowed and results in no box being opened. If the bomb is in one of the first k boxes, the subject will earn 0; otherwise, the subject would earn m cents per opened box or km cents. Notice, the subject is choosing between lotteries of the form $L(k) = [\$km, p(k), \$0, 1 - p(k)]$, where $[1 - p(k)] = k/100$. A risk-neutral theory agent using a CRRA utility function would pick $k = 50$, while a risk-averse subject will pick $k<50$.

What are risk elicitation mechanisms measuring?

A common finding is that different risk elicitation mechanisms result in different estimates of risk preferences. This finding is consistent with the experimental economics body of literature that the choice of institutional rules will cause different behavioral responses. For example, Isaac and James (2000) and Berg, Dickhaut, and McCabe (2005) found that measured risk preferences are different when estimated from bidding behavior in different auction rules. In their data, Berg, Dickhaut, and McCabe found that a subject measured as risk averse in first-price auctions will be risk-neutral in the Becker, DeGroot, and Marschak (1964) procedure and risk loving in English-Clock auctions. More recently, Friedman, Habib, James, and Crockett (2018) and Pedroni, Frey, Bruhin, Dutlih, Hertwig, and Rieskamp (2017) ran experiments where subjects participate in a variety of risk elicitation mechanisms. Both studies found that estimates or risk preference vary across instruments. Comeig, Holt, and Jaramillo (2019) provide an explanation for contextual differences in risk-preference measurements based on probability weighting. An overweighting of low probability of a large gain will cause subjects to exhibit risk seeking, and an overweighting the low probability of a low payoff will trigger risk aversion. These tendencies are clearly observed in the data, along with a clear increase in risk aversion caused by increases in payoff scale.

Looking at the evidence, Holt and Laury (2014) conclude:

> Taken as a whole, the evidence suggests that one should be cautious about using a risk aversion estimate obtained in one context to make inferences about behavior in another (unrelated) context. It is not altogether surprising that estimates of the coefficient of risk aversion differ across elicitation methods, but it is troubling that the rank-order of subjects in terms of their risk aversion coefficient differs across elicitation methods.
>
> *(Holt and Laury, 2014, p. 173)*

More recent research has used a latent variable approach (see Beauchamp, Cesarini, and Johannesson, 2017) or an instrumental variable approach (see Gillen, Snowberg, and Yariv, 2019), to estimate risk coefficients. Both of these approaches assume that the experimental institutions and subject decisions produce errors in measurement. Once these are accounted for, they found more consistent measures of risk coefficients.

Simulating a random utility model with noise

Crosetto and Filippin (2016) studied the effect of a random utility model on the estimation of risk preferences in the HLM, the Eckel and Grossman (2002) ITM, and their BERT mechanism. They hypothesized that the noisy random utility model used to make decisions will interact differently with the different risk elicitation mechanisms, resulting in task-dependent errors that would affect the estimate of risk coefficients. For each mechanism, Crosetto and Filippin ran a Monte-Carlo simulation with n = 100,000 agents, each of whom is randomly assigned a risk coefficient, r, drawn from the

Normal Distribution with mean .8 and standard deviation .3. The coefficient r is then used in the utility function $U(m) = m^{1-r}$, to reflect the agent's true preferences. The simulation considers three different decision rules.

Rule 1: agents decide using their true r without error using EUT

Rule 2: agents decide using EUT and a stochastic $r' = r + \varepsilon$, where the noise term ε is drawn from a Normal Distribution with mean 0 and a standard deviation of .3 or .6.

Rule 3: 90% of the time, agents decide using Rule 1, 10% of the time agents make uniformly random choices.

Their simulations showed that each of the mechanisms is subject to different measurement errors and result in different inferred risk coefficients for the same underlying r. They follow up with an experimental study that show human subjects produce the same ordering of risk aversion estimates as the simulation study.

Conclusions

The Holt-Laury paper has accumulated over 6,000 citations on Google Scholar for at least two reasons. First, it introduces a mechanism that continues to serve as a computational method for measuring risk preferences and a focal point of comparison to other risk elicitation mechanisms. Second, the paper makes an experimental contribution by showing that subjects exhibit increasing relative risk aversion as lottery payoffs increase. Further, Holt and Laury show that subjects' risk aversion does not change with increases in hypothetical payoffs. Subsequent research suggests that the institutional details used to run the inference mechanism and the identifying restrictions used in measuring risk coefficients will affect the estimates of risk coefficients. Still, numerous replications have verified Holt and Laury's results.

Other review articles discuss in more detail the modifications and uses of the Holt-Laury Mechanism as well as comparisons to other inference mechanisms. These reviews include the edited volume by Harrison and Cox (2008); and the more recent studies by Charness, Gneezy, and Imas (2013); Holt and Laury (2014); Friedman, Isaac, James, and Sunder (2014); Eckel (2019); and Holt (2019). Many of these reviews act as guides to choosing the most appropriate mechanism for measuring risk preferences, according to the experimenter's design goals.

References

Andersen, S., Harrison, G.W., Lau, M.I., Rutstrom, E.E., 2006. Elicitation using multiple price lists. *Experimental Economics* 9(4), 383–405.

Beauchamp, J.P., Benjamin, D.J., Laibson, D.I., Chabris, C.F., 2019. Measuring and controlling for the compromise effect when estimating risk preference parameters. *Experimental Economics*. DOI: 10.1007/s10683-019-09640-z

Beauchamp, J.P., Cesarini, D., Johannesson, M., 2017. The psychometric and empirical properties of measures of risk preferences. *Journal of Risk and Uncertainty* 54(3), 203–237.

Becker, G.M., Degroot, M.H., Marschak, J., 1964. Measuring utility by a single-response sequential method. *Behavioral Science* 9(3), 226–232.

Berg, J.E., Daley, L., Dickhaut, J., O'Brien, J., 1986. Controlling Preferences for Lotteries on Units of Experimental Exchange, *Quarterly Journal of Economics*, 101(2), 281–306.

Berg, J., Dickhaut, J., McCabe, K., 2005. Risk preference instability across institutions: A dilemma. *Proceedings of the National Academy of Sciences* 102(11), 4209–4214.

Charness, G., Gneezy, U., Imas, A., 2013. Experimental methods: Eliciting risk preferences. *Journal of Economic Behavior and Organization* 87, 43–51.

Chetan, D., Eckel, C.C., Johnson, C.A., Rojas, C., 2010. Eliciting risk preferences: When is simple better? *Journal of Risk and Uncertainty* 41(3), 219–243.

Comeig, Irene, Holt, C.A., Jaramillo, A., 2019. Dealing with risk: Gender, stakes, and probability effects. Discussion Paper, University of Virginia.

Crosetto, P., Antonio Filippin, A., 2013. The "bomb" risk elicitation task. *Journal of Risk and Uncertainty* 47(1), 31–65.

Crosetto, P., Antonio Filippin, A., 2016. A theoretical and experimental appraisal of four risk elicitation methods. *Experimental Economics* 19(3), 613–641.

Dickhaut, J., Houser, D., Aimone, J.A., Tila, D., Johnson, C., 2013. High stakes behavior with low payoffs: Inducing preferences with Holt–Laury gambles. *Journal of Economic Behavior and Organization* 94, 183–189.

Drichoutis, A.C., Lusk, J.L., 2016. What can multiple price lists really tell us about risk preferences? *Journal of Risk and Uncertainty* 53(2–3), 89–106.

Eckel, C.C., 2019. Measuring individual risk preferences. IZA World of Labor, June.

Eckel, C.C., Grossman, P.J., 2002. Sex differences and statistical stereotyping in attitudes toward financial risk. *Evolution and Human Behavior* 23(4), 281–295.

Friedman, D., Habib, S., James, D., Crockett, S., 2018. Varieties of risk elicitation. Discussion Papers, Research Professorship Market Design: Theory and Pragmatics SP II 2018–501, WZB Berlin Social Science Center.

Friedman, D., Isaac, R.M., James, D., Sunder, S., 2014. *Risky Curves: On the Empirical Failure of Expected Utility*. Milton Park: Routledge.

Gillen, B., Snowberg, E., Yariv, L., 2019. Experimenting with measurement error: Techniques with applications to the Caltech cohort study. *Journal of Political Economy* 127(4), 1826–1863.

Gneezy, U., Potters, J., 1997. An experiment on risk taking and evaluation periods. *The Quarterly Journal of Economics* 112(2), 631–645.

Harrison, G.W., Cox, J.C., 2008. *Risk Aversion in Experiments*. Bingley: Emerald Group Publishing.

Harrison, G.W., Lau, M.I., Rutstrom, E.E., Sullivan, M.B., 2005. Eliciting risk and time preferences using field experiments: Some methodological issues. In: Carpenter, J., Harrison, G.W., List, J.A., (Eds.). *Field Experiments in Economics* (Volume 10, Research in Experimental Economics). Greenwich, CT: JAI Press, 125–218.

Harrison, G, W., Johnson, E., McInnes, M.M., Rutström, E.E., 2005. Risk Aversion and Incentive Effects: Comment. American Economic Review, 95(3), 897–901

Harrison, G.W., Rutström, E.E., 2008. Risk aversion in the laboratory. *Research in Experimental Economics* 12(8), 41–196.

Holt, C.A., 2019. *Markets, Games, and Strategic Behavior: An Introduction to Experimental Economics* (Second Edition). Princeton, NJ: Princeton University Press.

Holt, C.A., Laury, S.K., 2002. Risk aversion and incentive effects. *American Economic Review* 92(5), 1644–1655.

Holt, C.A., Laury, S.K., 2005. Risk aversion and incentive effects: New data without order effects. *American Economic Review* 95(3), 902–904.

Holt, C.A., Laury, S.K., 2014. Assessment and estimation of risk preferences. In: Machina, M., Viscusi, K. (Eds.). *Handbook of the Economics of Risk and Uncertainty 1*. Amsterdam: Elsevier, 135–201.

Hurwicz, L., 1973. The design of mechanisms for resource allocation. *The American Economic Review* 63(2), 1–30.

Isaac, R.M., James, D., 2000. Just who are you calling risk averse? *Journal of Risk and Uncertainty* 20(2), 177–187.

Kahneman, D., Tversky, A., 2012. Prospect theory: An analysis of decision under risk. In: MacLean, L.C., Ziemba, W.T. (Eds.). *Handbook of the Fundamentals of Financial Decision Making, World Scientific Handbook in Financial Economics Series*, Volume 4. Singapore: World Scientific, 99–127.

Kogan, N., Wallach, M.A., 1964. *Risk Taking: A Study in Cognition and Personality*. Oxford: Holt, Rinehart and Winston.

Lejuez, C.W., Read, J.P., Kahler, C.W., Richards, J.B., Ramsey, S.E., Stuart, G.L., Strong, D.R., Brown, R.A., 2002. Evaluation of a behavioral measure of risk taking: The balloon analogue risk task (BART). *Journal of Experimental Psychology Applied* 8(2), 75–84.

Murnighan, J.K., Roth, A.E., Schoumaker, F., 1988. Risk aversion in bargaining: An experimental study. *Journal of Risk and Uncertainty* 1(1), 101–124.

Pedroni, A., Frey, R., Bruhin, A., Dutilh, G., Hertwig, R., Rieskamp, J., 2017. The risk elicitation puzzle. *Nature Human Behaviour* 1(11), 803–809.

Saha, A., 1993. Expo-power utility: A 'flexible' form for absolute and relative risk aversion. *American Journal of Agricultural Economics* 75(4), 905–913.

Selten, R., Sadrieh, A., Abbink, K., 1999. Money does not induce risk neutral behavior, but Binary lotteries do even worse. *Theory and Decision* 46, 211–249.

Smith, V.L., 1982. Microeconomic systems as an experimental science. *The American Economic Review* 72(5), 923–955.

Wilcox, N.T., 2008. Stochastic models for binary discrete choice under risk: A critical primer and econometric comparison. *Research in Experimental Economics* 12, 197–292.

16

DOES MARKET EXPERIENCE ELIMINATE MARKET ANOMALIES? (BY JOHN A. LIST)

Matthias Sutter

Introduction

There is no doubt that John A. List can be considered the pioneer of field experiments, establishing them as an indispensable tool for economic research. His early survey with Glenn Harrison (Harrison and List, 2004) provided the first taxonomy of experiment types, identifying the potential strengths and weaknesses of these different types. Although List's own work covers practically all the different types of experiments (from the lab to the field, and all variants in between), his strong advocacy of field experiments has triggered a shift of experimental work from the lab to the field over the past 15 years or so. His strong push for field experiments has paved the way for many scholars to study economic behavior in naturally occurring environments and under natural conditions (i.e., in the field). For this reason, it is no surprise that most experimental methods PhD-courses around the globe devote considerable room to discussing how to design and run field experiments. It is even less of a surprise that I don't know of any of these courses that do not include papers by John List.

The paper reviewed here (List, 2003) is one of the key and earliest contributions on how field experimental work can inform economic theory and practitioners alike. With its more than 1,200 citations on Google Scholar, it is a natural candidate for inclusion in this volume of foundationally important papers in our field of experimental economics. Therefore, it is a pleasure – and great honor – to review this paper for this collective volume.

List (2003) starts with the observation that human behavior is prone to many different kinds of anomalies. Richard Thaler's series of articles in the *Journal of Economic Perspectives* (e.g., Thaler, 1987, 1988; Kahneman et al., 1991) about behavioral anomalies and biases in economic decision making had questioned whether neoclassical economics would be a good framework to understand how markets work, given that individual human behavior

DOI: 10.4324/9781003019121-16

showed so many deviations from the standard assumptions. Upon this question, List built a whole research program that studied how robust such anomalies and biases were and in particular whether markets themselves might be able to eliminate them. In a sense, List turned the sentiment that prevailed around 20 years ago upside down. Rather than asking whether anomalies and biases in human behavior would require new theories about how markets work, he examined whether markets themselves correct anomalies, making the development of new theories about how markets work less urgent or perhaps even redundant.

List (2003) investigates the famous endowment effect (Thaler, 1980), which causes a gap between someone's willingness to pay (WTP) and willingness to accept (WTA) for a certain good. In simpler words, the endowment effect indicates people are more willing to retain a good once they own it than they are willing to pay for the exact same good to get it (when they don't own it yet). Numerous studies in the laboratory have confirmed that the endowment effect exists.

List (2003) examines whether this is also the case in naturally occurring environments. In the first experiment reported in his paper, participants trade memorabilia on the floor of a sports-card show. The participants are either dealers (with lots of experience in trading) or non-dealers (with much less experience, but still quite some variation in the level of trading). As a reward for filling in a survey, participants receive one of two memorabilia. Then, all of a sudden, they are given the choice to trade in the reward that they already own for the other of the two. According to the endowment effect, less than 50% of participants would be expected to trade. This is, in fact, what List (2003) finds in the aggregate (with slightly over 30% make trades). Yet, this aggregate result hides a key feature of the data. Dealers (with much more market experience) trade significantly at a higher rate than non-dealers. In particular, the likelihood of dealers trading is not significantly different from 50%. Even among non-dealers, List (2003) reports much higher trading frequencies for experienced non-dealers (indistinguishable from 50%) than for inexperienced non-dealers (around 7%).

This first evidence in favor of market experience eliminating market anomalies (i.e., the endowment effect) is corroborated in a second field experiment, staged at the collector pin market in Walt Disney World's Epcot Center in Orlando. Only non-dealers were considered as participants because there are only a few dealers in this market. Again, the more experienced participants were – in the aggregate – immune to the endowment effect, while inexperienced ones showed clear signs of an endowment effect.

Because the first experiment leaves open the possibility that the non-existence of the endowment effect in case of large market experience is due to a selection effect (only subjects without an endowment effect engage in more market experience) versus the treatment effect (of getting more market experience), List (2003) added a third field experiment by returning to the participants of the first field experiment after about a year. By doing so, he could condition the behavior of participants on their subsequent market experience after the first field experiment, thereby showing that the treatment effect is most likely the driving force (rather than the selection effect).[1] While everyone should read the whole paper, Figure 1 in the paper (on page 62) conveys the influence of market experience on the level of the endowment effect in a single, compelling graph. The figure shows the proportion of trades contingent on the number of trades per month of the different participants. The proportion of trade increases almost linearly from around 15 to 50%, showing that increased market experience drives down the endowment effect to practically zero.

As the next piece of evidence of the influence of market experience, List (2003) reports on a fourth field experiment at a sports-card show in Tucson where 120 dealers and non-dealers could submit their WTA or WTP, depending upon whether they already owned a specific piece of memorabilia (University of Wyoming basketball trading cards) or not. Here, the results show no statistical difference between WTA and WTP for dealers ($8.15 vs. $6.27), but a strong and significant difference for non-dealers ($18.53 vs. $3.32).

While an already very good paper would have stopped here – message delivered – this one continues by presenting complementary evidence from the laboratory, making the contribution truly outstanding. In the laboratory experiment, participants are allowed to trade mugs, candy bars, pens, markers, and the like. Totally consistent with previous laboratory work, List (2003) finds a good deal of an endowment effect in the subjects' trading decisions, but again he also finds that, with more experience, this effect becomes considerably smaller.

List uses a smart ABCD-DCBA design where two groups face four different settings (A to D or D to A) over the course of four weeks, but in inverse order. This allows, in particular, a comparison between behavior in setting A when it's either the first (for group 1) or the last setting (for group 2), and likewise for setting D when it's last or first. From the results of the laboratory experiment, List (2003) concludes that cognitive capital – which reduces the endowment effect or completely eliminates it – builds up slowly, but steadily, over weeks and perhaps years. This is certainly slower, however, so eradicating the endowment effect in the course of a one-hour long laboratory experiment is not easy.

Before concluding, List (2003) cites complementary findings from outside experiments by resorting to work that, for instance, shows strong differences in the valuation of houses between investors and owner-occupants (Genesove and Mayer, 2001). Work like this shows that the endowment effect is real, and that it prevails under a wide set of circumstances. However, List (2003) summarizes his novel insight nicely in the last sentence of his paper: "These results provide initial evidence consistent with the notion that market experience eliminates market anomalies" (p. 71).

The enormous number of citations of this paper indicates that List (2003) has become a cornerstone in the study of anomalies and the potential of markets to ameliorate them (see also List, 2001, for an even earlier contribution). For economics – a discipline that rests, to a large extent, on an analysis of markets – it is essential to understand not only how individual behavior shapes market outcomes, but also how markets themselves affect individual behavior. List (2003) also contributes to the question of how behavioral insights from the lab or in the theory manifest themselves in the field – one of the most important questions experimentalists face. List's (2003) early result that market experience matters has paved the way for many important subsequent contributions. By and large, both in the lab and the field, most of them have replicated the thrust of his experience results (see, e.g., early followers' contributions: Feng and Seasholes, 2005; Dhar and Zhu, 2006; Kermer et al., 2006; Choe and Eom, 2009; Gächter et al., 2009; Greenwood and Nagel, 2009; Engelmann and Hollard, 2010; Seru et al., 2010).

One of the main methodological strengths of List's paper is his choice of field environments. As such, the field sites – be it the collector pin markets or the sports-card shows – create an ideal testbed for the question at hand. The sites provide an environment where it is possible and comparatively easy to measure the different degrees of market experience of market participants (albeit with some caveats with respect to the issue of self-selection; see above and List, 2011). Moreover, the randomization of experimental conditions to the memorabilia that can be traded allows a clean identification of treatment (i.e., market experience) effects. The laboratory experiment with its ABCD-DCBA design, spread out over four weeks, generates additional and controlled insights about how cognitive capital accumulates. Using both laboratory and field sites for his study, List also set an example of how both types of experiments can fruitfully complement each other; a complementarity which I would like to see even more (in order to overcome the growing divide between lab and field experimentalists).

In addition to being impressed with the scientific insights produced by the different field and lab experiments in List (2003), I admire the passion and creativity that I see in every line of the paper. The field experiments have obviously been influenced by John List's personal (leisure time) interests. Most of the memorabilia used in the experiments he collected himself when attending several of the events where they could be collected. This nicely illustrates how personal interests and hobbies can shape a scholar's research program, so that personal and scientific enthusiasm for a subject or event are combined in a fruitful way.[2]

The story how he collected these memorabilia years before running these field experiments also illustrates how a brilliant mind is always looking for ways to transform everyday situations into scientifically exciting questions. This requires an admirable degree of creativity. Gary Charness told me that reading the newspaper generates many research ideas for him. Obtaining ideas and conceiving of good field experiment designs requires good knowledge about the conditions in the field. Consequently, going to the field (e.g., baseball field) – even when it's not directly research related – helps. This is another lesson we should learn from this paper: Field experience improves field experiments.

What does all of this mean for the future?

In terms of content, List (2003) has triggered a whole research agenda on how markets can correct anomalies. Gigerenzer (2018) has recently criticized behavioral economics for the bias of spotting biases in decision making even when there are none, which, according to him, ascribes to biases the status of truisms. The work of List (2003) and subsequent authors confronts this criticism by investigating whether behavioral patterns observed in the lab – often called anomalies or biases – persist in real markets. One body of literature tends to support the conclusion that individual behavior is prone to biases and anomalies, but another body indicates that market experience attenuates or even eliminates those many of those biases and anomalies.

Work like that of List helps keep our experimental community from being inclined toward blindly accepting the proposition that decision-makers are biased, encouraging us to adopt a more nuanced view that investigates when biases occur and when they do not. Having found market experience to be important, we face another question of first-order import: How do markets assimilate individual behaviors? Or, how significantly do behavioral preferences affect market outcomes? We have yet to flesh out this aspect of the List (2003) paper.

Obtaining more insights about how individual behavior maps into market outcomes will make behavioral and experimental economics more important for policy-makers. We will, however, only be successful in soundly advising politicians if our research designs are clean, parsimonious, and powerful. This book is intended to illustrate how the experimental method can – and should – be used to answer questions that are important for the research community, on the one hand, and overall society, on the other. John List's works repeatedly illustrate how a well-crafted design, original and creative research questions, and a good choice of field sites to study one's questions can make a difference. List (2003) is a prime example of the art, and it will continue to retain attention for years to come.

Notes

1 In List (2011), he reconsiders the issue of self-selection and confirms the influence of market experience also in a setting where market experience is exogenously manipulated. In Tong et al. (2016), he reports how experience shapes the encoding of gains and losses in the human brain.
2 I know how rewarding it is to combine one's hobbies with one's research. When watching the Round of 16 match in the FIFA World Cup 2006 between Switzerland and Ukraine – the latter won the penalty shootout (played in the event of a tie after 120 mins of play) 3:0 – I started wondering what drives success in penalty shootouts, and this interest as a soccer fan led to a later publication about potential first-mover advantages in soccer penalty shootouts (Kocher et al., 2012).

References

Choe, H., Eom, Y., 2009. The disposition effect and investment performance in the futures market. *Journal of Futures Markets* 29: 496–522.

Dhar, R., Zhu, N., 2006. Up close and personal: Investor sophistication and the disposition effect. *Management Science* 52: 726–740.

Engelmann, D., Hollard, G., 2010. Reconsidering the effect of market experience on the "endowment effect". *Econometrica* 78: 2005–2019.

Feng, L., Seasholes, M. S., 2005. Do investor sophistication and trading experience eliminate behavioral biases in financial markets? *Review of Finance* 9: 305–351.

Gächter, S., Orzen, H., Renner, E., Starmer, C., 2009. Are experimental economists prone to framing effects? A natural field experiment. *Journal of Economic Behavior and Organization* 70: 443–446.

Genesove, D., Mayer, C., 2001. Loss aversion and seller behavior: Evidence from the housing market. *Quarterly Journal of Economics* 116: 1233–1260.

Gigerenzer, G., 2018. The bias bias in behavioral economics. *Review of Behavioral Economics* 5: 303–336.

Greenwood, R., Nagel, S., 2009. Inexperienced investors and bubbles. *Journal of Financial Economics* 93: 239–258.

Harrison, G. W., List, J. A., 2004. Field experiments. *Journal of Economic Literature* 42: 1009–1055.

Kahneman, D., Knetsch, J. L., Thaler, R. H., 1991. Anomalies: The endowment effect, loss aversion, and status quo bias. *Journal of Economic Perspectives* 5: 193–206.

Kermer, D. A., Driver-Linn, E., Wilson, T. D., Gilbert, D. T., 2006. Loss aversion is an affective forecasting error. *Psychological Science* 17: 649–653.

Kocher, M., Lenz, M. V., Sutter, M., 2012. Psychological pressure in competitive environments: New evidence from randomized natural experiments. *Management Science* 58: 1585–1591.

List, J. A., 2001. Do explicit warnings eliminate the hypothetical bias in elicitation procedures? Evidence from field auctions for Sportscards. *American Economic Review* 91: 1498–1507.

List, J. A., 2003. Does market experience eliminate market anomalies? *Quarterly Journal of Economics* 118: 41–71.

List, J. A., 2011. Does market experience eliminate market anomalies? The case of exogenous market experience. *American Economic Review, Papers and Proceedings*, 101 (2): 313–317.

Seru, A., Shumway, T., Stoffman, N., 2010. Learning by trading. *Review of Financial Studies* 23: 705–739.

Thaler, R. H., 1980. Toward a positive theory of consumer choice. *Journal of Economic Behavior and Organization* 1: 39–60.

Thaler, R. H., 1987. Anomalies: The January effect. *Journal of Economic Perspectives* 1: 197–201.

Thaler, R. H., 1988. Anomalies: The winner's curse. *Journal of Economic Perspectives* 2: 191–202.

Tong, L., Ye, K. J., Asai, K., Ertac, S., List, J. A., Nusbaum, H. C., Hortacsu, A., 2016. Trading experience modulates anterior insula to reduce the endowment effect. *Proceedings of the National Academy of Sciences* 113: 9238–9243.

17

PROMISES AND PARTNERSHIP (BY GARY CHARNESS AND MARTIN DUFWENBERG)

Urs Fischbacher and Franziska Föllmi-Heusi

Introduction

Promises increase cooperation, and guilt aversion is a possible explanation for why promises work. This is the main result of Charness and Dufwenberg's paper (2006) (hereafter referred to as CD). The paper is a role model for an experimental economics study as it addresses a highly relevant research question – whether and how promises function – from empirical and theoretical points of view.

People often make promises. They promise to reward a service. Politicians make promises in their campaigns. Standard theory considers promises cheap talk. CD explain why they are not and why they are instead quite useful. Promises are credible commitments that allow partnerships to be established when legal enforcement is not possible. Promises recognize the existence of positive reciprocation, conveying the message that the receiver of a promise can rely upon the sender's reciprocal behavior.

In their experiments, CD demonstrate that promises enhance cooperation, and they explain why. They base their theory on guilt aversion, which assumes people try to avoid disappointing other people. It implies people are kinder when expected to be kind. That is, the mechanism of promises is the modification of expectations. If someone makes a promise, the recipient of the pledge has higher expectations concerning the trustworthiness of the first person, increasing their incentive to keep the promise.

We present the experiment and discuss its crucial features. We then discuss the contribution of the paper. Finally, we consider the influence of the paper on the further development of experimental and behavioral economics.

DOI: 10.4324/9781003019121-17

The experimental design

The experiment is a binary variant of a trust game. In this two-player game, Player A decides whether to trust (which CD call "move IN") or not trust ("move OUT"). If Player A chooses OUT, both players receive $5 payoff. If Player A chooses IN, Player B can decide to be trustworthy ("move ROLL") or not ("move DON'T"). If Player B is not trustworthy and chooses DON'T, Player B gets $14 and Player A gets nothing. If Player B is trustworthy and chooses ROLL, Player B receives $10 and a die is rolled to determine the payoff of Player A. This chance move is introduced so Player A cannot infer with certainty whether Player B was trustworthy or not. With a probability of 1/6, Player A gets nothing, else (probability of 5/6) he gets $12. The two players can establish a Pareto-improving partnership by choosing IN and ROLL. However, opting for IN is risky for Player A because a selfish Player B prefers not to be trustworthy and will choose DON'T.

The main treatment variation contains a new stage at the beginning of the game where Player B can choose to send or not send a message to Player A. This allows Player B to make a promise to Player A about his future move.

CD also run a treatment variation with an outside option. In this variant, both players receive $7 instead of $5 if player A does not trust and chooses OUT. The treatments are called (7,7) treatment and (5,5) treatment, respectively. This variation tests the robustness of the effect. A further treatment in which Player A (instead of Player B) can send a message allows testing whether it is the mere possibility of communication in general or, in fact, the option to send a promise that increases partnerships.

To test the guilt aversion model, first- and second-order beliefs concerning the decision of Player B subjects were assessed. Player A subjects had to guess the proportion of Player Bs who would be trustworthy. Player B subjects had to guess what Player Bs on average would guess in this regard. CD restricted the elicitation of Player B beliefs to those Player As who chose IN, for guilt is only relevant to a trusting Player A. For all belief elicitation responses, subjects received an additional payment if the guess did not differ more than 5% points from the realization.

Discussion of the design features

Some design features deserve special mention. We first discuss the features specific to this experiment. Then, we discuss more generally used methods in economic experiments.

The significant treatment variation is the availability of *communication*. Technically, the messages were written on a sheet of paper and transmitted by the experimenter. Thus, communication was controlled and only one-way. Nevertheless, communication was free, meaning the approach does not favor the delivery of a promise. In comparison to face-to-face communication, the method of using written texts is more controlled and less confounded. In particular, mutual communication is undesirable in this setting because promises are only relevant for Player Bs. It matters who can transmit messages. The variation of the sender of the message is a nice feature of the design and allows testing whether it is relevant that Player B can send a message or whether communication, in general, is cooperation-enhancing.

The trustworthy move (ROLL) involves a random component. With a probability of 1/6, Player A receives nothing – the same outcome as the not trustworthy move (DON'T). Since Player A is not informed about the decision of Player B but only about the payoff, Player A cannot conclude for sure whether Player B was trustworthy.

There is a theoretical argument that equilibrium assumptions on second-order beliefs are questionable. Because a (first-order) belief cannot be observed, it is unclear how consistency between first- and second-order beliefs could emerge. Conscious of this problem, CD collected the first- and second-order beliefs, allowing them to test the equilibrium belief prediction and investigate the relationship between beliefs and decisions. CD chose to use average behavior as a benchmark for the assessment of the beliefs, which has two main advantages. Subjects are less exposed to randomness as compared to a design where they have to guess the belief in their interaction, and the hedging problem is also smaller (Blanco et al. 2010).

For Player B, the strategy method was applied, meaning they had to decide whether to be trustworthy or not before knowing whether Player A trusted them. This is a method invented by Selten (1967) and has since been used frequently (see the discussion in Brandts and Charness 2011). In the experiment discussed here, the use of the strategy method increased the efficiency of the design. Had CD used the direct-response method, many more subjects would have had to participate in order to collect enough data since Player B was the target decision-maker.

Key results

Communication is more than cheap talk – it increases trust and trustworthiness. This key result characterizes the impact of communication, and CD relate it to promises. Promises increase the frequency of trustworthy decisions from Player B. In the (5,5) treatment without B messages, 20 of 45 (44%) Bs were trustworthy. However, when B could send a message to A, 28 of 42 (67%) Bs were trustworthy. In the (5,5) treatment, trust is profitable in expected terms if at least 50% of Player Bs are trustworthy. Indeed, 25 of 45 (56%) trusted in the treatment without messages, while 31 of 41 (74%) trusted in the condition with messages. Overall messages increased the share of successful interactions (A trusts [IN] and B is trustworthy [ROLL]) increased from 9 of 45 (20%) to 21 of 42 (50%). The effects were similar in the (7,7) treatment. Messages increased trustworthiness from 25 to 49%, trust from 23 to 47%, and fruitful mutual interactions from 8 to 31%.

The option to send messages increased trust and trustworthiness, and it was more specifically the possibility to make promises that made the difference. Two results support this claim. First, when Player As had the option to send messages rather than Player Bs, trustworthiness actually decreased (though insignificantly, from 44 to 39%), and trust increased only slightly and (though not significantly, from 56 to only 67%). Second, messages that contained explicit promises were more likely to induce trustworthiness and trust. Overall, 53% of the subjects made a promise. Of the Player Bs who made a promise, 79% were trustworthy; of those who did not make a promise, only 33% were trustworthy. This result can be interpreted in two ways: (i) those who made the promise increase the belief in trustworthiness and – due to guilt aversion – they did not want to disappoint Player A and (ii) many people are generally honest and do not want to make promises that they do not intend to keep. In both cases, there is a potential selection effect that selects different people into making promises or not. Promises were also effective on Player A – where a selection effect was absent. Of the Player As who received a promise, 79% trusted; of those who did not receive a promise, only 37% trusted.

CD showed not only the relevance of the promises, but also that guilt aversion is a potential mechanism through which promises work. Since guilt aversion can create many equilibria, a test of the model based on behavior only would not be convincing. Thus, subjects had to report their first- and second-order beliefs about Player B. There is a strong correlation between beliefs and behavior. Player A subjects with a higher belief in trustworthiness were more likely to trust, which is in line with rationality. Player B decisions were correlated with their second-order beliefs. Neither selfish players nor players who care only about the outcome should be affected by their belief in the expectation of their partner. Guilt aversion makes exactly this prediction and, in all treatments, second-order beliefs of the trustworthy Player Bs were significantly higher than the second-order beliefs of Player Bs who were not trustworthy.

The contribution of Charness and Dufwenberg

Along with Ellingsen and Johannesson (2004), CD were among the first to investigate promises. Promises increase cooperation – or partnerships, as suggested in the title of CD. This key finding is relevant in a general context. It shows the vital role communication can play, and it illustrates how communication can interact with social preferences. CD present a specific mechanism – guilt aversion – to explain their results, which is interesting in its own, but their work is also a role model for how to incorporate psychological behavior into Game Theory.

On promises and honesty. The CD paper was one of the first to address the element of new social preferences regarding how messages interact with decisions. Another remarkable phenomenon in this domain is honesty (Brandts and Charness 2003; Gneezy 2005). Honesty and promises are clearly related, and further work of this type may help delineate the relationship.

On the role of communication. CD demonstrate the importance of communication for cooperation. It was previously known that communication increases cooperation. For example, Dawes, McTavish, and Shaklee (1977) showed it in a multi-player prisoners' dilemma, while Isaac and Walker (1988) showed it in a public-goods-game. These studies and others offer a variety of mechanisms through which communication facilitates cooperation. Communication can trigger sympathy, which could lead to an increase in cooperation out of greater concern for the other. Communication can help conditional cooperators (Fischbacher, Gächter, and Fehr 2001) to coordinate their behavior. In simultaneous cooperation games like the public goods game, it is not possible to distinguish between defection based on an unwillingness to cooperate and defection that is driven by pessimistic expectations concerning the cooperativeness of other subjects. CD solve this problem by using a sequential game, such that they can distinguish these two motivations, and they can isolate the promise as the cooperation enhancing mechanism. The design allows them to show that promises work – they increase both trust and trustworthiness. In contrast, their design also allows them to show simple pleas to trustworthiness, which is what Player A can transmit in his messages, do not work; they neither increase trust nor trustworthiness.

On communication and social preferences. Promises provide a particularly notable example of how communication interacts with social preferences. With selfish preferences, promises are nothing but cheap talk because Player B will not act in a trustworthy manner, irrespective of any promise. CD set the stage for this kind of research and suggest – with guilt aversion – a specific mechanism of how communication interacts with social preferences. Another mechanism builds upon honesty. If someone has a preference for honesty, then communication can reveal information about that social preference. In the trust game, for example, it means at least some people who do not plan to be trustworthy will not dare to make a promise, and people who make a promise feel committed to it.

On guilt aversion. Guilt aversion is one example of a psychological phenomenon that takes (higher-order) beliefs into account. The idea was abstractly introduced by Geanakoplos, Pearce, and Stacchetti (1989), and it was applied in reciprocity models (Rabin 1993; Dufwenberg and Kirchsteiger 2004; Falk and Fischbacher 2006). Guilt aversion is a particularly simple example. The CD paper demonstrates that guilt aversion is a possible mechanism that explains why promises increase trust and trustworthiness: A promise raises Player A's expectations about whether Player B will repay them. Not repaying makes Player B feel guilty – and even more so if they made a promise – because a promise initially raised the expectation of Player A. This mechanism implies that the promise increases the second-order belief of Player B, i.e., what Player B believes about what Player A believes about whether Player B will repay. If the theory is correct, this belief is related to whether Player B repays. CD find evidence for this kind of mechanism.

On measuring higher-order belief. Second-order beliefs are crucial for the test of the guilt aversion model. Because more than one equilibrium exists, the model cannot be tested based upon behavior only. The paper was the first to measure experimentally higher-order (second-order) beliefs in an incentive-compatible way. They used a recursive procedure in which first-order beliefs were rewarded if they were consistent with the other players' behavior, and second-order beliefs were rewarded if they were consistent with the other players' first-order belief.

The influence of the paper

The CD paper is very influential; hundreds of other papers cite it. Its most important contribution was to set the stage for studying promises. Many studies investigate institutional and socioeconomic determinants of promise-making and promise-keeping. The importance of guilt-aversion is not especially evident, but the paper inspired a broad discussion of its role, in general, and its specific role for promise-keeping.

The trust game is ideal for studying promises. The first mover depends on the pro-sociality of the second mover, and the latter can signal the pro-sociality with a promise. This structure is particularly prevalent in the political domain, where campaign promises are a crucial element of competition. Several scholars have investigated how campaign promises affect behavior in office (Geng, Weiss, and Wolff 2011; Bernheim and Kartik 2014; Corazzini et al. 2014; Feltovich and Giovannoni 2015). In these experiments, candidates make promises of how much to share with voters in a subsequent dictator game. Even when candidates are forced to make a promise, they are effective. Greater promises increase the probability of being selected and increase the actual amount transferred. In these experiments, subjects could choose the level of transfer. It turns out that subjects must have at least some choice options when making promises. As Charness and Dufwenberg (2010) show, bare promises do not work. In their experiment, subjects could only choose whether to make a promise or not. There are other interesting details, for example, Born, van Eck, and Johannesson (2018) find that the credibility of promises is inverted U-shaped, which means that very high promises are less credible, and Feltovich and Giovannoni (2015) show that broken promises are punished.

Because of the sequential structure of the game, it is evident that the promises have to come from the second mover, and since the second mover can condition the decision on the first mover's decisions, expectations about the behavior of the first mover are irrelevant for the first mover. In simultaneous games like the simultaneous prisoner's dilemma, this is different. In this type of game, lack of cooperation can be due to selfishness or due to lack of trust. Thus, people might also be reluctant to make promises if they expect the other player to defect. Consequently, most studies that focus on promises use a sequential structure in the sense that keeping the promise would not depend on others. Notable exceptions are papers on game-show behavior where the game is exogenously given (Belot, Bhaskar, and van de Ven 2010; Turmunkh, Assem, and Dolder 2019).

CD classify the messages themselves. They use open messages, and their definition includes any statement of intent to choose the trustworthy move. Open messages have the advantage that the experimenter demand is almost absent. This is indeed important as Belot, Bhaskar, and van de Ven (2010) show in a study on promises in a high-stakes prisoner's dilemma that was conducted in a game show. If the presenter of the show explicitly asks for a promise, it is ineffective. The definition of a promise in CD is based on the intent of the message, while Belot, Bhaskar, and van de Ven (2010, p. 399, Footnote 11) make the definition even more precise and require that "the statement includes the word 'I' and a clear statement of the intention to share." Turmunkh, Assem, and Dolder (2019) extend the definition and use a two-by-two typology with implicit vs. explicit promises and unconditional vs. conditional statements as dimensions. These distinctions refer to how malleable the statements are. They find that the more malleable a message is, the less effective it is, showing that there are different degrees of promises.

Guilt aversion is not the only mechanism that can explain why people make and keep promises. People could dislike breaking a promise not only because they do not want to disappoint others, but also because they do not want to lie (Chen, Kartik, and Sobel 2008; Kartik 2009). Vanberg (2008) addressed this question in an experiment. The key idea of this experiment was that promises were exchanged. The game was simplified, but the critical idea consists of informing Player A either about the promise of the actual Player B or of another Player B. Player A did not know the situation, but Player B knew. If expectations drive promise-keeping, then Player B should also keep the promise of another Player B because a stranger's promise also raises the expectation of Player A. However, in the experiment, only one's own promises were relevant. Player B only kept the promise if he made it himself and if it was transmitted to A. This shows that the honesty motivation seems more relevant for keeping promises than guilt aversion.

Conclusion

The paper from CD is a role model for how papers in experimental economics should be conducted and presented. It is motivated by theory as well as by a relevant real-world phenomenon. Concerning the latter, it shows the relevance of promises. Concerning the former, it shows that the data is in line with the theory. Strictly speaking, theories cannot be confirmed, only falsified. The results in CD falsify a broad class of behavior models. They are not in line with the assumption of selfishness and contradict all models of social preferences that are purely outcome-oriented. The study is beautiful because it does not restrict the test of the model to behavior but goes beyond and shows that also the reported pattern of beliefs is in line with the model of guilt aversion. This paper inspired much work on promises and guilt aversion. Ironically, most of the citations refer to the paper as an example of demonstrating a preference for honesty, which was not the primary intention of it in the beginning.

References

Belot, M., Bhaskar, V., van de Ven, J., 2010. Promises and cooperation: Evidence from a TV game show. *Journal of Economic Behavior and Organization* 73, 396–405.

Bernheim, B.D., Kartik, N., 2014. Candidates, character, and corruption. *American Economic Journal: Microeconomics* 6, 205–246.

Blanco, M., Engelmann, D., Koch, A.K., Normann, H.T., 2010. Belief elicitation in experiments: Is there a hedging problem? *Experimental Economics* 13, 412–438.

Born, A., van Eck, P., Johannesson, M., 2018. An experimental investigation of election promises. *Political Psychology* 39, 685–705.

Brandts, J., Charness, G., 2003. Truth or consequences: An experiment. *Management Science* 49, 116–130.

Brandts, J., Charness, G., 2011. The strategy versus the direct-response method: A first survey of experimental comparisons. *Experimental Economics* 14, 375–398.

Charness, G., Dufwenberg, M., 2006. Promises and partnership. *Econometrica* 74, 1579–1601.

Charness, G., Dufwenberg, M., 2010. Bare promises: An experiment. *Economics Letters* 107, 281–283.

Chen, Y., Kartik, N., Sobel, J., 2008. Selecting cheap-talk equilibria. *Econometrica* 76, 117–136.

Corrazini, L., Kube, S., Marechal, M., Nicolo, A. 2014. Elections and deceptions: An experimental study on the behavioral effects of democracy. *American Journal of Political Science* 58, 579–592.

Dawes, R.M., McTavish, J., Shaklee, H., 1977. Behavior, communication, and assumptions about other people's behavior in a commons dilemma situation. *Journal of Personality and Social Psychology* 35, 1–11.

Dufwenberg, M., Kirchsteiger, G., 2004. A theory of sequential reciprocity. *Games and Economic Behavior* 47, 268–298.

Ellingsen, T., Johannesson, M., 2004. Promises, threats and fairness. *The Economic Journal* 114, 397–420.

Falk, A., Fischbacher, U., 2006. A theory of reciprocity. *Games and Economic Behavior* 54, 293–315.

Feltovich, N., Giovannoni, F., 2015. Selection vs. accountability: An experimental investigation of campaign promises in a moral-hazard environment. *Journal of Public Economics* 126, 39–51.

Fischbacher, U., Gächter, S., Fehr, E., 2001. Are people conditionally cooperative? Evidence from a public goods experiment. *Economics Letters* 71, 397–404.

Geanakoplos, J., Pearce, D., Stacchetti, E., 1989. Psychological games and sequential rationality. *Games and Economic Behavior* 1(1), 60–79.

Geng, H., Weiss, A.R., Wolff, I., 2011. The limited power of coting to limit power. *Journal of Public Economic Theory* 13, 695–719.

Gneezy, U., 2005. Deception: The role of consequences. *The American Economic Review* 95(1), 384–394.

Isaac, R.M., Walker, J.M., 1988. Communication and free-riding behavior: The voluntary contribution mechanism. *Economic Inquiry* 26, 585–608.

Kartik, N. 2009. Strategic communication with lying costs. *Review of Economic Studies* 76, 1359–1395.

Rabin, M., 1993. Incorporating fairness into game theory and economics. *The American Economic Review* 83, 1281–1302.

Selten, R., 1967c. Die Srategiemethode zur Erforschung des eingeschränkt rationalen Verhaltens im Rahmen eines Oligopolexperiments. In: Sauermann, H. (Ed.). *Beiträge zur experimentellen Wirtschaftsforschung*, Vol. I. Tübingen: J.C.B. Mohr (Paul Siebeck), 103–168.

Turmunkh, U., van den Assem, M.J., van Dolder, D., 2019. Malleable lies: Communication and cooperation in a high stakes TV game show. *Management Science* 65, 4795–4812.

Vanberg, C., 2008. Why do people keep their promises? An experimental test of two explanations. *Econometrica* 76, 1467–1480.

18

THE HIDDEN COSTS OF CONTROL (BY ARMIN FALK AND MICHAEL KOSFELD)

Laura Razzolini and Rachel Croson

Introduction

In the United States, couples marrying for the first time have approximately a 50% chance of divorcing (American Psychological Association: www.apa.org/research/action/marital). Prenuptial agreements would greatly simplify the terms of divorce and save couples thousands of dollars in attorneys' fees and court costs. Yet, less than 10% of married couples choose to enter into a prenuptial agreement. Why do individuals abstain from prenups that would save them so much later?[1]

More generally, we observe incomplete contracts in all areas of economic life. Falk and Kosfeld (2006) consider labor contracts, where we often see vague employment agreements. But incomplete contracts have been observed (and decried) in sourcing, international trade, and many other domains.

The typical explanation justifying incomplete contracts involves transactions costs; it's complicated and takes significant effort to write down (and to enforce) every possible contingency (Coase 1937, Williamson 1975, 1985). Some authors have argued that it's impossible to write a complete contract (e.g., Grossman and Hart 1986, Hart and Moore 1990, Hart 1995), while others have suggested that, with a sufficiently complex contract, anything can be achieved (Maskin and Tirole 1999). There is wide agreement, however, that observed contracts are more incomplete than would be expected, even given the transactions costs, possibility of renegotiation, and hold-up problems.

This paper puts forward a simple, yet innovative and compelling explanation. Contracts between parties are self-fulfilling prophecies. The more complete your contract, the more strongly you are signaling to the other party that you don't trust them; you believe that, given the opportunity, they

DOI: 10.4324/9781003019121-18

will try to take advantage of you. This signal reduces the desire of the other party to act in a trustworthy way. Thus, the more complete your contract, the less trustworthy your counterpart will behave. Falk and Kosfeld (2006) call this the "hidden cost of control." Complete contracts backfire, crowding out trustworthy behavior and leaving the controller in a worse situation than they would have been had they not tried to control in the first place.

The relationship between the agent who has to decide on his activity level and the principal who has the opportunity to control the agent is a situation of conflict. The agent has an interest in behaving selfishly and the principal has an incentive to control the agent to ensure higher earnings. Deci (1971) argued that control may serve as a disciplinary device by limiting shirking, but it may also crowd-out the agents' intrinsic motivation to perform. Which effect dominates depends on the specific relationship between the two parties. Frey (1993) suggested that the "disciplining effect" would dominate when the relationship was abstract, while the "crowding-out effect" would dominate in more personal relationships. In their seminal paper, Falk and Kosfeld (2006) argue and demonstrate that the crowding-out effects are substantial, even in abstract relationships, and are easily significant enough to outweigh the positive effects of control. They also demonstrate that most principals realize this and act accordingly.

Summary of the paper

The experimental design is a simple, one-shot game between a principal and an agent. The agent will be choosing an activity level x, such as working time, output, effort, or fidelity. The action is costly to the agent, with $c(x) = x$, and is beneficial to the principal, with $b(x) = 2x$. Thus, social value is created with higher values of x; activity costs the agent x, but benefits the principal 2x.

Before the agent decides their level of activity, the principal is given the opportunity to "control" the agent's choice by imposing a *minimum* level of activity x or not (no control, leaving the choice of x entirely up the agent). In the experiment, the agent could choose x between 0 and 120. In three treatments, the levels of x are (respectively) 5, 10, or 20. If the principal chooses to control in the first treatment, for example, the agent's choice of x would be restricted to being between 5 and 120.

Traditional utility maximization theories, as well as the reciprocity model from Falk and Fischbacher (2006), would suggest that the principal should control the agent, because agents are expected to act selfishly. Surprisingly, instead, Falk and Kosfeld (2006) find that the overwhelming majority of principals chose not to exercise control and not to impose a minimum level of activity. As they predicted, this trust, on average, generates significantly higher levels of activity (choice of x) than does control, which signals distrust.

The paper reports three main treatments, all implemented in a neutral frame. The experiment uses the *strategy method* where agents are asked to choose their level of activity (x) with and without an imposed minimum

before actually knowing whether the principals chose to impose the minimum. Under the low and medium treatments of 5 and 10, principals earned
a higher payoff without the control. When x = 5, the average activity (x) chosen is 12.2 with control and 25.1 with no control. When x = 10, the average
activity (x) chosen is 17.5 with control and 23 with no control. Both these
comparisons are statistically significantly different. For the highest level of
control x = 20, the agents' choices with and without control are not significantly different, but they remain directionally consistent: 25.4 with control
versus 26.7 without.

Falk and Kosfeld (2006) implemented three robustness check-treatments
to confirm the validity of their results. The first checked whether the elicitation of preferences via the strategy method could have affected the agents'
choices by placing too much attention on the "control-versus-trust" aspect
of the decision. In this robustness check, for the x = 10 case, agents made
their choice of x only *after* having learned the principal's decision to control
or not. The results support their findings. Even without the strategy method,
when agents are trusted (and not controlled), they engage in more activity
(higher x).

A second robustness test nailed down the causality assumed by the experimenters. Here the minimum activity level of x = 10 was artificially set
by the experimenter, rather than being chosen by the principal. When the
experimenter sets the minimum level of activity, the average level of activity
(28.7) is the same as when no control is set (and significantly greater than
when the principal chooses to control which was 17.5). This demonstrates
that it is the *intentions* of the principal in setting the control to which the
agent is reacting.

The third robustness test was done to check the validity of the results
in an economically richer environment, where the relationship between the
agent and the principal is modeled as an employer-employee relationship.
In this case, a gift-exchange treatment was implemented, with the principal
not only determining whether or not to exercise control, but also choosing a
wage to pay the agent. The principal offered the agent a payment (wage w ∈
{10, 30, 60, 120}) in hopes of inducing positive levels of activity. The agent's
payoff becomes (w − x), and the principal's payoff is (2x − w). At the same
time, the principal may choose to impose a minimum activity level of x = 10
or not. The results indicate that the principal's decision to control reduces
the agent's reciprocity, so that the slope of the agent's choice of activity as a
function of the offered wage is reduced. Indeed, control on the part of the
principal reduces the agents' motivation to reciprocate a high wage with
high activity (higher x).

In addition to the experiments and robustness checks, Falk and Kosfeld
also administered a post-experimental questionnaire to all the participants
and an additional (separate) questionnaire to 403 subjects not involved in
the previous experiments.

The post-experimental questionnaire was intended to assess subjects'
beliefs and perceptions about the consequences of control. Among the

questions it asked the agents was, "What do you feel if participant B (the principal) forces you to transfer at least x points?" Free-form answers were then categorized in six categories. The most common response was "distrust," especially among those agents who reacted negatively to control (i.e., those who chose a lower x when controlled than when they were not controlled by the principal). Similarly, the principals' elicited beliefs and expectations about the agents' performance were accurate: principals who chose to control expected to get less from the agents than those who chose to trust.

The additional questionnaire presented 403 participants with five everyday, work-related, real life scenarios. In each scenario, subjects read about two conditions: one where the principal (employer) trusted the agent (employee) and one in which the principal controlled the agent, setting explicit minimums or other limits to their behavior. For instance, one scenario was inspired by Hewlett-Packard's policy of keeping store rooms open and printers easily accessible. In the control treatment, the copy room is locked, while in the trust treatment the room with the copy machine is open. Respondents were asked to rate on a five-point scale from "very low" to "very high" their motivation to work under each condition. The questionnaire confirmed the results from the experiments. In all scenarios, control significantly reduced work motivation. Confirming the main result of the paper with every-day work situations adds realism and robustness to the results found in the lab.

Strengths of the paper

This paper has been cited 1,062 times according to Google Scholar (12/3/2019). It has also been replicated many times: Kessler and Leider (2016), Charness et al (2012), and Ziegelmeyer et al (2012) are just three examples. Fehr and List (2004) have even shown similar results using real-world CEOs.

The paper's main strengths are its innovation and creativity. It explains an important real-world anomaly with an innovative and intuitively compelling mechanism. The experimental design is simple, yet it elegantly captures the underlying situation and tensions. The decision that principals must make replicates the dilemma faced – to impose control on the other party. While control can reduce uncertainty, Falk and Kosfeld show that it also generates resentment and destroys goodwill and trust, reducing productivity and social welfare. The paper further shows a wide range of conditions (much wider than previously hypothesized) under which this negative effect outweighs the positive ones.

The robustness checks importantly eliminate alternative explanations and provide further evidence for the causality of the results. The authors also expand their methods beyond the traditional experimental economics methods, by coding survey responses from the post-experimental questionnaire, and through the use of realistic scenario studies in addition to traditional incentivized methods. This multi-method approach allows triangulation and provides important evidence in favor of the authors' explanation of the results.

Weaknesses of the paper

While this paper is extremely strong, every study can be improved. Here we identify three areas where we feel the paper could have been enhanced.

The first addresses the robustness check on the strategy method elicitation of preferences. The strategy method is extremely useful for gathering experimental data; however, there always remains the question of whether behavior would be different if it were allowed to proceed "naturally" and whether learning occurs as multiple choices are elicited. The authors recognize and address this in the paper via their robustness check, but this check only involves one treatment ($x = 10$). Providing data for all three treatments would have strengthened the paper.

Additionally, in their primary experiment each participant experiences all three treatments with no counterbalance for order. The possibility of order effects could have been considered and checked for.

Finally, the results of this paper are well documented in its Tables 1 and 2. Unfortunately, their Figure 1 (a replica of which is provided here as Figure 18.1) uses cumulative distribution functions to depict the data, and it is quite difficult to interpret. The values are hard to read and, other than showing that the lines are far from each other, it is not clear what the readers are supposed to take away from the figure. We recommend consulting sources like Tufte (2001) to consider how to best visually present experimental (or any) data.

Future directions

This paper focuses on and excellently documents the negative effect of control in situations of moral hazard, when the activity choice of x is not controllable. An important extension, however, would be to examine the selection effect. The ability to exit a relationship (or never to enter it in the first place) is important in the field, but not present in the experiment.[2]

Intuitively, would you work for a firm who locked up their printers? Would you marry a person who insisted on a prenup? This experiment examined the choice of activity (x), but not whether to engage in it in the first place. This reality is especially true in the labor and marriage markets, where there are multiple possible employers/partners. We would hypothesize that, in addition to choosing higher levels of activity when trusted, agents would choose to transact or partner with principals who trust. This would be an interesting and important extension to this work.

Overall, however, this paper was and remains innovative and insightful. The anomaly of incomplete contracts is intuitively explained and compellingly demonstrated to be a result of the hidden costs of control.

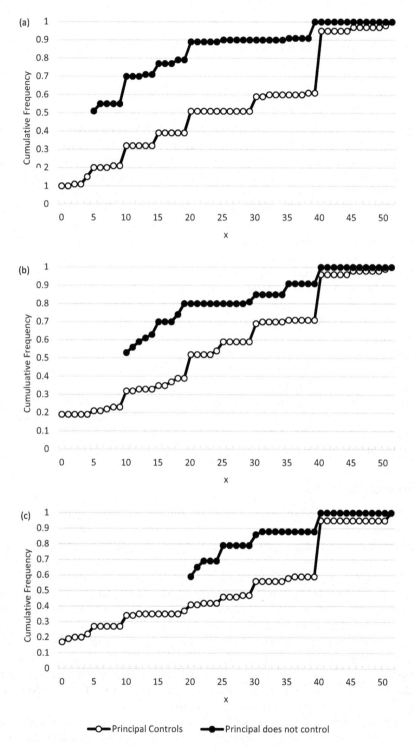

FIGURE 18.1 Cumulative distribution of agents' choices in treatment C5 (panel a), C10 (panel b), and C20 (panel c) (Falk and Kosfeld, 2006).

Furthermore, individuals in the experiment easily grasp this concept; when given the choice, most principals chose to trust their agent, and then reap the rewards.

Notes

1 One alternative explanation, of course, involves overconfidence. No couple entering marriage believes that they will get divorced. However, it is hard to generalize this explanation to the other domains in which we see incomplete contracts.
2 Some may argue that if the agent chooses activity level of 0, then that this is the equivalent of exiting. However, note that an activity level of 0 still implies earnings for both sides (under the particular parameterization in the experiment, the agent would earn 120 and the principal would earn 0). This is quite different from not engaging in the exchange at all, or finding another partner.

References

Charness, G., Cobo-Reyes, R., Jiménez, N., Lacomba, J., Lagos, F., 2012. The hidden advantage of delegation: Pareto improvements in a gift exchange game. *American Economic Review* 102, 2358–2379.

Coase, R., 1937. The nature of the firm. *Economica* 4, 386–405.

Deci, E., 1971. Effects of externally mediated rewards on intrinsic motivation. *Journal of Personality and Social Psychology* 18, 105–115.

Falk, A., Fischbacher, U., 2006. A theory of reciprocity. *Games and Economic Behavior* 54, 293–315.

Falk, A., Kosfeld, M., 2006. The Hidden Costs of Control. *American Economic Review*, 96(5): 1611–1630.

Fehr, E., List, J., 2004. The hidden costs and returns of incentives – Trust and trustworthiness among CEOs. *Journal of the European Economic Association* 2, 743–771.

Frey, B., 1993. Does monitoring increase work effort? The rivalry with trust and loyalty. *Economic Inquiry* 31, 663–670.

Grossman, S., and Hart, O., 1986. The costs and benefits of ownership: A theory of vertical and lateral integration. *Journal of Political Economy* 94, 691–719.

Hart, O., 1995. *Firms, Contracts and Financial Structure*. New York, NY: Oxford University Press.

Hart, O., Moore, J., 1990. Property rights and the nature of the firm. *Journal of Political Economy* 98, 1119–1158.

Kessler, J., Leider, S., 2016. Procedural fairness and the cost of control. *Journal of Law, Economics, and Organization* 32, 685–718.

Maskin, E., Tirole, J., 1999. Unforeseen contingencies and incomplete contracts. *The Review of Economic Studies* 66, 83–114.

Tufte, E., 2001. *The Visual Display of Quantitative Information*, Second Edition. Cheshire, Connecticut: Graphics Press.

Williamson, O., 1975. *Markets and Hierarchies: Analysis and Antitrust Implications*. New York, NY: Free Press.

Williamson, O., 1985. *The Economic Institutions of Capitalism*, New York, NY: Free Press.

Ziegelmeyer, A., Schmelz, K., Ploner. M., 2012. Hidden costs of control: Four repetitions and an extension. *Experimental Economics* 15, 323–340.

19

DO WOMEN SHY AWAY FROM COMPETITION? DO MEN COMPETE TOO MUCH? (BY MURIEL NIEDERLE AND LISE VESTERLUND)

Katherine B. Coffman and Alvin E. Roth

Introduction

Among the qualities that contribute to making an experiment important is that it should use an appropriately crafted experimental design to ask and answer a key question – a question whose answer may unlock a significant puzzle – in a convincing, replicable and generalizable way. Niederle and Vesterlund (2007, hereafter NV) does each of these things.

The general question that motivates NV (2007) is how do women's choices contribute to the fact that fewer women than men are observed to be in the highest paying and most powerful positions in the labor market? NV start with a hypothesis that this has to do with *competitiveness*, i.e., with gender-correlated differences in personal attitudes towards engaging in competition. This hypothesis arises in part from the earlier experiment by Gneezy, Niederle, and Rustichini (2003) that presented evidence that women and men may perform differently in competitive compared to non-competitive environments, and they may (therefore) have different preferences over participating in competitive environments. (In that experiment, which involved solving mazes, women performed the task on average less well than men did in a competitive environment, and with a gender gap in performance significantly larger than in a non-competitive environment.)

A laboratory experiment is an appropriate way to begin such an investigation, because it can potentially control away other reasons for the scarcity of women in competitive positions. These other reasons could involve discrimination, investment in human capital, innate skills, signaling, etc., and these can be excluded from the experimental environment.

DOI: 10.4324/9781003019121-19

The experimental design

NV (2007) employ an experimental task that involves adding five two-digit numbers displayed horizontally, with the performance criterion being the number of correct sums produced in five minutes. The experimental design is "within subject," and has each participant engage in this task under four different experimental conditions. Each condition varies how participants will be paid for their number of correctly computed sums. In each condition, participants receive feedback only on how many sums they have computed correctly (not on how their performance compares to that of the others). Finally, at the conclusion of the session, one of the payment treatments was randomly selected to be the one for which participants were actually paid.

Throughout the experiment, participants are assigned to a group of four, each containing two men and two women. Participants could see each other, and hence gauge each other's apparent gender, but it is never indicated that gender is of interest to the experimenters, reducing experimenter demand concerns.

The first payment condition ("Task 1") pays for correct sums with *piece-rate* compensation: if Task 1 is randomly chosen, each participant receives 50 cents per correct sum she computed.

Task 2 employs competitive tournament payoffs: if Task 2 is randomly selected for payoff, the participant who solves the largest number of correct sums in the group of four receives $2 times the number of correct sums she computes, while the other three participants receive no payment. (In case of ties, the winner is chosen randomly from among those tied for the largest number of correct sums, and only the tournament winner is paid in each group.)

The key condition is Task 3. Task 3 gives participants a choice of payoff methods. They again have five minutes to compute sums, but before beginning their computations, they make a choice either (i) to be paid according to a piece rate of 50 cents for each correct sum they compute, or (2) via a competitive tournament. A participant who chooses the tournament receives $2 per correct sum if her score in Task 3 is the highest of the group members *in the Task-2 tournament they have just completed.* That is, the new computations a participant makes in Task 3 are entered into a tournament with the results *already recorded in Task 2 by the other group members.* This is an important element of the design to which we'll return shortly. (Ties were broken randomly, as before.)

Task 4 does not involve any further computation of sums. Instead, participants are asked how they wished to be paid if Task 4 is chosen for payment, based on the number of correct sums they have (already) computed in Task 1. They could choose either to be paid a piece rate of 50 cents per correct sum, or to be paid according to a tournament payoff among the already recorded sums by each of their group members in Task 1, so that they would receive $2 per correct answer if their Task 1 performance had been the highest in their group, etc.

After participants have completed these four tasks, they are asked to guess their rank within their group in the Task 1 piece rate and the Task 2 tournament. Each participant selects a rank between 1 and 4 and is paid $1 for each correct guess.

Results and analyses

Tasks 1 and 2 established that, although there is considerable individual variability in the number of correct sums individual participants can produce in five minutes, that number is not strongly correlated with either gender or payment method. That is, on a first approximation, men and women do on average equally well, and they do about equally well under piece rate and tournament payoffs.

Nevertheless, in Task 3, there was a substantial difference in choice of payoff method: *73% of the men chose to enter the tournament, while only 35% of the women did* (i.e., 65% of the women chose to be paid the piece rate, and only 27% of the men did). The choice to enter the tournament was not highly correlated with earlier performance in Tasks 1 and 2: most men entered and most women did not, regardless of performance. Thus, too many low-performing men entered the tournament (they would have earned more by choosing piece rate) and too few high-performing women entered, despite the fact that they would have had higher expected tournament payoffs than they earned by piece rate.

What could account for this?

One of the most important jobs of an experimental design is to control for plausible alternative hypotheses to the one being investigated – which in this case is that taste for competition, i.e., "competitiveness" – accounts for the differences in behavior. But a difference in tournament entry might be due to other things than a simple taste or distaste for competing.

For example, one might worry that a reluctance to enter the tournament might not be a distaste for competitive payoffs, but rather a rational calculation about the chances of winning against a self-selected group of competitors – other individuals who all opt into competition. But the experiment avoids that possibility, because each participant who chose tournament payoff in Task 3 was competing against *the Task 2 performance of their whole group*, and not only against those who chose to enter the tournament.

Notice also that in Task 3 it is possible for everyone to win the tournament, since everyone is competing against the fixed results of their other group members in Task 2. No participant need be concerned that their participation in the tournament could have a negative effect on other participants (by causing them to lose the tournament), i.e., the design removes this potential part of a distaste for competition from consideration.

The inclusion of Task 4 in the design plays a critical role in assessing other plausible explanations for the gender gap in tournament entry observed in

Task 3. Task 4 does not involve any tournament performance, but only a choice of payoff mechanism for computations made previously. So observing the difference between tournament participation in Tasks 4 and 3 allows NV to separate attitudes towards tournament *participation* from attitudes towards tournament payoffs.

A key factor that might influence the choice of whether to compete is risk aversion, but in Task 3 elements of simple risk are confounded with concerns about performance. Entry in the Task 3 tournament is a complex choice that involves more than confidence in one's own performance, which might be affected by performing under tournament conditions. It also depends on the performance of others, which might also be influenced by the tournament conditions. Task 4 isolates the risky part of the decision unconfounded with the performance part, since it involves a choice of how to be paid for the sums computed in Task 1, which were performed under a piece-rate payoff. That is, the choice of tournament *payoff* in Task 4 does not involve any tournament *performance* (either by the participant making the choice, or by the other participants, since what will be compared are payoffs from computations made by players who were all working for piece rates). It just requires a choice between a sure piece-rate payoff (the participants were reminded of their Task 1 score) or a risky payoff that depends on whether the participant's Task 1 score was the highest in his/her group. Of course, the perceived risk of choosing tournament pay in Task 4 also depends on the participant's confidence, i.e., on beliefs about where his or her performance ranked, which were assessed following the completion of the four tasks. The Task 4 choice involves risk preferences and confidence, just as Task 3, but separates them from issues concerning active performance in the tournament environment.

Another reason an individual might choose to avoid entering the tournament in Task 3 or choose piece-rate payoffs in Task 4 is feedback aversion – a desire to avoid learning how one's performance compares to that of others. By choosing piece-rate compensation, rather than compensation that depends on relative ranking, a participant can avoid finding out how her Task 3 performance compared to others' Task 2 performances.

By design, then, Task 4 removes preferences for *performing* under competitive conditions, while leaving intact other factors, depending only on tournament versus piece rate payoff schemes that might influence the (Task 3) choice of choosing tournament participation. These other factors could include confidence, risk preferences, and feedback aversion, as well as other, not specifically named factors. As a result, by comparing choices across the two tasks, NV can assess the role played by preferences for performing competitively. If the main drivers of the gender gap in tournament entry in Task 3 were confidence, risk preferences, feedback aversion, and/or any other preferences related to how payoffs alone were determined, we would expect a similarly sized gender gap in compensation choice in Task 4. If not, that is, if there is a residual gender gap in tournament entry in Task 3 compared to Task 4 choices, it would point strongly to a role for preferences for performing in competitive or piece-rate environments.

This analysis leads Niederle and Vesterlund to the following, nuanced conclusions

> Overall, we find that about 57 percent of the original gender effect can be accounted for by general differences in overconfidence and risk and feedback aversion while the residual "competitive" component is 43 percent. This makes clear that the gender gap in choice of compensation scheme is exacerbated when individuals subsequently have to perform under the selected compensation scheme. Controlling for the Task-4 decision as well as believed tournament rank, the marginal effect of gender on the decision to enter the tournament is still 16 percent. This suggests that the gender gap in tournament entry is influenced by men and women differing in their preference for performing in a competitive environment.
>
> *(p. 1096)*

Replication, generalization, and broader conversations

Many researchers have chosen to use nearly identical designs when replicating and building upon this work – perhaps another compelling testament to the strength of their experimental design. Across a large number of studies using similar paradigms, several independent teams of researchers have replicated the results of NV (2007) (see Niederle and Vesterlund 2011, and Niederle 2016 for a review). Expanding beyond exact replications, there are several other "robust replications" that find similar patterns – women entering competitive environments less often than equally capable men – in distinct experimental paradigms (see, for instance, Booth and Nolen 2012; Gneezy et al. 2009; Vandegrift and Yavas 2009; Andersen et al. 2013; Ertac and Szentes 2011; Dohmen and Falk 2011; Gupta et al. 2013; Shurchkov 2012). These papers have demonstrated that these results hold across a variety of subject populations and contexts.

NV (2007) and the torrent of work that followed conveys a clear message about the critical role that laboratory experiments can play in understanding significant phenomena outside the laboratory. One motivation central to NV (2007) is understanding the underlying causes of gender gaps in labor market outcomes, in particular gender gaps in compensation and the underrepresentation of women at the very top tiers of business, government, and academia. NV (2007) hypothesized that a gender difference in willingness to opt-in to competition could contribute to these gaps, as women may be less willing to enter more competitive and higher-paying fields or to compete for selective positions or promotions. While a superficial view might say that a laboratory experiment could not tell us much about workplace dynamics, NV (2007) provides a perfect example of the important contribution of laboratory experiments. By cleanly, clearly (and quite cheaply!) demonstrating a gender gap in competitiveness within the laboratory, NV (2007) provided the spark that accelerated a stream of research linking competitiveness with educational and career outcomes.

Just over a decade after the publication of NV (2007), there is now a rather substantial body of work documenting the external relevance of their laboratory measure of willingness to compete. Buser, Niederle, and Oosterbeek (2014; BNO) explore how the willingness to compete, as measured by the NV (2007) experimental task, predicts the choice of academic track among high-school students in the Netherlands. In particular, conditional on academic ability, more competitive students are more likely to choose the more prestigious – and likely more lucrative – tracks of math and science. Importantly, Buser et al. (2014) estimate that gender differences in competitiveness account for approximately 20% of the gender gap in academic track choice, suggesting a significant role for competitiveness in determining educational trajectories. Similar results correlating competitiveness with the choice of more ambitious academic paths have been found in studies in Norway (Almås et al. 2016) and Switzerland (Buser et al. 2017). In the United States, Kamas and Preston (2018) report that competitiveness is predictive of the choice of major, with more competitive students more likely to opt for business and STEM majors.

Competitiveness has also been linked to earnings. Reuben, Wiswall, and Zafar (2017) find that more competitive undergraduate students, as measured by the NV (2007) task, report greater earnings expectations for their careers. Kamas and Preston (2018) measure the competitiveness of college seniors and then track their early careers following graduation. They find that more-competitive women later self-report higher compensation in their early careers compared to less-competitive women; within this study, competitiveness is not predictive of men's self-reported earnings. Reuben, Sapienza, and Zingales (2015) find that willingness to compete predicts both earnings and industry choice among MBA graduates. Moving beyond the United States, Berge et al. (2015) find that the measured competitiveness of entrepreneurs in Tanzania is predictive of their business size and decision-making – more competitive entrepreneurs employ more individuals and invest more in their businesses.

This body of work illustrates very directly the foundation that laboratory experiments can provide for investigating questions of first-order importance across a variety of contexts of economic significance. In this case, those subsequent investigations include "lab in the field" experiments in which an experimental indicator (choosing tournament versus piece rate in a laboratory task) is found to be predictive of high-stakes choices like those involving course of study, made in the naturally occurring field environment.

Given that gender differences in competitiveness contribute to gender gaps in educational and labor market outcomes, a crucial next question to consider is, what can be done about it? Broadly speaking, one could consider two classes of "solutions" to the issue of the competitiveness gap. First, one could seek to change the behavior of women (or men), encouraging, particularly, more talented women to behave more competitively. Of course, this path has some challenges. It is not particularly clear *how* to change the behavior of women, or whether this would even be individually or socially welfare-increasing. The second class of solutions avoids these issues not by asking, "How can we change the women?," but rather, asking the market design question, "How can we change our institutions?"[1] That is, can we design institutions (like college admissions processes, academic track selection processes, promotion decisions, etc.) such that they select based less on who is most competitive, and more on underlying talent and capacity to excel? In environments in which competitiveness itself is *not* a skill that is important for success, this seems like a promising path.

A number of studies have begun to explore these questions of institutional design. Niederle, Segal, and Vesterlund (2013) and Balafoutas and Sutter (2012), using the NV design, find that affirmative action policies, in which the tournament designer implements quotas for the number of female winners, increase willingness to compete among women, without reducing average quality among tournament winners. Institutions could also choose to provide increased feedback to candidates prior to them having to make choices about whether to opt-in to competition; under this paradigm, more talented individuals are more likely to be aware of their relative talent, reducing inefficiencies in who chooses to compete. Cason et al. (2010), Ertac and Szentes (2011), and Wozniak et al. (2014) all find that increased feedback on performance prior to tournament entry decisions can help reduce the gender gap in tournament entry. Outside the laboratory, researchers have shown that framing positions as more cooperative and less competitive in job advertisements can increase the number of female applicants (Samek 2019; Liebbrandt and List 2015; Flory et al. 2015).

More broadly, NV (2007) jump-started a conversation among economists about how the preferences and beliefs of individuals on the supply-side of the market (students, job candidates, employees) might contribute to gender gaps in labor market outcomes. A large body of work in economics and other fields has focused on the role of discrimination in contributing to gender disparities: statistical discrimination, employer preferences over whom to hire, teacher and employer bias in candidate evaluation, etc. In many ways, NV (2007) prompted renewed consideration of the role of individual choices, absent discrimination, in contributing to gender gaps. Abstracting away from the role of bias, what opportunities do women choose to pursue? When do women choose to volunteer their ideas? Beyond simply gender differences in competitiveness, are there gender differences in preferences for "opting in" or "speaking up" more generally?

Recent work in this area has spanned decision-making in educational, political, and professional contexts. Within the realm of test-taking, Baldiga (2014) uses a laboratory experiment to show that women are less willing to guess on multiple-choice tests than men when there are penalties for wrong answers. Using data from the national Chilean college entry exam, Coffman and Klinowski (2020) show that this gender difference in willingness to guess explains approximately 9% of the gender gap in test scores. The impact of the gender gap in willingness to guess on test scores is largest among high-ability test-takers and in domains in which women have been historically underrepresented (math, social science, and chemistry, compared to verbal skills and biology).

Researchers have documented differences in the propensity to volunteer ideas in group decision-making contexts as well. Coffman (2014) finds that, conditional on measured knowledge, women are less likely than men to contribute their ideas to the group in stereotypically male-typed domains. As a result, groups miss out on good ideas from talented women in male-typed domains, and they have a more difficult time recognizing female experts as knowledgeable, simply because they speak up less often.

Within the political realm, researchers have identified a stark gender difference in willingness to run for political office. Kanthak and Woon (2015) use a series of laboratory experiments to show that women are equally willing to serve as a group representative when the representative is chosen at random, but they are significantly less willing than men to enter themselves into an election for group representative. Similarly, Born, Ranehill, and Sandberg (2019) and Coffman, Flikkema, and Shurchkov (2019) find that women are significantly less likely to put themselves forward to represent their team in a group decision-making problem, particularly when they are in the minority. Moving to the field, Preece and Stoddard (2015) find that, among politically active individuals, women are more deterred from political engagement than men when its competitive nature is emphasized. Finally, Wasserman (2018) finds that women are much less likely than men to run again for local political office after suffering an initial close loss in an election. Each of these points to gender differences in the propensity to opt for leadership positions.

Researchers have also begun to consider these types of opt-in decisions in the workplace, asking whether there are gender differences in the propensity to apply for job openings, or to self-promote more generally. Niederle and Yestrumskas (2008) show gender differences in the propensity to select challenging tasks, both among low- and high-performing participants. Coffman, Collis, and Kulkarni (2019) find that talented women are less likely to apply for more challenging, higher-return work than equally talented men, suggesting that women may be more reluctant or may wait longer to put themselves up for promotion. Similarly, Exley and Kessler (2019) show that even conditional on holding the same objective beliefs of their own ability, women are less likely to self-promote, and that they describe their performance more conservatively on a subjective scale.

The results of NV (2007) also inspired conversations around the role of self-confidence and beliefs in driving these types of gender differences in behavior. While the main finding of NV (2007) is that there is a gender gap in competitiveness (even conditional on measured self-confidence), their clean experimental paradigm highlights a clear gender gap in self-confidence as well. They find that, conditional on performance, women hold much more pessimistic beliefs about their performance relative to others. These biased beliefs contribute, in part, to the gender gap in competitiveness, and represent an important topic of study, independent of their relationship to competitiveness itself.

Mobius, Niederle, Niehaus, and Rosenblat (2013) show that women not only hold different perceptions than men about their own ability, but also update those differently when provided with feedback. Coffman (2014) and Bordalo et al. (2019) explore gender differences in beliefs about one's own ability in more detail, and find an important role for self-stereotyping in predicting beliefs. Replicating the findings in NV (2007), they find that women are less self-confident than men in male-typed tasks, such as math. But, this gender difference is not universal. Rather, stereotypes play a large role in predicting self-confidence: men are more self-confident than women on average in more stereotypically male-typed domains, while women are more self-confident than men on average in more stereotypically female-typed domains.

Further work on competitiveness reveals similar patterns. As Niederle (2016) points out in her review, despite the fact that men and women perform similarly in the math task used in NV (2007), participants may still perceive it as a male-typed math task. The gender-type of the task may contribute to the gender gap in competitiveness, through its impact on beliefs or on preferences for competition. In fact, laboratory studies have shown that the gender gap in competitiveness can be reduced or reversed when a more female-typed "verbal" task is used (Kamas and Preston 2009; Grosse and Reiner 2010; Shurchkov 2012; Dreber et al. 2014).

These results led to increased understanding of the sources of the gender differences that many studies have documented; many of these results may not reflect fundamental differences between men and women (i.e., men are more self-confident, men are more competitive, or men are more willing to self-promote). Rather, these results may reflect that many of the economically significant contexts of interests that researchers have sought to study carry with them strong gender norms and stereotypes, with individuals associating many of these domains with male talent more than with female talent. In this way, these gender differences reflect how the norms and stereotypes associated with a given domain shape beliefs and behavior, both for men and women (i.e., individuals are more self-confident, more competitive, or more likely to self-promote in more gender-congruent domains). The fact that beliefs and behavior are responsive to norms and stereotypes has important implications for understanding the types of policy interventions that are likely to be most effective in reducing gender gaps.

Conclusion

NV (2007) brought a clever and rigorous experimental design to a novel question of first-order economic importance. Its careful design tackles alternative explanations with precision (and serves as an outstanding model for effective experimental design). And their creation of an easily elicited laboratory measure of competitiveness set the stage for an exploration of the role of competitive preferences in shaping educational and professional outcomes beyond the laboratory. The success of this endeavor likely increased the credibility and appeal of laboratory studies to the world of researchers outside experimental economics. Finally, their striking results have inspired an explosion of work on gender differences in beliefs and preferences, focusing not only on competitiveness, but also on assertiveness and self-confidence more broadly, leading to an increased understanding of the causes of gender gaps in labor market outcomes.

Note

1 On market design, see, e.g., Roth (2016, 2018).

References

Almås, I., Cappelen, A.W., Salvanes, K. G., Sørensen, E. Ø., Tungodden, B., 2016. Willingness to compete: Family matters. *Management Science* 62(8), 2149–2162.

Andersen, S., Ertac, S., Gneezy, U., List, J. A., Maximiano, S., 2013. Gender, competitiveness, and socialization at a young age: Evidence from a matrilineal and a patriarchal society. *Review of Economics and Statistics* 95(4), 1438–1443.

Balafoutas, L., Sutter, M., 2012. Affirmative action policies promote women and do not harm efficiency in the laboratory. *Science* 335(6068), 579–582.

Baldiga, K. (2014). Gender differences in willingness to guess. *Management Science* 60(2), 434–448.

Berge, L. I. O., Bjorvatn, K., Pires, A. J. G., Tungodden, B., 2015. Competitive in the lab, successful in the field? *Journal of Economic Behavior & Organization* 118, 303–317.

Booth, A., & Nolen, P. (2012). Choosing to compete: How different are girls and boys? *Journal of Economic Behavior and Organization* 81(2), 542–555.

Bordalo, P., Coffman, K., Gennaioli, N., Shleifer, A., 2019. Beliefs about gender. *The American Economic Review* 109(3), 739–773.

Born, A., Ranehill, E., Sandberg, A., 2019. A Man's World? The impact of a male Dominated Environment on Female Leadership. Available at SSRN: https://ssrn.com/abstract=3207198 or http://dx.doi.org/10.2139/ssrn.3207198

Buser, T., Niederle, M., Oosterbeek, H., 2014. Gender, competitiveness, and career choices. *The Quarterly Journal of Economics* 129(3), 1409–1447.

Buser, T., Peter, N., Wolter, S. C., 2017. Gender, competitiveness, and study choices in high school: Evidence from Switzerland. *The American Economic Review* 107(5), 125–130.

Cason, T. N., Masters, W. A., & Sheremeta, R. M., 2010. Entry into winner-take-all and proportional-prize contests: An experimental study. *Journal of Public Economics* 94(9–10), 604–611.

Coffman, K. B., 2014. Evidence on self-stereotyping and the contribution of ideas. *The Quarterly Journal of Economics* 129(4), 1625–1660.

Coffman, K. B., Collis, M., & Kulkarni, L., 2019. When to apply? Working Paper.

Coffman, K. B., Flikkema, C. B., Shurchkov, O., 2019. Gender stereotypes in deliberation and team decisions. Working Paper.

Coffman, K. B., Klinowski, D., 2020. The impact of penalties for wrong answers on the gender gap in test scores. *Proceedings of the National Academy of Sciences*, 117 (16), 8794–8803.

Dohmen, T., Falk, A., 2011. Performance pay and multidimensional sorting: Productivity, preferences, and gender. *The American Economic Review* 101(2), 556–590.

Dreber, A., von Essen, E., Ranehill, E., 2014. Gender and competition in adolescence: Task matters. *Experimental Economics* 17(1), 154–172.

Ertac, S., Szentes, B., 2011. The effect of information on gender differences in competitiveness: Experimental evidence (No. 1104). Working Paper.

Exley, C. L., Kessler, J. B., 2019. The gender gap in self-promotion. National Bureau of Economic Research (w26345).

Flory, J. A., Leibbrandt, A., List, J. A., 2015. Do competitive workplaces deter female workers? A large-scale natural field experiment on job entry decisions. *The Review of Economic Studies* 82(1), 122–155.

Gneezy, U., Leonard, K. L., & List, J. A. (2009). Gender differences in competition: Evidence from a matrilineal and a patriarchal society. *Econometrica* 77(5), 1637–1664.

Gneezy, U., Niederle, M., & Rustichini, A. (2003). Performance in competitive environments: Gender differences. *The Quarterly Journal of Economics* 118(3), 1049–1074.

Grosse, N. D., Reiner, G., 2010. Explaining gender differences in competitiveness: Gender-task stereotypes. Jena Economic Research Papers, 2010–017.

Gupta, N., Poulsen, A., Villeval, M.C. (2013). Gender matching and competitiveness: Experimental evidence. *Economic Inquiry* 51(1), 816–835.

Kamas, L., Preston, A., 2009. Social preferences, competitiveness and compensation: Are there gender differences. Working. Paper, Santa Clara Univ.

Kamas, L., Preston, A., 2018. Competing with confidence: The ticket to labor market success for college-educated women. *Journal of Economic Behavior and Organization* 155, 231–252.

Kanthak, K., Woon, J., 2015. Women don't run? Election aversion and candidate entry. *American Journal of Political Science* 59(3), 595–612.

Leibbrandt, A., List, J. A., 2015. Do women avoid salary negotiations? Evidence from a large-scale natural field experiment. Management Science 61(9), 2016–2024.

Mobius, Markus M., Niederle, M., Niehaus, P., Rosenblat, T., 2013. Managing self-confidence: Theory and experimental evidence. Working Paper.

Niederle, M., 2016. Gender. In J. Kagel and A. E. Roth (Eds.). *The Handbook of Experimental Economics*, Vol. 2, Princeton, NJ: Princeton University Press, 481–562.

Niederle, M., Segal, C., Vesterlund, L., 2013. How costly is diversity? Affirmative action in light of gender differences in competitiveness. *Management Science* 59(1), 1–16.

Niederle, M., Vesterlund, L., 2007. Do Women Shy away from competition? Do men compete too much? *The Quarterly Journal of Economics* 122(3), 1067–1101.

Niederle, M., Vesterlund, L., 2011. Gender and competition. *Annual Review of Economics* 3(1), 601–630.

Niederle, M. Yestrumskas, A.H., 2008. Gender differences in seeking challenges: The role of institutions, NBER Working Paper No. 13922. Available at: https://web.stanford.edu/~niederle/Niederle.Yestrumskas.2008.pdf.

Preece, J., Stoddard, O., 2015. Why women don't run: Experimental evidence on gender differences in political competition aversion. *Journal of Economic Behavior & Organization* 117, 296–308.

Reuben, E., Sapienza, P., Zingales, L., 2015. Taste for competition and the gender gap among young business professionals. National Bureau of Economic Research (No. w21695).

Reuben, E., Wiswall, M., Zafar, B., 2017. Preferences and biases in educational choices and labour market expectations: Shrinking the black box of gender. *The Economic Journal* 127(604), 2153–2186.

Roth, A.E., 2016. Experiments in Market Design. In: Kagel, J.H., Roth A.E. (Eds.) Handbook of Experimental Economics, Volume 2, Princeton, NJ: Princeton University Press, 290–346.

Roth, A.E., 2018. Marketplaces, markets, and market design. *The American Economic Review* 108(7), 1609–1658.

Samek, A., 2019. Gender differences in job entry decisions: A university-wide field experiment. *Management Science* 65(7), 3272–3281.

Shurchkov, O., 2012. Under pressure: Gender differences in output quality and quantity under competition and time constraints. *Journal of the European Economic Association* 10(5), 1189–1213.

Vandegrift, D., Yavas, A., 2009. Men, women, and competition: An experimental test of behavior. *Journal of Economic Behavior and Organization* 72(1), 554–570.

Wasserman, M., 2018. Gender differences in politician persistence. Available at SSRN 3370587.

Wozniak, D., Harbaugh, W. T., Mayr, U., 2014. The menstrual cycle and performance feedback alter gender differences in competitive choices. *Journal of Labor Economics* 32(1), 161–198.

20

GROUP IDENTITY AND SOCIAL PREFERENCES (BY YAN CHEN AND SHERRY X. LI)

Marie Claire Villeval

Introduction

I cannot visit a museum exhibiting paintings of Klee or Kandinsky without thinking immediately of Yan Chen and Sherry Li. Of course, the Klee-Kandinsky protocol used for inducing minimal group identity in the lab was introduced in 1971 by social psychologists H. Tajfel, M. Billig, R. Bundy, and C. Flament, decades before the publication of "Group Identity and Social Preferences" in the *American Economic Review* in 2009. But if my reference point on group identity is Yan and Sherry's paper, it is not because of an in-group bias in favor of economists! It is because their paper tends to have a huge impact on any scholar interested in understanding the impact of group biases and social preferences on individual decision-making. This is only one of many possible indicators of its impact: since its publication, the paper has received more than 1,380 citations (Google Scholar), an impressive achievement!

In the 1970s, social psychologists developed a theory of social identity to explain the foundation of intergroup discrimination (Tajfel and Turner, 1979). Social identity is a perception of the self that is grounded in the affiliation with a social group. People derive self-esteem from being identified with a community, as they value sharing common roots, values, and language. Categorization is also central in this theory, capturing the notion that humans put themselves and others into categories. The numerous empirical tests of the theory of social identity have revealed that in-group bias is an omnipresent feature of intergroup relationships (see surveys by Tajfel and Turner, 1986; Brewer, 1999; Abdelal et al., 2009; Balliet et al., 2014). Individuals bias their behavior in favor of the group they identify with or by discriminating against the group they do not identify with. However, in these psychological studies, subjects are not incentivized and protocols only

DOI: 10.4324/9781003019121-20

involve other-other allocation tasks. Thus, being generous or punishing others is costless to the subjects.

By introducing monetary incentives and decisions that impact players' own payoffs in the experimental design, economists could have ruined such well-established results in psychology. This is not what happened... Chen and Li first made a theoretical contribution by introducing identity in economic models of social preferences. By incentivizing decisions, by introducing self-other allocation games in which helping or punishing others entailed a personal cost, and by increasing the number of games, they provided more robust evidence of the role of social identity in shaping preferences. By removing step by step each element of the protocol that could drive the results, not only were they able to identify the mechanism of categorization behind "group-contingent social preferences" (I borrow this expression from Charness and Chen, 2020), but they also made important methodological contributions. Finally, I would like to insist on how inspiring this paper has been for further research programs on group-contingent preferences.

In-group favoritism in distribution, reciprocity and welfare-maximizing preferences

Economists have taken up the topic of group identity by means of two different approaches. They first developed preference-based theoretical models, reconceptualizing the notion of group identity. In Akerlof (1997), preferences are affected by exogenous social norms and individuals gain utility by conforming to these norms. Extending this model, Akerlof and Kranton (2000, 2005) proposed a theory of group identity and self-identification in which utility depends on conformity to prescriptions and violations of the norm prescribed by group identity cause disutility. The alternative approach of identity is, instead, cognitive, based on individuals' beliefs. In Bénabou and Tirole (2011), individuals invest in beliefs and identity management, depending on their confidence of being moral persons. This affects, in turn, their pro-sociality.

Chen and Li's contribution is in line with the preference-based models of identity initiated by Akerlof and Kranton rather than with the belief-based approach. In contrast to these models, however, their focus is not on conformity to social norms. They modelled group-contingent social preferences by incorporating group identity in the two-person model of social preferences from Charness and Rabin (2002). They extended this model by varying the relative weight put on a match's payoff in the individual's utility function, depending on whether this match shares or does not share the same group identity. By doing so, they contributed to endogenizing the norms that were exogenous in Akerlof and Kranton (2000) (Charness and Chen, 2020). Teaching this paper in economic classes is, thus, a good way to introduce the beliefs- vs. preferences-based theories of social identity.

Beyond this group-contingent social preferences model, the main reason why this paper merits being incorporated in this volume is its major empirical contribution on how and why group identity changes the weight people put on others' payoffs. In the same period, other economists tested the impact of group identity but they focused on other dimensions, such as trust (Hargreaves Heap and Zizzo, 2009), redistribution (e.g., Luttmer, 2001; Klor and Shayo, 2010); patience and risk attitudes after priming ethnic identity (Benjamin et al., 2010); coordination (Charness et al., 2007; Efferson et al., 2008); contributions in public goods games after priming gender identity (Cadsby and Maynes, 1998; Croson et al., 2003); discrimination (Fershtman and Gneezy, 2001; Hoff and Pandey, 2006); cooperation in prisoner's dilemma games (Goette et al., 2006; Charness et al., 2007) or in teams (Montmarquette et al., 2004; Eckel, and Grossman, 2005); altruism and third-party punishment (Bernhard et al., 2006a,b). Instead, Chen and Li focused on social preferences with an ambitious perspective encompassing distribution, reciprocity, and welfare-maximizing preferences.

This is a fundamental paper also because it identified which aspect of group identity (categorization, attachment, communication, etc.) modifies social preferences and to what extent efficiency is impacted. To that purpose, the experimental design of Chen and Li consists of four stages. In the first, subjects were assigned to groups. Inspired by the method of Tajfel et al. (1971), subjects had to review five pairs of paintings, one painted by Klee and the other by Kandinsky, and to report their preferences in each pair. Based on their preferences they were then assigned either to the Klee group or to the Kandinsky group. The second and third stages of the experiment were used to enhance group attachment and measure a possible identity bias. In the second stage, subjects had to identify which artist painted each of two new paintings. Before entering their answers individually, they had the opportunity to exchange information and opinions during ten minutes with the members of their own group via an online chat. The third stage consisted of five periods of an other-other allocation game where subjects had to decide how to allocate tokens between two other participants under three scenarios. The number of tokens to be allocated increased across periods. The scenarios varied whether the allocation had to be made between two in-groups, two out-groups, or between an in-group and an out-group.

The core of the experiment (and its major departure point from previous literature) is the sequential allocation games implemented in the fourth stage. In the main treatment, each subject played from seven to ten games out of 24 sequential two-person games. These included 5 dictator games and 16 response games taken from Charness and Rabin (2002), which varied the conflict of interests between pair members. The other three games were variations of a game of Charness and Rabin (2002) used to test Player B's cost sensitivity. There were three types of response games: according to the game, Player B could help or sanction Player A's entry decisions at no cost, or they incurred a cost to help, or they sacrificed to sanction. These games helped characterize charity (generosity driven by advantageous inequality aversion), envy (punishment motivated by disadvantageous inequality aversion), reciprocity, and efficiency concerns. Each game was played under the strategy method: subjects had to make decisions in two scenarios, varying whether the match was an in-group or an out-group.

This describes the original treatment. Group-contingent social preferences were identified by comparing behavior in this treatment with a control that included only the self-other allocation games without inducing group identity. I will mention the five other treatments when discussing the methodological contribution of the paper. In total, the experiment was run with 566 subjects from the University of Michigan. The structure of the experiment – the four stages and the five treatments – makes this paper a perfect tool for explaining the principles of the experimental methodology to students. The beauty of its design lies both in the large diversity of games used to characterize group-contingent social preferences and in the diversity of treatments that helps identify the mechanism underlying these preferences by omitting each stage step-by-step. It is indeed crucial to identify which mechanisms trigger the phenomenon under study.

This elegant design delivers clear-cut results. First, the data replicated those from experiments in social psychology: the other-other allocations revealed significant in-group favoritism, showing the importance of identification and comparisons. Subjects allocated significantly more tokens to the in-group than to the out-group match in mixed pairs, whereas no difference was found in homogenous pairs. It is important to replicate previous findings under stricter conditions, as it gives more credence to the novel results.

Second, in the self-other allocation games used to measure distributional preferences, subjects put more weight on their match's payoff when they shared the same group identity. Maximum likelihood estimates revealed that when matched with an in-group, charity increased (by 47%) whereas envy decreased (by 93%), compared to an out-group match. The magnitude of the effects is large. Third, positive and negative reciprocity were also affected by group identity. In response games where the first mover's entry signaled good intentions, second movers were more likely (by 18.6%) to reward an in-group than an out-group, although envy reduced positive reciprocity. In games where entry signaled selfish intentions, they were less likely (by 12.8%) to punish an in-group, especially with charity concerns, and punishment was less cost-sensitive than with an out-group match. Such leniency toward in-groups should be highlighted because one might have anticipated higher expectations from an in-group match and, thus, a higher willingness to retaliate when being let down.

If people put more weight on the payoff of an in-group than on the payoff of an out-group, is this neutral in terms of efficiency? The news is not so good here. Group identity increased concerns for social welfare maximization in homogenous groups but not in heterogenous ones. As a result, when group identity was induced, earnings in homogenous groups in terms of identity were higher on average than in the absence of identity, but this did not compensate for the loss of earnings in heterogenous groups. The fact that people were not better off in heterogenous groups when identity was made salient compared to a neutral environment has policy implications for organizations. It may be efficiency-enhancing for an organization to highlight a common culture, but if one wants to promote diversity, it might be better not to make it too salient. This dimension has been further investigated in Chen et al. (2014) in organizations with a diverse workforce, priming a common identity (the organization identity) rather than a fragmenting identity (like ethnic identities) is efficiency-enhancing.

Methodological contributions

When investigating the impact of group identity on decision-making, one often hesitates over procedures: Should one enhance group attachment by allowing subjects to communicate with their in-groups and perform a preliminary joint exercise? Should one use a between-subject or a within-subject design to compare attitudes towards in-groups and out-groups while avoiding experimenter-demand effects? Should one assign individuals to groups based on their preferences (about paintings or any topic orthogonal to the preferences and beliefs under investigation) or is it sufficient to randomly assign subjects to groups identified by any neutral attribute? Is it better to use a natural group identity (as in, e.g., Bernhard et al., 2006a, b; Goette et al., 2006; Hoff and Pandey, 2006; Goette et al., 2012) or to induce artificial identity? By muting some of the possible channels behind group-contingent social preferences, the different treatments in Chen and Li (2009) help address these questions.

In social psychology, minimal groups respond to the following principles: subjects are randomly assigned to non-overlapping artificial groups, group members are anonymous and do not interact, and there is no link between economic self-interest and in-group favoritism (Tajfel and Turner, 1986). As they acknowledge, Chen and Li deviated from several of these principles: decisions were monetarily incentivized; the assignment to groups was not random but was based on painting preferences; subjects could chat with their group members; they had not only to allocate money in other-other pairs but also in self-other pairs; etc. The test was, thus, more demanding since in some games subjects had to suffer a personal monetary cost or forego a personal gain to help or sanction another player. Still, the results held.

The Klee-Kandinsky method of inducing group identity is usually enjoyed by the subjects, but it is time consuming and group assignment is based on preferences. Would using random allocation to groups identified by any meaningless feature be sufficient to induce group-contingent social preferences? The paper is informative on this point. In additional treatments group assignment was random. No significant difference was found in any games. Therefore, the authors recommend a random allocation procedure since it increases the chance of forming similar groups. It may also avoid possible cultural effects in the evaluation of paintings.

Is it crucial to let in-groups communicate in a problem-solving task (solving puzzles, finding a name for the group, coordinating) to enhance group attachment? In one treatment, the chat between group members was withdrawn. They find that, in one of the 24 games, chat leads to a significant difference in group-dependent decisions; by comparison, self-reported group affinity is significantly higher with chat than without. Based on these results, they recommend that "[t]o enhance and strengthen group identity, a problem-solving stage, such as an online chat or puzzle-solving, can increase group attachment and might have a moderate effect on behavior" (p. 452). Other papers have found that minimal group alone may not be sufficient to change behavior (e.g., Eckel and Grossman, 2005; Charness et al., 2007) and that a team-building exercise can be more effective in improving coordination and cooperation (e.g., Chen and Chen, 2011; Charness et al., 2014).

To test whether making other-other allocation choices to strengthen group identity before the main task matters, another treatment removed both the chat and the other-other allocation stage. The resulting differences in behavior were hardly significant and went in the direction of increased group identity effects when this stage was omitted. The authors did not determine whether this results from crowding out or from the fact that artificially induced group identity is short-lived but they suggested that this task could be omitted.

The main treatments implemented a within-subject design: the same subjects made allocation decisions when matched with an in-group and with an out-group. However, the reference to different categories might be interpreted as a signal of the experimenter's expectation of discrimination. Therefore, in additional treatments, subjects had only out-group or only in-group matches. No significant differences were found with the initial results. This refutes the suspicion of an experimenter-demand effect driving the different decisions in in-group and out-group matches when using a within-subject design.

An inspiring line of research

In the decade following its publication, Chen and Li's paper has been replicated and has continued to inspire research. Several authors have explored further the impact of group identity on distributional preferences (e.g., Fehr et al., 2013; Grosskopf and Pearce, 2017; Kranton et al., 2018) and on reciprocity (e.g., McLeish and Oxoby, 2011; Gneezy and Fessler, 2012; Currarini and Mengel, 2016). The literature has also dramatically broadened its scope. It has investigated other sources of naturally occurring or artificially induced group identity, the heterogeneity of biases, and a larger range of strategic and non-strategic games, from cooperation, coordination, and competition among individuals to trust, gift-exchange, and reciprocity in principal-agent relationships. Costa-Font and Cowell (2015), Lane (2016), Pechar and Kranton (2018), Charness and Chen (2020), and Li (2020) provide recent surveys of the literature on group identity. It is now clearer when group identity affects decision-making and when it does not. In particular, while minimal group identity generates in-group favoritism and out-group discrimination in non-strategic settings, it may not be strong enough – if not reinforced – to change decisions in strategic settings (such as in contests or public goods games). The salience of group affiliation is, thus, an important vector.

Chen and Li themselves have explored other dimensions through which group identity affects social interactions, increasing our knowledge of the conditions in which group bias improves cooperation and welfare. Chen and Chen (2011) have shown how group identity contributes to equilibrium selection through a change in the potential function. Theoretically, group identity should facilitate coordination on higher equilibrium effort levels, which is confirmed experimentally in the minimum-effort game. Group identity also contributes to solving the moral hazard problem in principal-agent relationships with hidden action (Jiang and Li, 2019). Instead of inducing artificial group identity, Chen et al. (2014) primed the subjects' natural identities either through names revealing ethnicity (fragmented identity) or through their university affiliation (common identity). While the fragmented ethnic identity reduced effort in the minimum-effort game, priming the common identity increased cooperation in the prisoner's dilemma game. Li et al. (2017) found, however, more contrasting results, suggesting that the effect of common identity on individuals' contributions to local charities is sensitive to the environment. Also, Li and Liu (2019) showed that the positive impact of group identity on cooperation with in-groups in infinitely repeated prisoner's dilemma games is conditional on a high probability of future interactions. This suggests a role of group identity in the ability to build long-term partnerships.

More than ten years after Chen and Li's (2009) paper was published and despite the vast literature on the topic that followed, many questions have still not been definitively answered. First, in line with Akerlof and Kranton (2000), Chen and Li developed a preference-based interpretation, while Bénabou and Tirole (2011) advocated a belief-based approach but on purely theoretical grounds. There is relatively little empirical evidence of the role of beliefs on group identity (e.g., Ockenfels and Werner, 2014; Le Coq et al., 2015; Coffman et al., 2017). A systematic confrontation of these approaches by designing novel experiments capturing both preferences and motivated beliefs in the management of identity would be helpful.

Second, we still know relatively little about the multiple dimensions of group identity (e.g., Chen et al., 2014) and about the extent to which group identity is sensitive to individual traits. For example, Kranton et al. (2018) identified recently "groupiness" as a crucial individual trait influencing the size of the in-group bias. There may be multiple group identities in the same person that coexist, peacefully or not. Which dimensions of group identity are more salient depending on the environment and how do individuals manage this coexistence?

Third, many studies adopt a static view of group identity. However, people may change groups over time, either by force (e.g., Bauer et al., 2018), because of social mobility (Suchon and Villeval, 2019), or because they select their group and the associated norms of behavior. The mechanisms behind the endogenous selection of the dominant group identity, notably through the selection of peers and reference group, have been so far insufficiently explored (e.g., Shayo, 2009; Chiang et al., 2019).

Finally, it would be helpful to investigate more systematically how institutions and organizations can favor the welfare-enhancing effects of group identity without encouraging parochialism. Team competition is one of the possible triggers (Ai et al., 2016; Chen et al., 2017; Charness and Holder, 2019; Charness and Chen, 2020), but there may be others. This research program is more relevant than ever in our highly segmented societies, which are torn between more individualism and higher risks of community ghettoization.

References

Abdelal, R., Herrera, Y.M., Johnston, A.I., McDermott, R., 2009. *Measuring Identity: A Guide for Social Scientists*. Cambridge: Cambridge University Press.

Ai, W., Chen, R., Chen, Y., Mei, Q., Webb, P., 2016. Recommending teams promotes prosocial lending in online microfinance. *Proceedings of the National Academy of Sciences* 113 (52), 14944–14948.

Akerlof, G.A., 1997. Social distance and social decisions. *Econometrica* 65, 1005–1027.

Akerlof, G.A., Kranton, R.E., 2000. Economics and identity. *The Quarterly Journal of Economics* 115 (3), 715–753.

Akerlof, G.A., Kranton, R.E., 2005. Identity and the economics of organizations. *Journal of Economic Perspectives* 19 (1), 9–32.

Balliet, D., Wu, J., De Dreu, C.K.W., 2014. Ingroup favoritism in cooperation: A meta-analysis. *Psychological Bulletin* 140(6), 1556–1581.

Bauer, M., Cahlíková, J., Chytilová, J., Želinský, T., 2018. Social contagion of ethnic hostility. *Proceedings of the National Academy of Sciences* 115 (19), 4881–4886.

Bénabou, R., Tirole, J., 2011. Identity, morals and taboos: Beliefs as assets. *The Quarterly Journal of Economics* 126, 805–855.

Benjamin, D.J., Choi, J.J., Strickland, A.J., 2010. Social identity and preferences. *American Economic Review* 100 (4), 1913–1928.

Bernhard, H., Fehr, E., Fischbacher, U., 2006a. Group affiliation and altruistic norm enforcement. *American Economic Review* 96 (2), 217–221.

Bernhard, H., Fischbacher, U., Fehr, E., 2006b. Parochial altruism in humans. *Nature* 442, 24.

Brewer, M.B., 1999. The psychology of prejudice: Ingroup love and outgroup hate? *Journal of Social Issues* 55 (3), 429–444.

Cadsby, C.B., Maynes, E., 1998. Gender and free riding in a threshold public goods game: Experimental evidence. *Journal of Economic Behavior and Organization* 34, 603–620.

Charness, G., Rigotti, L., Rustichini, A., 2007. Individual behavior and group membership. *American Economic Review* 97(4), 1340–1352.

Charness, G., Cobo-Reyes, R., Jiménez, N., 2014. Identities, selection, and contributions in a public-goods game. *Games and Economic Behavior* 87, 322–338.

Charness, G., Chen, Y., 2020. Social identity, group behavior and teams. *Annual Review of Economics* 12 (1), https://doi.org/10.1146/annurev-economics-091619-032800.

Charness, G., Holder, P., 2019. Charity in the laboratory: Matching, competition, and group membership. *Management Science* 65 (3), 1398–1407.

Charness, G., Rabin, M., 2002. Understanding Social Preferences with Simple Tests. *Quarterly Journal of Economics* 117(3), 817–869.

Chen, Y., Li, S.X., 2009. Group identity and social preferences. *American Economic Review* 99 (1), 431–457.

Chen, R., Chen, Y., 2011. The potential of social identity for equilibrium selection. *American Economic Review* 101 (6), 2562–2589.

Chen, Y., Li, S.X., Liu, TX, Shih, M., 2014. Which hat to wear? Impact of natural identities on coordination and cooperation. *Games and Economic Behavior* 84, 58–86.

Chen, R., Chen, Y., Liu, Y., Mei, Q., 2017. Does team competition increase prosocial lending? Evidence from online microfinance. *Games and Economic Behavior* 101, 311–333.

Chiang, C.-F., Liu, J.T., Wen, T.-W., 2019. National identity under economic integration. *Journal of Population Economics* 32 (2), 351–367.

Coffman, K.B., Exley, C.L., Niederle, M., 2017. The role of beliefs in driving gender discrimination. Harvard Business School Working Paper 18–054.

Costa-Font, J., Cowell, F., 2015. Social identity and redistributive preferences: A survey. *Journal of Economic Surveys* 29 (2), 357–374.

Croson, R., Marks, M., Snyder, J., 2003. Groups work for women: Gender and group identity in the provision of public goods. *The Negotiation Journal* 24 (4), 411–427.

Currarini, S., Mengel, F., 2016. Identity homophily and in-group bias. *European Economic Review* 90, 40–55.

Eckel, C.C., Grossman, P.J., 2005. Managing diversity by creating team identity. *Journal of Economic Behavior and Organization* 58 (3), 371–392.

Efferson, C., Lalive, R., Fehr, E. 2008. The coevolution of cultural groups and in-group favoritism. *Science* 321 (5897), 1844–1849.

Fehr, E., Glätzle-Rützler, D., Sutter, M., 2013. The development of egalitarianism, altruism, spite and parochialism in childhood and adolescence. *European Economic Review* 64, 369–383.

Fershtman, C., Gneezy, U., 2001. Discrimination in a segmented society: An experimental approach. *The Quarterly Journal of Economics* 116 (1), 351–377.

Gneezy, A., Fessler, D., 2012. Conflict sticks and carrots: War increases prosocial punishments and rewards. *Proceedings of the Royal Society B: Biological Sciences* 279, 219–223.

Goette, L., Huffman, D., Meier, S., 2006. The impact of group membership on cooperation and norm enforcement: evidence using random assignment to real social groups. *American Economic Review* 96 (2), 212–216.

Goette, L., Huffman, D., Meier, S., 2012. The impact of social ties on group interactions: Evidence from minimal groups and randomly assigned real groups. *American Economic Journal: Microeconomics* 4 (1), 101–115.

Grosskopf, B., Pearce, G., 2017. Discrimination in a deprived neighbourhood: An artefactual field experiment. *Journal of Economic Behavior & Organization* 141, 29–42.

Hargreaves Heap, S.P., Zizzo, D.J., 2009. The value of groups. *American Economic Review* 99, 295–323.

Hoff, K., Pandey, P., 2006. Discrimination, social identity, and durable inequalities. *American Economic Review* 96 (2), 206–211.

Jiang, J., Li, S.X., 2019. Group identity and partnership. *Journal of Economic Behavior and Organization* 160 (C), 202–213.

Klor, E.F., Shayo, M., 2010. Social identity and preferences over redistribution. *Journal of Public Economics* 94, 269–278.

Kranton, R., Pease, M., Sanders, S., Huettel, S., 2018. Group and not groupy behavior: deconstructing bias in social preferences. *Mimeo.*

Lane, T., 2016. Discrimination in the laboratory: A meta-analysis of economics experiments. *European Economic Review* 90, 375–402.

Le Coq, C., Tremewan, J., Wagner, A.K., 2015. On the effects of group identity in strategic environments. *European Economic Review* 76, 239–252.

Li, S.X., de Oliveira, A.C.M., Eckel, C., 2017. Common identity and the voluntary provision of public goods: An experimental investigation. *Journal of Economic Behavior & Organization* 142, 32–46.

Li, S.X., Liu, T.X., 2019. Group identity and cooperation in infinitely repeated games. *Mimeo.*

Li, S.X., 2020. Group identity, ingroup favoritism, and discrimination. In: Zimmermann, K.F. (Ed.). *Handbook of Labor, Human Resources and Population Economics*. Springer, Cham.

Luttmer, E.F.P., 2001. Group loyalty and the taste for redistribution. *Journal of Political Economy* 199, 500–528.

McLeish, K.N., Oxoby, R.J., 2011. Social interactions and the salience of social identity. *Journal of Economic Psychology* 32(1), 172–178.

Montmarquette, C., Rullière, J.-L., Villeval, M.C., Zeiliger, R., 2004. Redesigning Teams and Incentives in a Merger: An Experiment with Managers and Students. *Management Science* 50 (10), 1379–1389.

Ockenfels, A., Werner, P., 2014. Beliefs and ingroup favoritism. *Journal of Economic Behavior & Organization* 108, 453–462.

Pechar, E., Kranton, R., 2018. Moderators of intergroup discrimination in the minimal group paradigm: A meta-analysis. *Mimeo.*

Shayo, M., 2009. A model of social identity with an application to political economy: Nation, class, and redistribution. *American Political Science Review* 103(2), 147–174.

Suchon, R., Villeval, M.C., 2019. The effects of status mobility and group identity on trust. *Journal of Economic Behavior & Organization* 163, 430–463.

Tajfel, H., Billig, M., Bundy, R., Flament, C.L., 1971. Social Categorization and Inter-Group Behavior. *European Journal of Social Psychology* 1, 149–177.

Tajfel, H., Turner, J.C., 1979. An integrative theory of intergroup conflict. In: Austing, W.G., Worchel, S. (Eds.). *The Social Psychology of Intergroup Relations*. Monterey: Brooks/Cole, 33–48.

Tajfel, H., Turner, J.C., 1986. The social identity theory of intergroup behavior. In: Worchel, S., Austin, W. (Eds.). *Psychology of Intergroup Relations*. Chicago, IL: Nelson Hall, 7–24.

21

LIES IN DISGUISE – AN EXPERIMENTAL STUDY ON CHEATING (BY URS FISCHBACHER AND FRANZISKA FÖLLMI-HEUSI)

Uri Gneezy and Marta Serra-Garcia

Introduction

Some people lie frequently. For example, Donald Trump's proclivity for spouting exaggerated numbers, unwarranted boasts, and outright false-hoods is remarkable. According to the *Washington Post*, during his four years as a president, Mr. Trump made 30,573 false or misleading claims.[1]

Whereas President Trump's lies are easy to detect, in many cases, verifying whether someone is lying is difficult. Unlike Trump, people may choose not to lie if they know their lies would be easily detected, for example, due to reputation concerns or fear of punishment. Hence, inherent to cheating is the fact that observers have a hard time detecting it. As a result, although cheating is an economic behavior with important consequences, research-ers face challenges when studying it. Fischbacher and Föllmi-Heusi (2013; FFH hereafter) offered a simple and ingenious way to study cheating be-havior. The design they introduced is simple, elegant, and extremely useful for further research. It builds on previous work on cheating, such as Gn-eezy (2005), who studied a deception game in which the experimenter, rather than the receiver of the lie, could observe the lying; Mazar et al. (2008), who studied cheating with a more complex design; and Serra-Garcia et al. (2011, 2013), who studied lying in a public goods game.

In the basic game in FFH's paper, a person rolls a die in private and then reports the outcome to the experimenter. The participant's payoff depends on the number he reports. Although the experimenter cannot verify whether a specific person is cheating, she can use statistics to infer. For example, if one uses a six-sided die, each number has a 1/6 chance of being reported. If a given number is reported significantly more than 1/6, the participants are probably lying when reporting it to the experimenter.

This simple game has become a workhorse for studying cheating. In this chapter, we discuss the importance of the game to the literature. Putting

DOI: 10.4324/9781003019121-21

such a paper in the more general context of behavioral economics is important. We discuss the usefulness of the game in generating new research, and we compare its contribution with two other games that appear in this book – the ultimatum and trust games. Although these three seminal papers are not perfect, they have changed the way behavioral economists think about the world, and have generated numerous new studies.

The Fischbacher and Föllmi-Heusi experiment

In FFH's basic experiment, a participant is asked to roll a six-sided die in private. She is told that her payoff will depend on the outcome she reports. The payoff in Swiss Francs (CHF) is equal to the number reported, except if the number reported is a 6; in that case, the participant would receive a payoff of 0 CHF.

An important element of the FFH experiment is that only the participant knows whether the report regarding the number is true or false. Lies cannot be detected at the individual level. Yet, by comparing the distribution of the numbers reported with the theoretical probability distribution of rolling a six-sided die, the researcher can test whether, on aggregate, a group of individuals have lied.

The privacy of lying decisions in the FFH experiment allows us to identify private lying costs. Whereas in a general setting people may decide not to lie for different reasons, such as reputation concerns or fear of retaliation, the FFH experiment ceases such strategic concerns with its private setting and provides us with a simple way of measuring lying costs without such strategic concerns. Although lying cannot be measured at the individual level, the distribution of outcomes can help us understand the structure of lying costs.

Theoretically, without lies, the frequency of each payoff reported should be around 16.7%. The data provide clear evidence of lying. Thirty-five percent of participants in FFH's experiment engaged in "maximal lying" by reporting a 5, a significantly higher percentage than the expected 16.7%. Others engaged in "partial lying": the percentage of participants reporting a 4 was 27.2%. Only 6.4% of participants reported a 6 and earned 0 CHF.

FH conducted a number of control treatments to explore the robustness of the distribution of lying costs identified in the main treatment. Though the experimenter cannot tell whether a participant has lied, she may update her beliefs about the participant's honesty based on the report he gives. For example, the experimenter's belief that a participant is lying may be higher if he reports a five rather than three. To increase privacy even further and reduce this concern, FFH provided complete anonymity by adding a double-blind treatment in which the experimenter was not able to link a report to any given individual. They found the distribution of reports was not significantly different from that in the main treatment.

FFH also changed the incentives. In one control treatment, they tripled the payoff of each report. In another, they increased the payoff from reporting a 4 to 4.9 CHF, instead of 4 CHF. In a third treatment, they introduced an externality, such as reporting a higher number reduced the payoff of a different participant. The distribution of reports was again robust. The numbers reported did not change significantly with higher payoffs or with the externality. The 4.9 CHF payoff treatment decreased the frequency of five reports and increased that of four, indicating that lying costs may depend on the size of the lie.

Examples of how this game is used in the literature

The FFH experiment has led to a new generation of papers in experimental economics. We are not reviewing the literature here, because Abeler et al. (2019) have published a comprehensive and highly useful meta-analysis of papers using the FFH experiment. They showed that in the relatively short time since its publication (2008 as working paper, 2013 in JEEA), the FFH experiment has been part of 90 papers, with more than 429 treatments or experiments, and has been run with more than 44,000 participants in over 44 countries worldwide.

A crucial advantage of the FFH game relative to other approaches is that it is easy to run and adapt to answer different questions. One way to vary the FFH game is to change the "size" of lies. Shalvi, Dana, Handgraaf, and De Dreu (2011) did so by introducing an "exit payment" in lieu of completing the experiment. In two different groups, participants could accept an exit payment of either €2.5 or €3.5, or instead play a die-rolling game. When the exit payment was €2.5, if the participant chose to roll the die, she could choose to report truthfully or lie minimally by reporting a 3, moderately by reporting a 4, or majorly by reporting a 5. However, when the exit payment was €3.5, if the participant chose to roll the die, she could choose to report truthfully, lie minimally by reporting a 4, or lie maximally by reporting a 5. Hence, the two treatments differed in the availability of different sized lies to choose from. In accordance with previous literature, Shalvi, Dana, Handgraaf, and De Dreu (2011) found people avoid major lies but embrace intermediate lies. They also found people avoid small lies, indicating that lying has an innate cost.

Related to the size of the lie, Gneezy, Kajackaite, and Sobel (2018) developed and tested a model of lying costs, showing the highest fraction of lies is from reporting the maximal outcome, but some participants do not choose the maximal lie. By introducing an "observed game," in which the roll of the die is not fully private, they show that more participants lie partially when the experimenter cannot observe their outcomes than when the experimenter can verify the observed outcome (see also Gneezy, Rockenbach, and Serra-Garcia, 2013). Partial lying also increases when the prior probability of the highest outcome decreases.

An important variation of the FFH game is the "mind game." This design takes the game in the opposite direction of the observed game. A potential concern in the FFH game is that the experimenter may (secretly) observe the real outcome of the die roll or that the die is manipulated. In the "mind game," participants first think about a number in private, then roll the die in private, and report whether the number that came up is the same as the one they thought of (Jiang, 2013; Shalvi and De Dreu, 2014; Potters and Stoop, 2016). Participants are paid if they report that the outcome of the die roll was the number they thought about.

Kajackaite and Gneezy (2017) used a version of the FFH game as well as the mind game to study the role of incentives in lying. In their version of the FFH game, the participant is paid X (=$1, $5, $20, or $50, depending to the treatment) if she reports rolling a 5, and nothing otherwise. In line with the previous results, cheating did not increase with X in these treatments. Comparing these results with a treatment using the mind game, participants lied substantially more than those playing the cheating game. Furthermore, the participants were responsive to incentives in the mind game and lied more when the incentives increased. Their findings, and those of others, have been informative for new theoretical models of lying costs that have tried to better understand why people suffer from lying costs and why lying does not respond strongly to incentives (e.g., Abeler et al., 2019; Gneezy et al., 2018; Dufwenberg and Dufwenberg, 2018; Khalmetski and Sliwka, 2019).

The FFH game has also been modified into a coin-flipping task, in which participants are paid more for the more "heads" outcomes they report. Cohn et al. (2014) used the coin-flipping task to investigate whether business culture fosters dishonesty. They first primed two different groups of banking professionals by either asking them questions related to their work, or questions unrelated to their profession. The authors concluded that banking professionals are generally honest when they are not primed with work-related questions, but they exhibit dishonest behavior when they are primed with work-related questions. Furthermore, they showed that this pattern does not hold for people who are not banking professionals. However, a recent study (Rawhan, Yoeli, and Fasolo, 2019) failed to replicate this finding, showing that priming effects may be fragile and may depend on banker culture.

Abeler, Becker, and Falk (2014) also used the coin-flipping task to investigate the differences in cheating behavior between a lab setting and a familiar setting, namely, the comfort of one's home. They used a representative sample of the German population, called them at home, and asked them to flip a fair coin four times. Each person was told they would receive €5 for each tail they reported. The same experiment was also run in the lab with a standard student population, to compare outcomes between the field and the lab. They found the students in the lab lied substantially more than the representative sample in the field, concluding that different norms apply when reporting private information at home than reporting in the lab, and that the level of lying costs seems to be influenced by the context in which people are asked to report a given outcome.

Cultural differences in regard to cheating have been explored by Dieckmann et al. (2016), who used the coin-flipping paradigm and compared cheating behavior across five different European countries. They found that people over-report profitable outcomes in all countries, but that significant differences exist in the levels of dishonesty between countries. In contrast to Dieckmann et al. (2016), when using a coin-flipping paradigm, Pascual-Ezama et al. (2015) found no significant differences in dishonest behavior across 16 different countries.

Gender disparities have also been found in regard to cheating using the FFH game. For example, Muehlheusser et al. (2015) divided participants into groups of two and varied the gender composition of the groups. They found no gender differences in cheating, but also found more cheating in male groups and mixed groups than in female groups. This result is in contrast to findings from the deception game that showed women lie less when the lie hurts the receiver (e.g., Dreber and Johannesson, 2008). Fosgaard, Hansen, and Piovesan (2013) found that increasing awareness of cheating as an option significantly increases the probability that women cheat, but not men. This result is consistent with the argument that risk-aversion differences between men and women may cause men to lie more than women in cheating games. They also reported that, following a suggestion that their peers have cheated, men cheat significantly more, whereas women do not.

The FFH game has led to a series of papers that have established the external validity of experimental measures of lying costs. For example, Dai et al. (2018) showed that cheating in the die-roll game predicts fraud in public transportation: higher reports in a variant of the FFH experiment are correlated with a higher likelihood of not paying for bus rides. Potters and Stoop (2016) found that cheating in the mind game predicts who will report receiving a higher payment for participation in an experiment than the one earned. Kroell and Rustagi (2017) studied cheating behavior by farmers who sell lower-quality milk by adding more water to it. Again, cheating behavior in the field correlates with cheating in a variant of the FFH experiment. These results also hold for children and adolescents. Cohn and Maréchal (2018) found that middle and high school students who submit higher reports are more likely to engage in misconduct at school.

The above are just a few examples of the burgeoning literature started by the FFH experiment.

Conclusion: putting FFH in the bigger picture of behavioral economics

This book of 20 top papers in behavioral economics includes three studies that have become workhorses in the literature; the other two are Guth et al.'s (1982) ultimatum game and Berg et al.'s (1995) trust game.

These papers share a few similar features. First, they are not perfect, and criticisms are easily found. In addition, although they all appeared in good journals, they did not make it to the "top 5" journals – probably because they were not perfect. FFH, for example, appeared first as a working paper in 2008, and took seven additional years to be published.

Such a delay in recognition begs the question of why the publication and review process failed to understand the importance of these games as workhorses that could revolutionize the field. First, this type of mistake is not unique to experimental economics. Gans and Shepherd (1994) give some classic examples of "How Are the Mighty Fallen: Rejected Classic Articles by Leading Economists," such as Akerlof's (1970) "market for lemons" paper. They cite Akerlof's comment that "I submitted it in June, 1967 to the *American Economic Review*. I got a reply from the editor which said that the article was interesting but the *American Economic Review* did not publish such trivial stuff." The review team at the *Journal of Political Economy* asserted the opposite: the paper was too general to be true. The *Review of Economic Studies* rejected it on the grounds, again, that it was "trivial."

These rejections raise the question of what can be done to reduce such oversights. Although, clearly, the quality of data is important, the review team should also ask, when considering the contribution of a paper, about its *usefulness*. Is it going to open up a field of investigation? A good paper should not be the last in the literature, but rather should open up a discussion. Having more open questions could be a good sign of the importance of a paper, and should not lead to an automatic rejection because the paper does not answer all of them.

We can only hope for more papers that introduce "imperfect" designs such as the original ultimatum, trust, and cheating papers. This type of contribution proves vital in starting new lines of research. We hope readers will consider this possibility the next time they evaluate a new contribution. Thus, 20 years from now, when someone edits the new volume of major contributions to the field, the papers in it will have been published in the top journals.

Fischbacher and Föllmi-Heusi's (2013) seminal paper has proven to be an extremely useful workhorse that has changed the way we study cheating. We can only hope for more like it in the future.

Note

1 www.washingtonpost.com/politics/how-fact-checker-tracked-trump-claims/2021/01/23/ad04b69a-5c1d-11eb-a976-bad6431e03e2_story.html

References

Abeler, J., Becker, A., Falk, A, 2014. Representative evidence on lying costs. *Journal of Public Economics* 113, 96–104.

Abeler, J., Nosenzo, D., Raymond, C., 2019. Preferences for truth-telling. *Econometrica* 87(4), 1115–1153.

Akerlof, G., 1970. The market for "lemons": Quality uncertainty and the market mechanism. *Quarterly Journal of Economics* 84(3), 488–500.

Berg, J., Dickhaut, J., McCabe, K., 1995. Trust, reciprocity and social history. *Games and Economic Behavior* 10(1), 122–142.

Cohn, A., Fehr, E., Maréchal, M.A., 2014. Business culture and dishonesty in the banking industry. *Nature* 516(7529), 86–89.

Cohn, A., Maréchal, M.A., 2018. Laboratory measure of cheating predicts school misconduct. *The Economic Journal* 128(615), 2743–2754.

Dai, Z., Galeotti, F., Villeval, M.C., 2018. Cheating in the lab predicts fraud in the field: An experiment in public transportation. *Management Science* 64(3), 1081–1100.

Dieckmann, A., Grimm, V., Unfried, M., Utikal, V., Valmasoni, L., 2016. On trust in honesty and volunteering among Europeans: Cross-country evidence on perceptions and behavior. *European Economic Review* 90, 225–253.

Dreber, A., Johannesson, M., 2008. Gender differences in deception. *Economics Letters* 99(1), 197–199.

Dufwenberg, M., Dufwenberg, M.A., 2018. Lies in disguise – A theoretical analysis of cheating. *Journal of Economic Theory* 175, 248–264.

Fischbacher, U., Föllmi-Heusi, F., 2013. Lies in disguise—An experimental study on cheating. *Journal of the European Economic Association* 11(3), 525–547.

Fosgaard, T.R., Hansen, L.G., Piovesan, M., 2013. Separating will from grace: An experiment on conformity and awareness in cheating. *Journal of Economic Behavior and Organization* 93, 279–284.

Gans, J., Shepherd, G., 1994. How are the mighty fallen: Rejected classic articles by leading economists. *Journal of Economic Perspectives* 8(1), 165–179.

Gneezy, U., 2005. Deception: The role of consequences. *The American Economic Review* 95(1), 384–394.

Gneezy, U., Kajackaite, A., Sobel, J., 2018. Lying aversion and the size of the lie. *The American Economic Review* 108(2), 419–453.

Gneezy, U., Rockenbach, B., Serra-Garcia, M., 2013. Measuring lying aversion. *Journal of Economic Behavior and Organization* 93, 293–300.

Guth, W., Schmittberger, R., Schwarze, B., 1982. An experimental analysis of ultimatum bargaining. *Journal of Economic Behavior and Organization* 3 (4): 367–388.

Jiang, T., 2013. Cheating in mind games: The subtlety of rules matters. *Journal of Economic Behavior & Organization* 93, 328–336.

Kajackaite, A., Gneezy, U., 2017. Incentives and cheating. *Games and Economic Behavior* 102, 433–444.

Khalmetski, K., Sliwka, D., 2019. Disguising lies – Image concerns and partial lying in cheating games. *American Economic Journal: Microeconomics* 11(4), 79–110.

Kroell, M., Rustagi, D., 2017. Measuring honesty and explaining adulteration in naturally occurring markets. mimeo.

Mazar, M., Amir, O., D. Ariely, D., 2008. The dishonesty of honest people: A theory of self-concept maintenance. *Journal of Marketing Research* 45(6), 633–644.

Muehlheusser, G., Roider, A., Wallmeier, N., 2015. Gender differences in honesty: Groups versus individuals. *Economics Letters* 128:25–29.

Pascual-Ezama, D., Fosgaard, T., Cardenas, J.C., Kujal, P., Veszteg, R., de Liano, B.G., Gunia, B., Weichselbaumer, D., Hilken, K., Antinyan, A., Delnoij, J., Proestakis, A., Tira, M., Pratomo, Y., Jaber-López, T., Branas-Garza, P., 2015. Context-dependent cheating: Experimental evidence from 16 countries. *Journal of Economic Behavior and Organization* 116, 379–386.

Potters, J., Stoop, J., 2016. Do cheaters in the lab also cheat in the field? *European Economic Review* 87, 26–33.

Rawhan, Z., Yoeli, E., Fasolo, B., 2019. Heterogeneity in banker culture and its influence on dishonesty. *Nature* 575, 345–349.

Serra-Garcia, M., Van Damme, E., Potters, J., 2011. Hiding an inconvenient truth: Lies and vagueness. *Games and Economic Behavior* 73(1), 244–261.

Serra-Garcia, M., Van Damme, E., Potters, J., 2013. Lying about what you know or what you do? *Journal of the European Economic Association* 11(5), 1204–1229.

Shalvi, S., Dana, J., Handgraaf, M., De Dreu, C., 2011. Justified ethicality: Observing desired counterfactuals modifies ethical perceptions and behavior. *Organizational Behavior and Human Decision Processes* 115(2), 181–190.

Shalvi, S., De Dreu, C., 2014. Oxytocin promotes group-serving dishonesty. *Proceedings of the National Academy of Sciences* 111(15), 5503–5507.

INDEX

absolute risk aversion 13
acquire-a-company game 56, 58
addict 47
adverse selection 56, 59, 61
affirmative action 204
agent 15
allocation game 212
alternating offer game 45
altruism 12, 47, 152
analogy-based expectation equilibrium 60
Andreoni, J. 5, 12, 65, 152
anonymity 18, 45
antisocial punishment 107
as-if 34
aspiration adaptation 34
aspiration formation 34
aspiration level 32
asset 77
asset market 26

backward induction 38
bargaining 7, 37, 103
bargaining games 38
Bayesian updating 6
beauty contest game 9
behavioral economics 37
behavioral type 42
belief 14, 66, 201, 211
Berg, J. 8, 119
bounded rationality 2, 9
boundedly-rational 34
best shot game 44
betting game 60

bias 176, 180
bilateral bargaining 90
boundary experiments 122
bubble 27

call-market method 33
categorization 17, 210
causal attribution 45
centipede game 43
certainty bias 163
CES (Constant Elasticity of
    Substitution) 153
Chamberlin, E. 1, 20
charitable giving 12, 66
charity 17, 213
Charness, G. 1, 4, 14, 53, 182
cheap talk 14, 182
cheating 18, 220
Chen, Y. 10, 17, 134, 210
clearing-house 33
Coase theorem 85
Coffman, K. 16, 198
cognitive capital 178
coin-flipping task 223
collaboration 6
common identity 216
common knowledge 66, 77, 122
common value auction 4, 53, 57
communication 14, 183
competition 16, 198
competitive market 1, 20
compromise effect 169
conditional cooperator 11, 186

congestion 67
contingent claim 6
contingent reasoning 60, 62
contingent thinking 61
control 15, 191
control treatment 222
cooperation 10, 14, 134, 182, 212
coordination game 38
critical cost efficiency index (CCEI) 153
Croson, R. 15, 191
crowding out 144, 192
culture 7, 18
cultural difference 46, 104, 224
currency effects 104
cursed equilibrium 60

deception 46
deception game 220
decision criteria 2
deliberation 10
deregulation 26
deterrence hypothesis 11
Dickhaut, J. 8, 119
dictator game 45, 152, 187, 212
direct response 16, 184
directional learning 110
discrimination 210
disguise 18
distributional preferences 213
dissolution 26
distrust 192
double auction 1, 77
double blind 18, 221
Dufwenberg, M. 14, 182

Eckel, C. 12, 152
efficiency 17, 153, 212, 214
effort 15
egoist 156
electronic mail game 60
elicit 13, 15
endogenous depth of reasoning 10, 114
endowment effect 14, 85, 177
enter 16
entitlement 45
environment 13
envy 17, 153, 213
evolutionary game analysis 33
excess cash 27
exit 16
exit payment 222
expectations 182
experience 7, 14, 24, 39, 54, 57, 59, 99, 105
experimenter effect 104, 214
extrinsic incentive 144

fair 8
fairness 3, 44, 47, 103, 158
Falk, A. 7, 15, 103, 191
feedback aversion 201
Fehr, E. 10, 134
field 17
field experiment 7, 10, 11, 14, 145, 177
financial incentives 22
fine 11, 144
first-order belief 187
first-price auction 54, 57
Fischbacher, U. 14, 18, 182, 220
flow chart 31
FMRI 46, 98, 116
Föllmi-Heusi, F. 14, 18, 182, 220
fragmented identity 216
framing 13, 204
free-ride 5, 10, 44, 65, 134
fundamental value 26

Gächter, S. 10, 134
Game 183
gender 12, 16
gender difference 203, 224
gender effect 202
gender gap 202
gender stereotypes 207
general axiom of revealed preference
   (GARP) 152
gift exchange 16, 48, 135, 193
giving 152
Gneezy, U. 11, 18, 144, 220
Grosskopf, B. 37
groupiness 216
group bias 210
group-contingent social preferences 211
group identity 17, 210
group size 5, 65, 69
guessing game 9, 109
guilt 11
guilt aversion 14, 182
Güth, W. 3, 37

heterogeneity 8, 13, 107
heuristic 79
Hicksian compensating surplus 92
Hicksian equivalent surplus 92
hidden cost 15, 191
higher-order belief 187
hold-up problem 191
Holt, C.A. 1, 13, 20, 162
homemade preferences 68
honesty 185, 221
human sociability 119
Hurwicz, L. 162

hypothetical incentive 13
hypothetical payoff 168
hypothetical thinking 61

Imas, A. 11, 144
impure altruism 5
impure public good 67
in-group 210
in-group bias 210
in-group favoritism 211
incentive 12, 13, 17, 144, 162, 222
incomplete contract 16, 191
incomplete information 45
induced preference 168
induced-value 87
inequity aversion 47
information 6, 76
information aggregation 76
information aggregation model 81
insider traders 77
institution 2, 13, 162
instructions 24
instrumental variable approach 172
insula 46
intention 193
intrinsic motivation 12, 144, 192
investment game 8
Isaac, M. 5, 6, 65, 76

Jonckheere test 24

k-level reasoning 10
Kagel, J. H. 4, 9, 53, 109
Keser, C. 2, 30
Kahneman, D. 7, 85
Kliemt, H. 2, 30
Knetsch, J. L. 7, 85
Kosfeld, M. 15, 191

lab experiment 7, 10, 14, 178
lab in the field experiment 203
language-driven effects 104
latent variable approach 172
Laury, S. 13, 162
learning 4, 47, 54, 71, 107
learning direction theory 47
learning effect 167
Leontief preferences 153
level-k reasoning 109
level-k thinking 60
Levin, D. 4, 53
Li, S. X. 17, 210
lies 18, 220
List, J.A. 7, 14, 85, 176
loss aversion 91

lottery 13
lying costs 221

Mann-Whitney test 25
marginal per capita return 68
market 7
market anomalies 176
market centralization 21
market experience 176
market game 106
market power 25
maximum likelihood 166
maxmin 6
McCabe, K. 8, 13, 119, 162
mechanism design 2, 23, 135
medial prefrontal cortex 10
men 198
merger 25
microeconomic system 13, 162
Miller, J. 12, 152
mind game 19, 223
minimum acceptance threshold 38
monetary incentives 26
monkey 47
mood 46
moral hazard 195, 216

Nagel, R. 9, 37, 109
Nash equilibrium 4, 9
negative reciprocity 16
neuroeconomics 46
neuroscience 10
new trust game 129
new ultimatum game experiments 129
Niederle, M. 16, 198
nim 90
nonparametric statistics 24
non-strategic setting 216
norms 206
normal-form 34

Okuno-Fujiwara, M. 7, 103
oligopoly 2, 30
opt-in 202
oral double auction 21
order effect 41, 168, 195
other-interest 9
other-regarding preference 126
out-group 212
overconfidence 16, 60, 202

p-guessing game 9
partial lying 18, 221
partnership 182
penalty 11

Penta, A. 9, 109
perfect competition 21
personality-psychology perspective 107
piece rate 16, 199
pilot study 43
Pingle M. 1
Plott, C.R. 6, 76
policy 14, 17, 18, 23, 26
positive reciprocity 16, 182
posted offer auctions 25
Prasnikar, V. 7, 103
preference ordering 12
preferences 162
price 11
price dispersion 20
pricing formula 32
principal 15
prior information 77
privacy 221
private information 77, 80
private signal 57
promise 14, 182
prosocial 148, 187, 211
protocol method 30
public good 5, 10, 65, 134
public goods game 48, 68, 220
public information 4, 53, 58
punishment 10, 127, 134, 212

questionnaire 193

random allocation 214
random utility model 172
rational expectations 6, 76
rationology 34
rationality 59
Razzolini, L. 15, 191
real donation 157
real effort 16
real incentive 13
reciprocity 8, 48, 103, 119, 186, 192, 211
reference point 5, 7, 53
reinforcement learning 107
reinforcement model 47
relative risk aversion 13, 167
repeated game 71
repetition 41
reputation 18, 70
resentment 194
response game 212
response time 46
review process 19
reward 122
risk-averse 13, 162, 164

risk aversion 162, 201, 224
risk elicitation 171
risk-loving 164
risk-neutral 164
risk neutral Nash equilibrium 54
risk preferences 163
robustness check 193
Roth, A. 7, 16, 103, 198
rule-following conduct 126
rules of thumb 61
Rustichini, A. 11, 144

salivary alpha-amylase 46
satisficing 34
Sauermann, H. 30
scenario studies 194
Schmittberger, R. 3, 37
Schwarze, B. 3, 37
second-order belief 187
second-price common-value auction 57
security markets 76
selection effect 60
self-confidence 205
self-interest 3, 8, 10, 18
selfish player 183
selfish preferences 153, 186
Selten, R. 2, 30, 42
sequential game 186
sequential rationality 34
serotonin 46
Serra-Garcia, M. 18, 220
signal 16, 59, 61, 148, 192
signaling game 60
simultaneous 186
Smith, A. 8, 9
Smith, V. L. 1, 20, 119
social identity 210
social market 149
social norm 5, 11, 140, 211
social preference 9, 12, 15, 17, 38, 44, 59, 73, 105, 120, 135, 137, 185, 210
social welfare 17
socialization 9
socio-psychological imperative 107
stake 13, 18, 46
state 13
statistical discrimination 204
stereotypes 206
strategic setting 216
strategy method 2, 16, 30, 42, 45, 47, 184, 192, 213
strategy tournament 33
strategy vector choice 42
strategy vector method 34, 44

subgame perfect equilibrium 38
subject pool 12, 46
substantive rationality 31
Sunder, S. 6, 76
surplus 12
Sutter, M. 14, 176

team competition 217
Testosterone 46
Thaler, R. H. 7, 85
tokens 104
tournament payoffs 199
tournament play 16
trading institutions 23
transactions cost 191
trust 8, 14, 119, 191
trust game 8, 48, 187, 224
trustworthiness 8, 119, 183

ultimatum bargaining 3
ultimatum bargaining game 3, 37, 104, 224
unhinged outcome 26

uniform distribution 53
utility function 13

Vesterlund, L. 16, 198
Villeval, M.C. 17, 210
voluntary contribution mechanism 5, 65, 68

Walker, J.M. 5, 65
warm glow 5, 65
wealth effect 167
willingness to accept 7, 85, 177
willingness to guess 204
willingness to pay 7, 85, 177
winner's curse 4, 53
within-subject design 199, 214
women 198

yes-no-game 45

Zamir, S. 7, 103
zero-intelligence trader 82

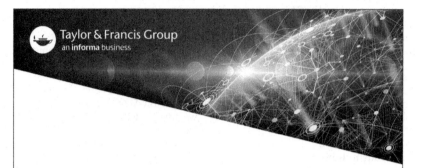

Printed in the United States
by Baker & Taylor Publisher Services